Mysteries OF THE
HUMAN JOURNEY

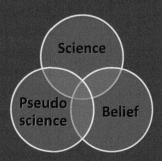

Science

Pseudo science

Belief

H. LYN WHITE MILES, PH.D.
UNIVERSITY OF TENNESSEE AT CHATTANOOGA

WITH CONTRIBUTIONS FROM VIVIAN JAMES, M.S.

SECOND EDITION

Kendall Hunt
publishing company

www.kendallhunt.com
Send all inquiries to:
4050 Westmark Drive
Dubuque, IA 52004-1840

Published in the United States of America

TABLE OF CONTENTS

PREFACE

Mysteries of the Human Journey is a unique alternative to a standard comprehensive four-field anthropology text. It is a combination text/workbook that presents basic introductory material from the four subfields of anthropology in a provocative and exciting manner by examining twelve "mysteries" of how our ancestors became human, including Sasquatch, Neanderthals, multi-gender societies, Kula trade, and even zombies!

Each chapter consists of anthropology fundamentals followed by background information on that chapter's mystery. Each chapter also has learning objectives, interesting websites and critical thinking questions, and a tear-out mystery worksheet for students to complete a written assignment for discussion, flipped classroom, or further group work in class. The book is especially designed for active learning but also works well with lecture courses. Instructors can select among the topics, add mysteries of their own, and supplement with readings, allowing this accessible workbook to be used as a stand-alone text or supplement. This second edition has had a major format uplift, updating throughout the chapters, and new mysteries to consider.

Mysteries begins with a clear distinction among science based on evidence, faith based on belief, and pseudoscience—a little science combined with a great deal of speculation. It presents the scientific method and the anthropological emphasis on evolution, culture, and the comparative method. Yet, it also honestly shows where anthropology orthodoxy has hampered our understanding, e.g., just dismissing the aquatic hypothesis without considering some swamp environmental factors; arguing that the Bering Land Bridge was the only route to the New World; showing a gender interpretive bias; or clinging to certain hominin species designations. No other introductory text takes this approach.

While the text/workbook discourages pseudoscience, it understands the curiosity of Bigfoot advocates and coasttocoastam.com fans, and asks students to keep an open mind using skeptical but open inquiry as scientific "possibilians," a term coined by neuroscientist David Eagleman. It works for students for whom an interesting puzzle can lead to more in-depth learning and who want more scientific direction than just the "ancient alien theorist" approach they find in popular culture. However, it does not take a sarcastic or mocking tone against pseudoscience or belief but rather calls for critical thinking.

Students today are bored with just received knowledge from lecture, and want to be active learners. They are fascinated with Steve Jobs whose "Here's to the Crazy Ones" Apple advertisement showed a series of rejected geniuses in their day. Bob Dylan who "couldn't sing," Martin L. King, Jr. who "had only a dream," and Albert Einstein who had "just a theory"—were all mocked by colleagues for their vision. Likewise, I was criticized in elementary school for not coloring a holiday wreath in an "anatomically correct manner," in high school for arguing for continental plate tectonics, and in graduate school by famous paleoanthropologist Sherwood Washburn for wanting to teach language to a silent orangutan who would "never learn." Even the greats can get it wrong sometimes. *Mysteries of the Human Journey* gives solid scientific tools of analysis while challenging orthodoxy and opening students to exciting inquiry and possibility.

H. Lyn White Miles, Ph.D.
Acworth, Georgia, USA, December 17, 2016

ACKNOWLEDGEMENTS

I was inspired by my own possibilian professors. At the University of Connecticut, Dennison Nash opened up the amazing world of anthropology and the social construction of knowledge for me. At Yale, Dame Alison Richard, DBE, taught me primatology and our common ancestry with apes, later to become the 344th Vice-Chancellor of Cambridge University. Philip Lieberman of Brown University encouraged me to explore the origins of language and cognition, and at the University of Oklahoma, Roger Fouts introduced me to the world of ape language and culture and the complexities of challenging human uniqueness.

Vivian James (Kennesaw State and SUNY Albany) and Warren Roberts and Shela Van Ness (University of Tennessee-Chattanooga) made great suggestions for this book with wit and irony. Bev Kraus, Terry Brennan, and Lara Sanders of Kendall-Hunt were kind and put in extra effort as deadlines closed in. My students in Anthropology 1000: Mysteries of the Human Journey gave great feedback on the first edition.

This book is dedicated to my grandmothers. Ida Bell Gaunya's ancestry began with the Coast Salish and Blackfoot First Nations of Canada, being raised in an Indian orphanage in Quebec, and finally making her way to Connecticut where I was born. Eight thousand miles away, Sofia Bik Dybas was raised in a thatched hut near Krakow and brought her cleverness and 13th century skills with her to the Americas. I am glad their children met. This book is also dedicated to my brother Robert Abraham Miles, Chantek "first orangutan person" and Star Russian Blue.

Finally, I pay tribute to the prehistoric Denisovans, whose non-*Homo sapiens* genes I carry. Being only 96% human gives me a great perspective from which to be an anthropologist.

1 ANTHROPOLOGY:
Bones, Stones, Phones, & Drones

Hands imprinted on a prehistoric cave wall...who made them and what do they tell us about the human species? Anthropology was born out of the intellectual freedom to look beyond the ideas of any one culture or time. We examine what it means to be human based on biocultural scientific evidence about all times and places. Anthropology places the human species *within* nature—not apart from it. Along the way, there have been a number of fascinating mysteries...

LEARNING OBJECTIVES

1. Understand how anthropology takes a biocultural view of the human species in all times and places, using concepts such as culture, adaptation, and evolution.

2. Describe the Age of Enlightenment which introduced a new way of knowing through human reason. The Enlightenment grew from the impact of social upheavals, scientific discoveries, and rejection of the views of authorities.

3. Show how discovering that the earth changes and is not the center of the universe led to the Scientific Revolution and the development of the scientific method based on evidence.

4. Describe how anthropology emerged from these revolutions and is now organized into four subfields: biological, archaeology, linguistic, cultural, and applied anthropology which solves problems in the real world.

5. Understand why humankind now faces the challenge of creating sustainability and developing a Type 1 Civilization.

6. Analyze the cultural roots and contemporary popularity of zombies from the perspective of the subfields of anthropology.

INTRODUCTION

Imagine you are on vacation with friends and family on beautiful Flores Island in Indonesia. Flores Island is hauntingly beautiful with white beaches, Komodo dragons, and pristine waterfalls—and a surprising early human ancestor. Villagers in the marketplace tell you legends about the 'little people' who were already on the island when they arrived thousands of years ago. The little people lived in the mountains and were starving so the villagers gave them food only to discover that they even ate the wooden bowls! The villagers called them the "poor starving people from hell." Your best friend is a fan of "ancient aliens" television shows, of which you are pretty skeptical, but you are intrigued. What a myth—could it be true?

You decide to go to the mountains and explore for yourself where you discover an international team of scientists already at work on the Liang Bua cave. The scientists found prehistoric human fossils of 3 ft. tall individuals along with crude stone tools and evidence of hunting of giant rats and elephants. You make the connection with the myths, and wonder if remnants of the little people could have provoked the stories. You sign up to volunteer to dig and sift for the summer.

The scientific team holds a press conference at your hotel, and announces the discovery of a new human species, *Homo floresiensis*. They hold up a skull with a brain only one third the size of modern humans today that they date at 95,000 years old. Since modern humans were also in this area, this means that two species of humans lived side by side for thousands of years in this area. Could *floresiensis* actually be the little people? Should they be viewed as microcephalic (small brained), a separate species, or just short humans?

You consider *floresiensis'* **BONES** and what common ancestry they share with modern humans—the concern of the subfield of biological anthropology. You see the need to investigate their tools made of **STONES** and how they lived—the subfield of archaeology. You already hypothesized a link between the legends about the little people with evidence of a real fossil ancestor. How did *floresiensis* think and what would be the **PHONES** or sounds of the language of another human species—the subfield of linguistic anthropology. Comparing the culture and technology with modern tools such as **DRONES**—would be the subfield of cultural anthropology. Now, you are thinking like an anthropologist!

Anthropology uses a combination of observation, evidence, excavation, fieldwork, experiments, and a set of concepts such as culture and evolution to reconstruct the human past, explore our diversity today, and go beyond the ideas of just our culture. We take a biocultural approach and study the bones, stones, phones, and drones of other societies in all times and places. Along the way we encounter puzzles, things that contradict current knowledge, that we can't explain or challenge current theories, and we explore the mysteries of the human journey!

AGE OF ENLIGHTENMENT

For thousands even millions of years, myths and story-telling were the primary way humans expressed our understanding about the world and our origins. Native Americans/First Nations saw humans as a part of nature and viewed all of creation as the unfolding of the 'good mystery.' Australian aborigines told about the eternal 'dreamtime', and the Ituri forest people of the DRC, Africa spoke of "molimo" the spirit of the forest that imbues both the animate and inanimate world. In the Middle East, people worshiped animal totems and deities and later a single creator that formed the basis of the Abrahamic religions (Judaism, Islam, and Christianity).

Just like the local people of Flores Island, all these cultures relied on ancient myths and stories to explain and navigate the world and deal with the challenge of death. With the invention of writing these myths became sacred scriptures and were further solidified. As societies developed food production and cities, wealthy elites emerged with strong religious and civil control and used these concepts to dominate the populace. Ancient empires like Sumer, Egypt, and Rome protected the status quo and their own power and created state religious systems that brought comfort and explained the unknown on the one hand, but also justified social injustice, wars, and oppression including torture and even death for challenging authority, on the other.

But, by the 17th century, a number of cultural factors converged in the West to create a whole new way of knowing based on individuals using their own minds to observe and collect information about the world. They explored concrete evidence independent of the views of the authorities. Called the Age of Enlightenment, it revolutionized how we thought about ourselves and nature and ultimately gave rise to the Scientific Revolution, and the birth of anthropology.

GREAT CHAIN OF BEING
Before the Enlightenment, the West viewed all life as a "Great Chain of Being," a composite of Greek philosophy and Judeo-Christian theology. The ancient Hebrews viewed the world as flat and all life was organized as links in a chain reaching up to the heavens with so-called 'lower' life forms on the bottom and 'higher' ones close to the heavens. Humans were at the top in the image of God. Scholars made calculations based on the ages of people in scriptures and concluded that the earth was created 6,000 years ago in 4004 BCE, at 9 am on October 23. Later interpretations expanded this by a few thousand years—but the point was to literally interpret the received knowledge of scripture. Medieval theologians argued that creation was perfect just the way God made it, with no new species and no extinctions. This static view of the universe paralleled the relatively static social order and authority of the church and monarchy.

SOCIAL UPHEAVAL
But social conditions began to change. In 1347, the bubonic plague killed a third to a half of all the people in Europe. People tried many belief-based remedies such as prayer, flowers, flagellation, putting a cross on your door, and even persecuting Jews, gypsies, or other groups, but nothing worked until people discovered improved hygiene and some natural immunity to the disease. They also noticed that the

wealthy and pious died as much as the outcasts which challenged civil authority. Royalty lost their lands and peasant farmers now had access to resources which provided opportunities for a new middle class.

An era of prosperity emerged which allowed middle class Europeans to think more independently and explore other continents. Sailors and some scholars already knew the earth was not flat and they sought routes to other lands. The prosperity also created demand for gold, spices, and export crops, and royalty commissioned expeditions to other parts of the world for exploitation of both natural resources and people. It is estimated that 90-95% of Native populations of the New World were destroyed by enslavement and disease, but it also made Europeans aware of other peoples.

In the 17th century, the Thirty Years' War created horrible destruction in Europe and writers began to call for a "different way." A philosophical movement grew up that advocated liberty, progress, reason and tolerance—and diminished some of the abuses and control of the Church and State. Through centuries of explorations and Crusades, western scholars also rediscovered ancient libraries and knowledge of Greece, Egypt, and the Arab world, and learned about other languages and culture.

By comparing manuscripts, they grew to recognize that scriptures had been copied and recopied with many conflicting passages, additions, and deletions that resulted. They determined that parts of *Genesis* were likely borrowed from the much older *Epic of Gilgamesh* around 1700 BCE. The scholars found that the gospels differed about the time of Jesus' death, place of birth, opening of tomb, and sayings of Jesus whose Aramaic name was really Yeshua. They learned that the early Church had many varying ideas about Yeshua and that other divine figures were also reported to have been born on December 25th, including Mithra, Dionysus, and even Krishna.

Not just Christianity, but the scriptures of other religions also had the same copying issues with errors and additions through the centuries. Scholars determined that they were important books of faith—but not necessarily literal history or scientific textbooks for all times. For example, the ancient scriptures assumed the earth was flat which scholar now knew was not true. They sought other ideas and alternatives based on interpretation of tangible evidence. The political revolutions for independence in the U.S. and France also showed growing impatience with injustice and a desire for embracing social change, freedom of thought, and challenge to authority. People reasoned: if all this social and cultural change could occur, maybe things were not as static as the authorities had maintained for centuries. Independent thought, although sometimes costly and resulting in torture and imprisonment, became highly valued among scholars.

4

SCIENTIFIC REVOLUTION

COPERNICUS

The Enlightenment paralleled the Scientific Revolution which began in 1543 when the Polish scientist Copernicus bravely calculated that the earth was not the center of the universe. This challenged the ancient worldview that the earth was at the center and was flat with the sun, moon, and stars all revolving around the earth just as it appears in the night sky. Copernicus' made his mathematical discovery because he was able to go beyond the appearance of the night sky and earlier dogma to see another possibility based on a broader perspective—that of the whole solar system.

Technology also helped this intellectual growth with the invention of the telescope. In 1604, astronomer Johannes Kepler recorded a new star (actually a supernova) which challenged the doctrine of a static universe. Galileo later confirmed Copernicus' conclusion that the earth revolved around the sun with actual observations. The authorities did not react positively. They imprisoned Galileo, put him on trial, and tortured him for his discovery. Three hundred years later, the Church apologized to Galileo, showing that ideas can take time to be accepted and religious authorities can change their views over time.

The scientific discoveries began to cascade. In 1642, Isaac Newton hypothesized gravitation, laws of motion, and helped develop telescope technology further. He posited natural laws and processes that could be systematically investigated. This allowed scientists to determine the great age and size of the universe and reject the idea it was small and only 6,000 years old.

Georges Cuvier argued for "catastrophism," the idea that a series of environmental disasters must have occurred to result in the fossil record of repeated extinctions. Charles Lyell developed the idea of "uniformitarianism," and showed that environmental processes had been changing the earth and its organisms for millennia. Robert Malthus argued that individuals and species engaged in a competition for resources and that there were trimming processes like famine that kept the earth in balance. But exactly how did this occur? The stage was set for yet another scientist to take a new perspective and address the issue of species change.

CHARLES DARWIN

In 1859, Darwin put all these ideas together, adding the concept of 'common ancestry' developed from linguistic scholars who compared languages in Europe and noticed that there were many similar words or cognates between French and Italian, and between Finnish and Hungarian. They reasoned that these languages were actually the descendants of an earlier common ancestor language that had split into several lineages. Modern European languages must have descended from the everyday Latin of different areas of the Roman Empire.

In like manner, Darwin reasoned that diverse life forms had descended from a distant common ancestor. All individual organisms varied slightly from each other, and some had traits better suited to the environment than others so they left more offspring. The next generation contained slightly more of those traits and over thousands of generations the changes accumulated would be enough that a new species, like a new language, was born. Darwin called his idea "natural selection" and said it occurred through 'descent with modification.'

Darwin over-estimated gradual evolution, and under-estimated chance factors. But, by taking a broader perspective over thousands of generations not just a human lifetime, he made a revolutionary scientific discovery that placed humans within nature because he surmised that humans had descended from earlier species thousands even millions of years ago. The obvious living cousin candidates were the great apes who explorers had brought back from Asia and Africa and who exhibited intelligence and human-like behavior. Darwin argued that apes and humans had a common ancestor many millions of years ago.

CULTURE LAG

Most developed nations ultimately accepted this scientific discovery, and in 1996, the Pope declared evolution to be a fact. However, the U.S. was unusually slow to accept human evolution, in part because of our puritanical origins and also because of the low level of science education in our schools. Many clung to a literal interpretation of the *Genesis* story rather than believe that God worked through nature to create new species which the majority of people concluded, mixing belief and science. Scholars call this a "culture lag."

For example, the 1925 Scopes Monkey Trial in Dayton, TN drew attention to this religious controversy after Tennessee enacted a law that creationism must be taught in the schools. Substitute teacher, John Scopes, was selected to test that law and bring much needed attention to southeast Tennessee during the depression. Scopes was convicted in the first nationally broadcast legal trial, Tennessee was mocked, and U.S. teaching of biology and genetics was set back further for decades. In the 1960s, President John Kennedy, competing with the Russian space achievements, introduced a stronger science curriculum in the public schools, although the South continued to lag behind in achievements. Although anthropology respected the views of all religions worldwide, it made human evolution the foundation of its investigations.

Today, there are five different positions most Americans take on human evolution. Young earth creationists believe the earth was created in six literal days about 6,000 years ago. Small changes might occur within species (microevolution) but no new species emerge over time. Old earth creationists agree that humans have not evolved from earlier animal species, but accept scientific evidence showing that the earth is billions of years old and that plants and animals have undergone microevolution, and perhaps even some macroevolution. Theistic evolutionists believe that God creates through natural processes and that all plants and animals, including humans, have developed from earlier species. Spiritual evolutionists see a higher power or meaning to the universe often influenced by beliefs from world religions, but also accept that humans descended from earlier species. Natural evolutionists leave religious or spiritual matters out and just focus on natural evidence of human descent from earlier species.

In culture lag, the U.S. still ranks at the bottom of 34 developed nations in the acceptance of human evolution (only Turkey ranks lower). About 55% of Americans embrace human evolution and Tennessee ranks lowest among the states with only 30-40% acceptance. A number of religious groups nationwide still attempt legal cases to insert the concept of "intelligent design" or other religious beliefs into school science curricula. However, over 98% of scientists accept human species change and the theory is no longer scientifically debated—only the processes and details. Thus, it is a religious controversy not a scientific one, and creationism is not taught in science courses because it is based on belief, not tangible evidence.

ORIGINS OF ANTHROPOLOGY

Anthropology had its origins in the Enlightenment and Scientific Revolution described above. As the Age of Exploration developed and Europeans ran out of resources, they 'discovered,' colonized, and exploited the New World and encountered people and cultures very different from their own. Westerners focused on furs, gold, cash crops like tobacco and sugar, and dominating and exploiting the indigenous people of Africa, Asia and the Americas.

Scholars wondered who these other people and cultures were—monsters, fallen angels, barbarians, or the lost tribes of the Bible. They speculated that the unfamiliar societies must be earlier stages of cultural evolution, always placing Euro-American culture at the top in the process. They were only dimly aware that Arab scholars had already started to address the description and origins of society centuries earlier.

Anatomists pondered the physical traits and skeletal structure of other people and developed techniques to measure skulls and other bones. When humanlike fossils were discovered, naturalists speculated where other humanlike types might belong on the tree of life. One scholar thought a skull found in the Caucasus Mountains was the most 'perfect' and claimed Europeans to be superior to all other groups, so these early studies were racist by today's standards because they promoted the biological inferiority of other groups.. Pope Paul III in the 16th century declared Native Americans to be human and to possess souls, and scholars called for fieldwork to systematically study other cultures.

By the 1800s, anthropology (*Anthropos* + *logos* = study of humans) was born out of this curiosity about our origins, our diversity, and how our humans developed over time. Early anthropologists focused on the concept of culture, the learned patterns of behavior passed on from generation to generation. They adopted a comparative method, tried to record and preserve Native American languages, and advocated against slavery and for human rights.

By 1902, the American Anthropological Association was founded. As a result, anthropology took the broadest approach to what it means to be human in all times and places of all the social sciences, incorporating both empirical evidence and humanistic interpretation. Most anthropologists work in teams with other scientists from geology, sociology, dentistry, and many other disciplines. Insight and expertise from these scientists from other fields adds to the richness of anthropological interpretation and ensures a more complete understanding of our species and all our cultural iterations.

American anthropology developed four integrated fields, which can be thought of in a memory device as bones (biological anthropology, stones (archaeology), phones (linguistic anthropology), and drones (cultural anthropology). A fifth field, applied anthropology, uses the insights and methods of the subfields to solve practical problems, and is now the fastest growing area of anthropology in the U.S.

This holistic approach especially equips anthropologists to study globalization, the worldwide interconnectedness of natural resources, trade, human labor, capital, information and disease. In the last century the pace of this interconnection increased and is now greatly aided by the internet and global news operations and scientific cooperation. You are witness to this exponential change in human culture. Just think of the South American fruit you eat, how your clothes may be made in factories in Indonesia, and how your cars are made in Asia. Americans are also more globally aware as we enter new eras of sociopolitical complexity involving views on trade, immigrants, and structural violence, e.g., genocide.

BONES: BIOLOGICAL ANTHROPOLOGY

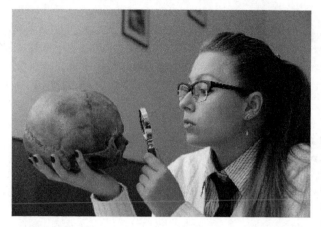

Biological anthropology includes five major areas of study. Paleoanthropologists find and analyze fossils and artifacts to reconstruct human evolution and prehistory. They are detectives who piece together evidence from skeletons and culture that is preserved in the rock layers of the earth. Paleoanthropologists make major fossil discoveries that change our view of human evolution and are heavily reported in the news media. Primatologists study the ecology, anatomy, and behavior of our closest biological relatives, monkey and apes, and consider the complexity of their social interactions and alliances and also whether they have culture.

Other biological anthropologists specialize in human growth and development and adaptation to the environment. Molecular geneticists study DNA, genes, and heredity and seek to understand the mechanisms of species change and how populations adapt over time. Comparisons of gene frequencies or types of specific genes can be used to trace ancestry not only for living populations, but also to reconstruct major population movements thousands of years ago. A recent discovery in this field is that many contemporary humans of European ancestry still carry Neanderthal genes, and those from the South Pacific carry Denisovan genes, a form of human not even known until a few years ago.

Many applied biological anthropologists specialize in forensics, the application of biological information in legal settings. They help law enforcement locate and identify bodies and investigate human rights abuses from racism, ethnic hatred, terrorism, war, and other forms of violence. They use statistical data about the traits of global populations, rate of decay, soil conditions, and other factors that might affect death issues and their techniques have been popularized in televisions shows such as the *CSI* series. For example, if an asteroid hit an island, biological anthropologists might excavate for prehistoric fossils, help identify the human remains, and monitor the health of the remaining people for any after-effects.

STONES: ARCHAEOLOGY

Archaeology studies the environment and material remains of human cultures for clues for reconstructing societies and understanding how cultures change. Archaeologists are interested in patterns of tool use, migration patterns, and how cultures adapt to changing circumstances. Archaeologists also engage in cultural resource management, helping to preserve the country's historic and prehistoric sites. Finding charred animal bones, pottery fragments, food preparation tools, and remains of a hearth on Sapelo Island, Georgia not only shows that our ancestors were cooking, it sheds light on the conditions of enslaved individuals from Africa. Applied archaeologists also help indigenous peoples reconstruct their past or establish old boundaries or treaties. Archaeology mysteries include Stonehenge, first domestication of plants and animals, and what happened to the colonist Roanoke colony of Virginia. If asteroid hit Sapelo Island, archaeologists would collect artifacts to preserve knowledge about the Island culture and help manage cultural resources as the Island was rebuilt.

PHONES: LINGUISTIC ANTHROPOLOGY

'Phones' refer to both the mobile devices we use to text with and connect with others as well as the linguistic technical term for the smallest units of sound in a language. Linguistic anthropologists describe the elements of language such as grammar, and study language families, writing, media, and texting and internet. A great mystery in linguistic anthropology is the very origin and evolution of language.

Linguistic anthropologists focus on how language relates to culture and society. While thought itself may be nonverbal, cultures certainly shape how we think about reality. By the same token, the terms we use for things reflects how we feel about them. Applied linguistic anthropologists are often involved in helping indigenous peoples document their language or develop written representations. This has even led to language revival where Native children become bi-cultural and learn the language and ways of their heritage as well as ways to communicate with the dominant society. In our asteroid and island example, linguistic anthropologists would collect the words and grammar of any languages, record oral stories and folktales, and look at how media communication worked post-disaster.

DRONES: CULTURAL ANTHROPOLOGY

About half of all anthropologists study contemporary human cultures and societies for patterns of human organization, behavior, beliefs, and technology. Culture is defined as a society's shared and socially transmitted ideas, values, behaviors, and perceptions. Just like genes determine biological characteristics, cultural memes serve as units of ideas or behavior that are passed down socially.

An example is the recent introduction of drones into our lives. Drones have three meanings which span the three levels of culture. Infra-structure refers to production, reproduction, and other life and death issues. Drones used by the military are programmed to kill targets during conflicts. The structure of a culture refers to the institutions of a society such as economy, education, and family. Drones have been used extensively by delivery services, and by construction, plumbers, and in real estate to inspect or reveal remote areas.

Finally, the super-structure refers to the symbolic area of society, including language, religion, arts, and entertainment. Now governments are seeking to restrict drones and where they are flown, which creates new laws and ordinances and affects our police, laws, and courts. This snowball effect from the invention of a new technology all through various parts of a society shows that culture is an integrated whole—most parts affect each other and a change in one has an impact on other areas. Cultural anthropologists would be key in our asteroid disaster example. They would study how the society worked, whether it was stratified into different groups, and how to best deliver health care to the survivors based on their belief system. They would also work on natural resources and restoring trade and the economy.

ANTHROPOLOGY CRITICAL THINKING

There are a number of skills to acquire from anthropology whether or not it becomes your career. Anthropologists develop social intelligence, great observational skills, problem-solving methods, and an appreciation for culture and diversity. They understand beliefs, behaviors, and subtle differences among cultural traditions which makes them good managers serving diverse populations. This broad perspective allows you to think in unconventional and creative ways about novel solutions in problem solving. Teamwork and ideas about social justice and the meaning of human activities are also important. Government, nonprofits and businesses of all kinds seek people with anthropology training out.

But because anthropology takes us beyond the ideas of our own culture it is also revolutionary because it challenges our culture by pointing out its convenient social fictions and inequalities. Interestingly, comedy also does this by making us aware of an absurd aspect of living or inconsistency in our cultural values. An example is Australian comedian Jim Jeffries observations on gun control in the U.S. versus Australia. He challenges the "reasons" Americans give to oppose the control most other developed nations have, e.g., "protecting" families with assault weapons or keeping guns unavailable in a safe! Exposing how culture essentially "makes it up," limits your choices, and even misrepresents or misleads can be extremely revealing and insightful.

We have come to rely on our culture to give us absolute categories of thinking as well as values and an intelligible picture of the world. To discover the very different choices of other cultures, that some have more than two genders, that great even apes have culture, and that human origins are in Africa, is startling to some but also an adventure in expanding horizons beyond what your particular culture may tell you. For example, learning that gender is culturally constructed and not inherent in our physical being, can liberate us to be who we are because we are "born this way." Besides, there are many more puzzles and mysteries of the human journey yet to be discovered and solved, and its only a very broad understanding of our species that will get us there.

BECOMING A TYPE 1 CIVILIZATION

An anthropological perspective can also help with the challenges we face in the future. According to the Kardashev Scale, we are currently a Type 0 civilization with use of fossil and even nuclear fuels by a collection of nation states. Now, we need to solve our social, political, and environmental problems to move toward becoming a Type 1 civilization with sustainability and harmonious use of earth's resources.

Our cities of the future will have to develop roof gardens and recyclable resources. Sustainability will have to become not just a nice idea, but a reality. The alternative is not pretty—extinction, especially if war, global health epidemics, poverty, population size, or other issues are not solved. After all, 99% of all life forms on earth have gone extinct—we want to be different and have better stewardship of the earth.

Anthropologists are documenting how our species went from common origins with great apes, to standing upright and using stone tools, to the development of fire and shelter, to the domestication of plants and animals, to creation of civilization, and now planting rovers on Mars and eventual exploration of the universe. Understanding this human journey will play a key role in figuring out how to survive.

But there is little question that our species will continue to explore and ask questions about our origins and diversity, as well as our future because we have done so in the past. Perhaps the ultimate mystery of the human journey will be how we shape our species as we terraform the moon and Mars, on our way to a journey to the stars.

MYSTERY: ZOMBIES!

You can't be aware of popular culture, participate in Halloween, or explore books, television, games, films, or the internet and not be aware of zombies. Are there such things as the "undead"? Where did the fascination with zombies and the zombie apocalypse come from?

Anthropologists recognize that this phenomenon has roots in at least four culture areas: Europe, Africa, Caribbean, and North America. The notion of zombies stems from a mix of many cultural factors: colonial oppression, folklore and religious belief, fear of the unknown, social and economic stress, corporate exploitation, alienating modern lifestyles—and the fun and drama of acting out against easy targets! It is a good example to illustrate the breath of anthropology's focus in time and across cultural boundaries, in order to better understand our species, how we have adapted to cultural and environmental changes, the problems we need to solve as a global society, and where we might be headed.

HAITI

The story starts in Haiti, "land of high mountains," a vibrant nation on the western side of the island of Hispaniola in the Caribbean. Haiti has a rich cultural tradition that is a blend of African, Native, and European cultures because of colonialism that began in the 16ᵗʰ century. Although 80% of the island is Catholic, it is common for cultures to create syncretic religion in which orthodox or imposed religious beliefs and rituals are blended with earlier indigenous traditions. In Haiti, this blend of global cultures due became the Vodou (or voodoo) tradition.

Haiti was the home of the indigenous Taino people who lived throughout the Caribbean and Florida and who probably migrated from northern South America and Mesoamerica. We have several words in English that come from the Taino, e.g., barbacoa "barbeque," kanoa "canoe," and juracan "hurricane." The Taino were matrilineal and engaged in fishing and harvesting cassava (yucca) roots. Their religion focused on spirit ancestors related to the moon, waters, fertility, and crops. One myth described how people once lived in caves and only came out at night, and another was that the souls of the dead would go to the underworld to rest by day, and roam the forests at night.

When Columbus arrived in 1492, he found five Taino chiefdoms on Hispaniola. The chiefs were advised by bohiques, shaman priests who could speak with spirit beings and were consulted at important events. Columbus' crew and subsequent expeditions commonly demanded tribute from the Taino and cut off their hands if they failed to comply. They raped Taino women which produced mixed race mestizo children and eroded the status of women and traditional Taino folkways. In addition, smallpox and other infections killed an estimated 90% of the Native Americans in the area.

The French ruled the area for the next two centuries and developed sugarcane plantations by importing thousands of slaves from Africa, one-third of whom died within a few years from disease and horrible treatment. Vodou developed when the French Catholic colonial power tried to suppress the languages and beliefs of West African slaves and forced them to convert to Christianity. The "conversions" resulted in a combination of the Taino and African cultural beliefs with the official Catholic overlay.

The West African traditions from the Dahomey, Yoruba, and Kongo cultures held that Loa are spirits who serve a monotheistic creator "Bondye." The Loa are helpers who are designed to bring humans back to God. Some, such as the Petro are very warlike while others such as Rada are old and wise family helpers. Through dance, song, prayers, and trances, believers can commune with the divine through invoking the Loa. The spirits might even use a "coco macaque" which is a stick that can walk on its own and even be sent on errands to attack an enemy who will die before dawn as a result. Priests called gangan and priestesses called mambo would lead processions in dancing and drumming to invoke these spirits, many of whom are associated with fertility or death. In Vodou, the spirits of the dead exist alongside the living and all of nature, e.g., rocks, trees, and streams all possess spirits. Some spirits are powerful and fit Catholic beliefs about the ability of saints, angels, and the Madonna to intercede between a believer and the Creator.

Amy Wilentz has argued that the zombie myth has its roots in this deep religious tradition under French colonial rule. She reasons that zombies were a reaction to the misery of slave life, and individuals may have projected their hope to be released from their lives by dying into a kind of afterlife in which they would be free to roam at will. A slave was a human spirit trapped inside a functionally dead body—a zombie. Even after slavery ended the folklore continued to circulate and practitioners, called bokor, could bewitch corpses into becoming undead and carry out their evil tasks.

ZOMBIES IN NORTH AMERICA

In the 19th century, western writers became aware of this Haitian syncretic religion and incorporated the idea that a corpse could be reanimated as an undead person. In 1932, a film *White Zombie* starred horror actor Bela Lugosi and presented zombies as undead Haitian slaves. In additional films, zombies morphed to become mindless operatives under the control of evil magicians. By the 1968 film, *Night of the Living Dead*, zombies had become hungry human flesh eaters, specializing in brains!

As fears about war, immigrants, nuclear power, and social conflict increased, zombies were conceived of as ushering in the "zombie apocalypse" in a further blend of Caribbean, African, and Euromerican Christian concepts of the end of the world. For example, in Michael Jackson's music video, *Thriller*, a global rise of hostile zombie attacks civilization, causes chaos, and turns their victims into zombies as society panics. Zombie fans now actually prepare for the apocalypse, create special weapons, and sell books and pamphlets showing how to survive an outbreak.

Neuroscientists have put forth serious scientific articles about the anatomy and functions of zombie brains. The Centers for Disease Control even used the zombie myth to create emergency-preparedness graphic novel, called *Preparedness 101: Zombie Apocalypse* as a fun way to inform the public! Merchandise, including masks, clothing, and zombie weapons have flooded the popular culture market, and a popular television series gained a massive audience. The *New York Times* reported in 2010 that one of the highest viewing audiences watched the first episode of "The Walking Dead" on AMC, stating that interest in zombies has steadily risen over the last 40 years.

This is an interesting cultural development since contemporary film zombies can't talk or think and just eat flesh. Writer Chuck Klosterman explains that is because zombies personify our fears and are actually easy to kill. In fact, monsters may function to project people's fears onto "the other." It might be a Navajo witch, the immigrants on the other side of town, Jews, or, you know, "THOSE people!" He points out that the stories of Frankenstein began as science was growing exponentially; Godzilla emerged from the atomic age after the hydrogen bomb was dropped on Japan; and werewolves symbolize the West's growing detachment from nature. Perhaps zombies today represent our fears about global pandemics or invasion?

Kosterman speculates that the current fascination with zombies may actually be more about how we feel about modern life—maybe we are the "walking dead" in an increasingly alienating world. He says, "a lot of modern life is exactly like slaughtering zombies," by dealing with 400 mindless emails a day, having to get through hours of rush hour traffic, or working through a computerized phone call! Just like endless rows of zombies approach us, we have to deal with daily life zombies of sorts. What allows this characterization is that zombies aren't like vampires in literature who have personalities ranging from boring, to vicious, to the erotic. Zombies are not really individuals, they are communal and archetypal. "The zombie you kill today will merely be replaced by the zombies of tomorrow."

In summary, anthropological analysis shows that the zombie craze began as real ethnic beliefs about the undead and possible altered state individuals in trance who were believed to be dead but who weren't. The myth was a way to cope with the abuses of slavery and colonialism and survive which was elaborated in folk stories and religious rituals and finally adopted by another culture looking for the monster of the decade. This ability to consider both biological and cultural aspects of the human experience, in all times and places, is the hallmark of anthropology and the key to its unique ability to address human problems today.

CRITICAL THINKING & WEBSITES

1. Describe why the subfields of anthropology require a broad perspective. Which subfield interests you?

2. How do most people combine both their scientific and belief systems to accept human evolution?

3. Discuss how the bubonic plague was horrific—but also led to productive change in the social order.

4. Historian Bart Ehrman, author of *Misquoting Jesus*, describes his development from fundamentalist to agnostic studying early Church history and the issue of suffering:
https://www.youtube.com/watch?v=4zymRzAzWnc&list=PLH6y1qJWoZZ8kfafz3OXhQ2hhe6PCFKNd&index=62.

5. Check out Australian comic, Jim Jeffries, perspective on gun control:
https://www.youtube.com/watch?v=0rR9IaXH1M0.

6. Pick a zombie film or game and analyze the attitudes and values reflected in them.

REFERENCES

Anonymous, & George, Andrew. (2003). *The Epic of Gilgamesh*. New York: Penguin Classics Reissue Edition.

Darwin, Charles. (2009). *On the Origin of Species*. New York: Signet/Penguin.

Dayan, Colin. (1998). *Haiti, History, and the Gods*. Berkeley: University of California Press.

Evans, Craig. (2010). *Holman QuickSource Guide to the Dead Sea Scrolls*. Nashville, TN: Holman Reference, B&H Publishing Group.

Grant, E. (1996). *The Foundations of Modern Science in the Middle Ages: Their Religious, Institutional, and Intellectual Contexts*. Cambridge, England: Cambridge University Press.

Haviland, William, Prins, Harald, Walrath, Dana, & McBride, Bunny. (2014). *Anthropology: The Human Challenge, 14th edition*. Belmont, CA: Cengage.

Jurmain, Robert, Kilgore, Lynn, Trevathan, Wenda, & Ciochon, Russell. *Introduction to Physical Anthropology, 2013-2014 edition*. Belmont, CA: Cengage.

Kardashev, Nikolai. (1997). Cosmology and civilization. *Astrophysics and Space Science* 252:25.

Kelly, John. (2006). *The Great Mortality: An Intimate History of the Black Death, the Most Devastating Plague of All Time*. New York: Harper Perennial.

Klosterman, Chuck. (2010). My zombie, myself: Why modern life feels rather undead. *The New York Times*, December 3, 2010. Retrieved from
http://www.nytimes.com/2010/12/05/arts/television/05zombies.html?pagewanted=all&_r=0, December 1, 2016.

Kramer, A., Durband, A. C., Weinand, D. C. (2009). Teaching the "E" Word in Tennessee. *Reports for the National Center for Science Education*, 29(6):18-22, 27.

Larson, Edward. (2008). *Summer for the Gods: The Scopes Trial and America's Continuing Debate Over Science and Religion*. New York: Basic Books.

Lyras, G. A., Dermitzakis, M. D., Van Der Geer, A. A. E. , Van Der Geer, S. B., & De Vos, J. (2008). "The origin of *Homo floresiensis* and its relation to evolutionary processes under isolation. *Anthropological Science*.

Mariani, Mike. (2015). The tragic, forgotten history of zombies. The Atlantic, October 28, 2015. Retrieved from:
http://www.theatlantic.com/entertainment/archive/2015/10/how-america-erased-the-tragic-history-of-the-zombie/412264/, December 1, 2016.

Miller, Jon, Scott, Eugenie, & Okamoto, Shinji. (2006, August). Public acceptance of evolution. *Science* 313:765-766.

Noll, Mark. (1992). *A History of Christianity in the United States and Canada*. Grand Rapids, MI: Wm. B. Eerdmans Publishing Company.

Pagden, Anthony. (2013). *The Enlightenment: And Why It Still Matters*. New York: Random House.

For each of the subfields below, describe how applied anthropologists might investigate reports of zombies on an island who have been terrorizing the population.

Biological Anthropology

Archaeology

Cultural Anthropology

Linguistic Anthropology

2 METHODS:
Science and Pseudoscience

Have ancient aliens landed on earth? Did they help build the pyramids of Egypt or landing strips in Peru? Early anthropologists dealt with ideas that nonwestern peoples were not advanced enough to build mounds, temples, and great stone monuments. We did this by embracing ways of knowing based on reason, evidence, and systematic methods of investigation.

LEARNING OBJECTIVES

1. Understand the significance of the new way of knowing based on evidence and contrast it with belief and pseudoscience.

2. Describe how beliefs are our oldest way of knowing, and how myths explain our world, e.g., hero myths.

3. Describe the scientific method based on hypotheses and theories that must be testable, replicable and falsifiable. Explain why science should be open-minded and creative when evidence suggests a paradigm shift.

4. Define pseudoscience and its basis in extraordinary claims based on a combination of some science and a lot of belief.

5. Explain why science needs to be both skeptical and also possibilian.

6. Illustrate the methods of science through the analysis of Otzi Iceman as a Copper Age herdsman— who ran into some serious trouble on a glacier 5,000 years ago.

WAYS OF KNOWING

Epistemology refers to a "theory of knowledge," or how you know what you know. You partly know through your personal experience, but a big part of your understanding of the world comes from your family, your community, and your culture. In fact, your culture gives you the tools for distinguishing and labeling your world by literally constructing it with concepts. Anthropology is not saying that your world doesn't exist, but rather that culture shows you how to divide up the color spectrum, name the parts of a car, or otherwise label and distinguish your world. In short, culture makes it up!

For example, in the film *My Big Fat Greek Wedding*, a white middle class American family brought a bunt cake which has a hole in the middle to a Greek family celebration. The Greeks thought the hole was a mistake and politely filled it up with a potted plant. Likewise, when an anthropologist took a horticultural Yanomamo man from Venezeula to the airport, the man thought he would be 'eaten' by a bird (the plane), and then dove into the interior of the car through a window, not the door. Both are cultural misunderstandings based on the ideas given by culture.

There are at least three ways of knowing about the world of common human experience:
1. Myth, belief and speculation
2. Systematic investigation of concrete evidence using the scientific method
3. Pseudoscience—a combination of some evidence and a lot of belief

BELIEF

Beliefs are the oldest way of knowing about the world and interpreting human experience. They are the way you think something is true or actual, whether or not you can demonstrate or prove it. Beliefs may be well thought-out and studied, revealed from a spiritual source, or they may be just a hunch or guess. Either way, they stem from a combination of individual thoughts and emotion and the teachings and models of one's family and society. Beliefs both shape and reflect culture and give our experience meaning through our ideas. Belief also reflect your place in society, and give you identity.

A myth is a legendary story, usually about a major event or a hero, that reflects the beliefs and worldview of the culture that created it. For example, Thor is a Norse god who wields a hammer and causes thunder and lighting and is also a symbol of strenth and protection of humankind. Our word Thursday means "Thor's day." Thor has many parallels with other Indo-European deities, for example, Indra of Hinduism who also has red hair and thunderbolt weapons.

These gods, who are real to the believer, may be based on real figures who lived thousands of years ago whose stories have been imbued with the supernatural, or they may be purely expressive of the idea of strength and fear of storms. But the gods and heroes are deeply worshiped and also have a presence in modern popular culture. Just think of Luke Skywalker, Harry Potter, or Superman.

SCIENCE

SCIENTIFIC METHOD

The scientific method which has its origins in the 17th century Age of Enlightenment consists of observations and techniques of step by step systematic analysis of evidence. Tentative conclusions are reported to other scientists who debate and provide alternative explanations. Eventually, most reach a consensus until a new discovery is made to cause a paradigm shift—a major change or new theory. Science is open-minded. Unlike belief which can present answers that are never challenged, the very foundation of science is to be open to questioning assumptions, evidence, and conclusions, and to create new knowledge.

Scientists start with something that gets their attention: maybe a new fossil discovery, an inconsistency in experimental results, or big questions such as whether monogamy is universal, or who build the Stonehenge. Next, science develops hypotheses which are good guesses to explain the phenomenon, for example, the idea that a large brain was the first human trait to evolve (one that proved to be incorrect).

Table 2.1. Hypotheses and Theory

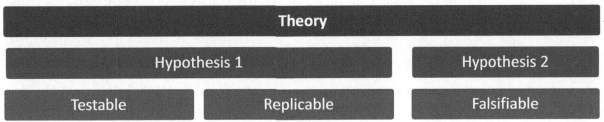

Science then attempts to test out an hypothesis and gather some concrete tangible evidence. Some natural sciences can do this experimentally, but astronomy and the social sciences also rely on quantitative and qualitative structured observations because you can't manipulate the variables of a whole society or the sky as you can a test tube. It is critical that an hypothesis be falsifiable. Consider an hypothesis that world leaders are being controlled by a mother space ship on the other side of the moon. How would you test this? You could travel to the moon to see if you can see the ship or detect its presence, but a space ship believer would say it is invisible to skeptics, or shielded from detection, or from another dimension, etc. These supernatural explanations might be true, but they are not testable.

The results then need to be interpreted and carefully evaluated. Were all factors considered? Are there any special circumstances that affected results? Were there any correlations with other observed phenomena? Any inconsistencies? Here is where scientists compare and contrast ideas. Other scientists attempt to replicate the experiment or observation results. Sometimes it is possible to have a second team study the exact same behavior or material. In other cases, the results are compare with other sites or cultures. For example, if a big megalithic stone structure in Peru is alligned with the summer solstice, is that true for structures in other parts of the world? If one monkey leaps from branch to branch in a certain way, do other closely related species do the same?

As more evidence is accumulated and new hypotheses are developed they begin to coalesce around a broader idea that incorporates all of them, called a theory. A theory is a widely confirmed body of knowledge that must be tested further. Sometimes new evidence just expands and improves existing theory. When scientists proceed step by step building up evidence to a theory—it's called induction. When you start with the theory and test it out on new evidence—it's deduction.

Scientists follow what's called Occam's Razor, a rule that you favor the simplest, least complicated non-supernatural explanation. For example, Thor may be sending down thunderbolts, but tangible evidence shows that electrical charges in the atmosphere are causing lightning and its product is thunder. Most theories are well confirmed before they are widely accepted.

But, when new evidence, perhaps from a different perspective, challenges a theory, a "paradigm shift," occurs. For example, with Einstein's theory and evidence we moved from a Newtonian to a quantum perspective in physics. Anthropology has undergone a number of such shifts with different dominant theories as we learn more about our biology and culture. This change frustrates some observers but it's really useful, as we get closer and closer to understanding the world.

CULTURE AFFECTS SCIENCE

Science has some inherent epistomological perspectives. Science has belief and philosophical foundations through the assumptions that the universe is knowable through human reason and that the world exhibits natural patterns or regularities such as gravity. Further, some latest scientific thinking is on the edge of philosophy, e.g., the evidence that order might itself be an emergent property of chaos. If the universe were totally random and eternally chaotic, and human reason could not understand it, hypotheses and theories would be inconsistent and useless. So, science has some belief foundations.

But, in addition to these inherent methodological issues, there are cultural factors that affect science as well. Scientists are people raised in a culture themselves with other beliefs and ways of knowing around them that can have a likely effect. Scientists are also ambitious and competitive as they struggle for research funds or promote their ideas. Schools of thought develop in science and powerful lineages of important researchers who train a large number of students will have disproportiate influence and may be reluctant to hear the views of smaller research operations or catch onto a new idea by a less well known individual.

In trying to understand and describe the world, scientists also become storytellers. Misia Landau (1993) addressed this issue in her controversial book on myth in biological anthropology, *Narratives of Human Evolution*. Landau adapted Campbell's hero myth schema and applied it to the scenarios constructed by paleoanthropologists about human origins: the hero who first stood upright or had a larger brain, or developed fire or monogamy.

Donna Haraway (1990) gave a similar critique in her book, *Primate Visions: Gender, Race and Nature in the World of Science*. She pointed out a western male bias in anthropological theories of human evolution and culture. For example, a Gulf Oil advertisement for chimpanzee research stated that Jane Goodall was "all alone" in the jungle, when she was actually in camp with African rangers, cooks, and research assistants, as well as her mother and son. Primatologist Shirley Strum also reported gender bias when she tried to show the role of male social dominance among baboons she studied and few listened. Twenty-five years later a male paleoanthropologist, Ian Tattersall, made the same point in tracing the cultural influences in models of human origins, and was praised. Science, like culture, changes slowly over time and what was once unaccepted or distrusted can later become the new "received knowledge."

An amusing example of science bias comes from the 19th century classic archaeology exploration of the Minoan society of Crete. Early scholars were fascinated with the romance of treasure and exotic religions and came across amazing crescent moon symbols in a temple structure. They speculated and argued about ancient religions, moon rituals, cults, and sacrifices, but it turned out they were toilet seats!

Today, archaeologists study less the lofty and more the mundane. In fact, they spend most of their time sifting through other people's garbage. That evidence actually gives us our best clues about subsistence and how people lived in the past—often people such as women, children, slaves, and the poor, whom history ignores.

On rare occasions, even science goes beyond interpretive storytelling to out and out fraud. A recent example is Marc Hauser, a former Harvard professor, who was found responsible for misreporting the behavior of monkeys he was studying, drawing conclusions not based on the evidence, and then attempting a coverup. Such examples are relatively rare, and with peer review and other scientists replicating studies, the truth eventually comes out. Although imperfect and affected by cultural context and ambition, science is still a powerful tool using human senses to give us a way of looking at the world through reason.

CREATIVITY AND IMAGINATION

But, scientists need to be a little crazy, too! Great scientists are also cultural creatives and artists with a vision and sense of awe and wonder at discovery. Nikola Tesla, a brilliant 20th century engineer and futurist, was such a scientist who now has cult status because he essentially inspired the 20th century by creating alternating current and other major discoveries. He was inaccurate on some things and used showmanship to attract attention and push the envelope to advanced science but he changed how we all live and think.

Steve Jobs, a computer visionary, was similarly creative. He enraged and infuriated his friends, co-workers, and rivals. He made the creative element in science and technology explicit when he praised "the crazy ones" stating that you need to dare to be different, even odd, and be tenacious in reaching your goals. Unlike Tesla, Jobs didn't directly invent a great deal but he had an uncanny way of imagining what we would want in the future and creating a tool we didn't know we needed.

Creativity is especially important in anthropology. In the early 1900s, Margaret Mead's studied societies in the South Pacific and challenged middle class American notions about sexuality and family life. One society encouraged teens to experiment sexually so they would become skillful marriage partners and another had gender role reversal with males being emotional and domestic and females being rational breadwinners. It was eye-opening and courageous, even if some of the details were challenged and corrected later. As new theories are developed, anthropological evidence may go against the grain.

21

PSEUDOSCIENCE

A third way of knowing about the world is pseudoscience, a combination of belief, a little evidence, and great imagination. You may be familiar with pseudoscience through several television programs and internet sites about "ancient alien theorists" and those who are "finding bigfoot." Pseudoscience (meaning "false science") starts out well enough, often with a tidbit of real evidence about a temple, odd artifact, drawings, or video or oral reports of observed puzzling phemonena. But, it derails quickly with drawing inappropriate conclusions, making fantastic claims for which there is no evidence, making connections with unrelated assumptions or ideas, or other wrong turn (see Table 2.2). Pseudoscience advocates say "this may…" or "ancient theorists believe…" but often avoid making direct claims that cannot be substantiated.

For example, science relies in credible sources and trained observers while pseudoscience tends to be less critical and discriminating in sorting out reports. For example, at one Bigfoot Conference in the state of Georgia, a legitimate researcher tried to present carefully recorded sonograms of alleged Bigfoot calls (which were inconclusive but at least systematically collected) while another participant said she meets regularly under a tree in the woods with ten-foot tall "Bubbah" and "Little Bit" who leave twig signs for her which she interprets. True believers often see skepticism and criticism as negative and hostile whereas that is part of the process of science. Finally, many pseudoscience explanations are odd and radical and do not fit with existing knowledge about the world.

Table 2.2. A comparison of science and pseudoscience.

SCIENCE	PSEUDOSCIENCE
Credible sources	Questionable or biased sources
Trained experts with credentials	Amateurs and true believers
Systematic accumulation of evidence	Highly selective and biased evidence
Change with new evidence	Fixed ideas and speculations
Extensive peer review	Little peer review; review by true believers
Invites criticism	Sees criticism as conspiracy
Verifiable, replicable, falsifiable, testable	Non-repeatable or falsifiable results
Conservative parsimonious claims	Exaggerations & "may be" explanations
Consistent worldview	Highly unusual disjointed explanations
Precise measurements	Ball-park measurements
Explanations based on natural causes	Resort to supernatural causes
Explanations fit with existing theory	Radical explanations & other odd claims
New theories explain more not less	Repetition of similar ideas
Independent belief systems	Supplements existing belief systems

Pseudoscience can be inductive and begin with a strange discovery or anomaly such as a hugh megalithic structure, inscriptions on a stone, or bizzare lights in the sky. But, rather than testing hypotheses, extensive investigation, and peer review, pseudoscience moves too quickly to speculations or the supernatural before simpler explanations are exhausted. Pseudoscience too often presumes that nonwestern peoples were too "primitive" or unintelligent to have created the achivement. For example, in the 1800s, Euro-Americans assumed Native Americans could not have made the large earthen mounds of southeast America. So lost tribes, ancient civilizations, Egyptians, Mayans, and others were given credit rather than the ancestors of local tribes.

Deductive pseudoscience starts with a school of thought based on myth or belief, e.g., astrology, numerology, or turning other metals or materials into gold. Even some scientists such as Issac Newton, were caught up in the effort to create gold out of nothing showing that some pseudoscience lives just at the boundaries of great science. Astrology is a good example. There are really movements of the sun, moon, constellations, etc. and there are gravitational and magnetic effects these bodies have on each other and earth's living organisms. But, there is a leap of faith to interpret positions of stars calculated thousands of years ago and relate it to a birthdate to predict who you will marry. Could heavenly bodies have some mysteries yet unknown affect on species? Yes, they could—but we need evidence.

Although ancient pseudoscience has a deep history, most people today are most familiar with the extreme claims of Erich von Däniken who wrote, *Chariot of the Gods* (1968). As teenagers, they were fascinated with wild claims of extraterrestrials repeatedly visiting the earth and interacting or guiding different societies. Däniken's book explained away wonders of the world and ancient temples with the same idea—that others from outer space had brought esoteric knowledge and architectural skills to earth.

But, few readers realized that this was written and revised while serving several terms in prison for forgery and financial crimes. Although certainly a productive use of his time, the book explained monuments and historic sites because he couldn't believe ancient cultures could have done this on their own. His writings are riddled with errors, speculation, false claims, and failure to credit and cite other authors, as is the practice in science. Georgio Tsukalos, von Däniken's protégée, also appears on ancient civilization and astronaut programs. He sports a tribal necklace, has waves of wild hair as if he is being electrified, and speaks dramatically and excitedly of exotic discoveries. A caption on one of his internet memes is "I didn't hear your question but the answer is aliens!" That is the enchantment of pseudoscience.

However, despite flaws, fraud, and false claims without evidence, Däniken and his followers did succeed in popularizing prehistory for the general public. Pseudoscience is now big business through books, conferences, and festivals. The grain of science appeals to our rationality and desire to understand our world and the speculation appeals to our emotions and imagination. It leads to intoxicated enthusiasm and childlike wonder of what could be, not necessarily what actually is. Pseudoscience becomes even more appealing when evidence is incomplete, withheld, confusing, or accidents occur. Conspiracy theories can ignite to fill the vacuum of real knowledge. For example, at a 1992 CONTACT conference about evaluating possible ET messages, a simple computer glitch led to immediate conspiracy theories that the U.S. was withholding information from the world. It's exciting but often incorrect.

POSSIBILIANISM

One inventive neuroscientist, David Eagleman, coined the term "possibilian" to refer to how scientists can be skeptical, but also keep an open mind regarding spectacular claims and ultimate causes of the universe that have not or cannot yet be tested by science. That might mean exploring an outlying hypothesis believed to be crazy or opposed to existing ideas, or working with eager amateurs who seek scientific input. It might even mean participating in documentaries shown on television, giving talks at local organizations, or giving TED Talks on you.tube, in the interest of promoting science to the general public.

Eagleman emphasized the need to consider new possibilities and to think outside the box whether the issue is the workings of our brain or the role of fire in cultural learning in our ancestors. This extreme degree of openness can be unpopular in some scientific circles. One envious scientist groused that famous astronomer Carl Sagan hadn't looked through a telescope in years, another complained that Jane Goodall gave the chimps she studied too many bananas, and primatologist Francine Patterson was criticized for over-interpreting the gestural signs her gorilla Koko was learning. But if these scientists had not considered new ideas and had not worked hard to present knowledge to school children and the general public, where would the next generation of scientists come from?

Other legitimate scientists with open minds use critical thinking to study extraordinary topics. Jeffrey Meldrum studies human anatomy and created the Relict Hominoid Inquiry, a scientific attempt to assess Sasquatch claims. Geneticist Brian Sykes has offered to test Bigfoot hair samples (only negative results so far). Smithsonian Institution scientists openly explored peopling of the New World from Europe rather than the Bering Land Bridge. Forensic scientist Clyde Snow attempted to find the outlaws Butch Cassidy and the Sundance Kid, and astronomer Seth Shostak searches for ET through the SETI project.

But, these researchers use careful methods within science and play devil's advocate with any and all hypotheses. They remain skeptical—but open and excited about cutting edge investigations into the unknown. In contrast, when pseudoscience goes against mainstream explanations that are widely accepted in science and connects with wider belief systems about extraordinary things it can fail to be skeptical and take on more of a true believer attitude. For example, the ancient Anazazi of the Southwest carved concentric circles in mesa walls and boulders.

Most archaeologists interpret these as sun watching stations, where Native Americans monitored the position of the sun on the horizon, marking the summer and winter solstice. However, some pseudoscientists sidestep overwhelming evidence for sun watching behaviors and locations and go immediately to interpret the circles as a representation of a spiral galaxy in space, speculating that ancient astronauts must have visited and informed native groups. That's a big speculative jump that shows imagination and is a *possibility*, but lacks evidence—and even a means to test the evidence. So the key seems to be to think imaginatively, not mock unpopular ideas, but remain a skeptical possibilian.

MYSTERY: OTZI ICEMAN

One of the ways to illustrate the scientific process is to examine an anthropological case study in greater detail. A fascinating example is the mummy of Otzi Iceman a prehistoric man found by accident in the mountains of Europe. Hikers discovered Otzi Iceman in 1991 while traveling in the Swiss-Italian Alps. He was found face down with his upper skeleton reaching out from the glacier. He was a frozen mummy who ended up in a crevasse so his body was perfectly preserved rather than being crushed by glacier movements. He had remained there for 5,000 years—who was he and how did he die?

Interdisciplinary teams of scientists over the next several decades investigated Otzi with the latest technologies and pieced together information about him like a CSI forensic case. They determined that he was a late Neolithic/early Copper Age man from 3350-3300 B.C.E. who could provide tantalizing clues about our ancestors' evolution, behavior, and social conflicts.

The remarkable level of preservation allowed them to examine his blood, clothing, tools, diet, and even his shoes. The Iceman stood about 158 cm (5'2") tall, and weighed about 134 lbs. He was rather short compared to most European males of the time, but sturdily built. He was in his mid-40s, and had strong leg muscles and good overall fitness, living in the Tyrolean Alps. He died about 5,200 years ago.

His health was fair for the period--he had arthritis in his joints and whipworm, a painful intestinal parasite. Otzi had several tattoos on his body, located near modern Chinese acupuncture points. These included a cross on the inside of his left knee; six parallel straight lines arranged in two rows on his back above his kidneys, each about 6 inches long; and several parallel lines on his ankles.

The Iceman carried a range of tools, weapons, and containers. An animal skin quiver contained arrow-shafts made of viburnum and hazel wood, sinews and spare points. A copper ax head with a yew haft and leather binding, a small flint knife and a pouch with a flint scraper and awl were all included in the artifacts found with him. He carried a yew bow, and there was evidence he spent a lot of time around animals. Otzi's clothing included a belt, loincloth, and goat-skin leggings with suspenders, not unlike lederhosen. He wore a bear-skin cap, outer cape and coat made of woven grass and moccasin-type shoes made from deer and bear leather. He stuffed those shoes with moss and grasses, no doubt for insulation and comfort. Most mysteriously, his penis was missing—was this at his death or a contemporary souvenir?

Table 2.3 summarizes the evidence to date that can be used to reconstruct the "story" of Otzi. For example, a recent forensic reconstruction of Otzi shows him as a middle aged man more accurately. Continuing research by teams of interdisciplinary scientists will add to Otzi's story.

Table 2.3 Otzi Iceman's Discovery, Body, Clothing and Tools

ITEM	EVIDENCE	CRITICAL THINKING
	Discovery & Location	
Discovery	1991, Italian-Swiss Alps near Austria	Who "owns" Otzi?
Dating	C14 dating showed 5,200 years old	What is his birth and death date?
Condition	Dried and ice-preserved glacier mummy, complete body, clothing, tools, but with genitals missing	Why missing genitals? How was the body preserved?
Location	Mountain slope near a valley; Body showed mountain pollen and dust and fresh valley pollen and dust	What brought him to the mountain slope? Did he live in a village? What season?
Artifact	Several large stacked stones near his body	A natural formation or grave marker?
	Body & Skeleton	
Size	5'5", 110 lbs.	Was he "average" for his community?
Age/Sex	Skull & pubic closures=45 years old; Male jaw and pelvis shape	Middle aged or old in the Copper Age?
Pelvis & tibia	X-rays show extensive wear on joints consistent with extensive bipedal locomotion & labor	Where was he going? Was it habitual?
Hair	Copper and arsenic found in his hair	Was Otzi a Copper Age smelter?
Skin	Geometric lines & 57 tattoos near acupuncture points on lumbar spine, behind R knee & R & L ankles	What was the significance of the tattoos? Did Otzi have health issues or diseases for which he was treated?
Nails	Beau's lines on fingernails indicating 3 illnesses	Was he repeatedly sick or dying?
Stomach	Contents were chamois, ibex & red deer meat, berries, wheat, herbs; Parasites: whipworm	What was his last meal?
Teeth	Cavities; minerals show birth near Brixen, Italy; adult life in valleys	High grain carb diet? Twig toothbrushes?
Lungs	Blackened with soot marks	Campfires? His occupation?
Genetic	DNA indicates rare Haplogroup K, found among Ashkenazi Jews in France, Austria and Middle East; Lactose-intolerant	Was he recently descended from farmers who migrated from the Middle East?
	Artifacts & Clothing	
Tools	99.7% pure Copper axe hafted on a long handle; Flint knife & leather sheath 13cm; Fire-making flint and moss kit, other flint points, needles, punches, 2 birch bark baskets, 2 medicinal mushrooms, etc.	What was the quality and complexity of Otzi's toolkit? What was Otzi's occupation? Was copper axe used? Made alone? Status symbol?
Weapons	Longbow, quiver + 14 arrows	Did they show any wear, usage, or repair?
Clothing	Woven grass cloak, leather vest, leather belt, leggings, loincloth, brown bear hat	How complicated was the weaving pattern or sewing—sophisticated clothes?
Shoes	Waterproof bearskin/deer hide snowshoes stuffed with birch grass; Shoes were mounted on a wooden frame with cross-hatch sinews making squares	Were the shoes simple or specially made by a cobbler craft specialist? Did the birch grass provide any medicinal purpose or just comfort?
	Cause of Death	
Blood	Otzi blood; Blood from 1 person on knife; Blood from 2 persons on arrow; Blood from 4th person on coat	Murdered? Buried? Chased? Did Otzi kill or injure anyone else?
Injury	Arrow found in Otzi's back; shaft removed *after* death; Bruises & cuts on hands, wrists, chest; Cerebral blow to the head	Who shot the arrow? Did it kill Otzi? Was there a struggle?
Death	Dried blood clot indicating lived a bit after injury	Did not die immediately?

CRITICAL THINKING & WEBSITES

1. Have you or anyone you know changed your beliefs based on new ones, evidence, or both?
2. Can you think of any positive aspects to pseudoscience?
3. Describe the steps of the scientific method. Why must it be testable?
4. Contrast how science and pseudoscience would investigate an unusual possibility, e.g., spaghetti found on Mars.
5. Explore Erich van Däniken's claims about extra-terrestrials or check out redditt.com for "I am Giorgio Tsoukalos" of History Channel Ancient Aliens fame and compare it with skepticalinquirer.com.
6. Check out the Baloney Detection Kit on you.tube to review the contrast between science and pseudoscience.

REFERENCES

Bradley, Bruce & Stanford, Dennis. (2004). The North Atlantic ice-edge corridor: A possible Paleolithic route to the New World. *World Archaeology* 36 (4): 459-478.

Carlson, W. Bernard. (20130. *Tesla: Inventor of the Electrical Age*. Princeton, NJ: Princeton Univ. Press.

Chagnon, Napoleon. (1968). *Yanomamo: The Fierce People*. Belmont, CA: Wadsworth Publishing/Cengage.

Eagleman, David. (2015). Why I am a Possibilian. Retrieved from http://www.eagleman.com/2015/11/27, December 9, 2015. [blog post].

Fowler, Brenda. (2000). *Iceman: Uncovering the Life and Times of a Prehistoric Man Found in an Alpine Glacier*. Chicago, IL: Chicago University Press.

Gauch, Hugh G. (2003). *Scientific Method in Practice*. Cambridge, Eng: Cambridge University Press.

Gay, Peter. (1996). *The Enlightenment: An Interpretation*. New York: W. W. Norton & Company.

Jobs, Steve. (2012). *Here's to the Crazy Ones*. Retrieved from https://www.youtube.com/watch?v=-z4NS2zdrZc/2015/11/27Landau, Misia. (1993). *Narratives of Human Evolution*. New Haven, CT: Yale University Press.

Johnson, Carolyn. (2014, May 20). Harvard Report Shines Light on Ex-Researcher's Misconduct. Boston Globe, May 30, 2014. Retrived December 4, 2015 from: https://www.bostonglobe.com/metro/2014/05/29/internal-harvard-report-shines-light-misconduct-star-psychology-researcher-marc-hauser/maSUowPqL4clXrOgj44aKP/story.html.

Lindow, John. (1978). *Swedish Folktales and Legends*. Berkeley, CA: University of California Press.

Mitchell, Melanie. (2011). *Complexity: A Guided Tour*. Oxford, Eng: Oxford University Press.

Shermer, Michael. (2001, November & December). Baloney Detection & More Baloney Detection. *Scientific American*.

Strum, Shirley. (1990). *Almost Human: A Journey into the World of Baboons*. New York: W. W. Norton & Company.

Tattersall, Ian. (2015). *The Strange Case of Rickety Cossack*. New York: St. Martin's Press.

Von Daniken, Erich. (1968; 1999). *Chariots of the Gods*. Berkley, CA: Berkley Books.

Go to the South Tyrol Museum of Archaeology website: www.iceman.it.

1. List three methods used by scientists to analyze Otzi and his artifacts.

2. When did Otzi live, how did he make a living, and how was his health?

3. What evidence from Otzi's artifacts (clothing, tools, etc.) or body are interesting to you, and why?

4. What additional evidence would you like to see and what issue would it resolve?

3 PERSPECTIVE:
Evolution and Culture

Anthropologists use a number of concepts and theories in studying our species such as culture, evolution, and adaptation. We also utilize excavation, fieldwork, and the comparative method and take a biocultural perspective about humans in all times and places.

LEARNING OBJECTIVES

1. Describe the four forces of evolution (natural selection, mutation, gene flow, and genetic drift) and the genetic code.

2. Explain the patterns of micro- and macroevolution, how a new species is created, and the common misunderstandings about evolutionary theory.

3. Explain the process of excavating and dating fossils and artifacts and the challenges of interpreting them.

4. Describe the infrastructure, structure, and superstructure of culture, the nature of cultural memes, and how culture is learned, shared, and symbolic to form an integrated whole.

5. Describe participant observation and emic versus etic views of culture, and identify three theories of idealism, cultural materialism, and evolutionary psychology.

6. Explain how rejected groups come to be defined as "the other," and how cooperation develops empathy and identification.

EVOLUTION

A key question of anthropology is how our ancestors adapted to the environment, underwent species change, and developed our physical and cultural diversity today. As people discovered fossils of earlier lifeforms they wondered how this change would occur. Linnaeus in the 1600s organized all known forms of life and saw that they formed hierarchical family groups based on similarities in their features. A growing number of scientists came to see that these groups must have shared descent from a common ancestor, much like a diversity of European romance languages share descent from Latin, or like the Protestant, Catholic, and Orthodox churches all share common descent from the first century Christians. This was later confirmed by the fact that all of life shares the same genetic system with four base pairs arranged in different combinations. But, the question was, how?

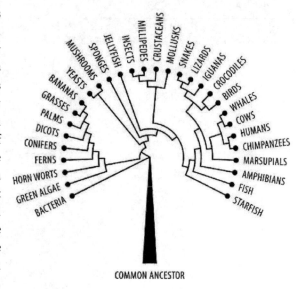

COMMON ANCESTOR

 In 1859, Charles Darwin developed the theory of evolution and described a set of processes that result in speciation—the systematic creation of new life forms and extinction of old ones. The theory is now well-confirmed and only the details are debated by scientists (evolution is not a scientific controversy, only a religious one for fundamentalists). Anthropologists today identify four major forces involved in the process of evolution: natural selection, mutation, gene flow, and genetic drift.

NATURAL SELECTION

Charles Darwin described the process of natural selection as descent with modification. He began with the observation that all members of a species vary in their physical and behavioral traits with some being taller or shorter, lighter or darker, and smarter or dumber. He hypothesized that individuals whose traits were well suited for a particular environment would have an advantage and likely get more food and mating opportunities, have an easier life, and leave more children. Those without any advantages would leave fewer offspring, so the next generation would have a slightly different proportion of traits, as would the generation after that. He stressed that species were not static and written in granite, but were fluid and flexible in the traits they exhibited. Multiplied by many generations, the percentage of advantageous traits would increase until the organisms were different enough from the original species it had morphed into a new species through the accumulated changes.

Darwin made this discovery by comparing life forms found on the Galapagos Islands off South American and comparing them with forms on the mainland. When the Galapagos finches, a type of bird, migrated to the islands some traits were better suited than others to the variety of environments found. Forested areas favored birds with longer beaks who could pluck insects out between the ridges of tree bark in the forest, get more food, and leave more children. But, long thin beaks would be a disadvantage at the seashore where birds cracked open shellfish—here a short strong beak would give an advantage. Over many generations, the proportion of long thin to short thick beaks would vary between the two populations and the original species that migrated to the island would be split into a seashore and forest group.

With additional habitat differences, a dozen or more different species would be descended from one common ancestor, so Darwin called it "descent with modification." Where we started with one species of finch, over thousands and millions of years they would end up with major trait frequency differences, ultimately becoming so different they no longer mated with each other. This process had begun with the simplest one celled organisms and eventually resulted in the creation of the diversity of life over millions of years.

MUTATION

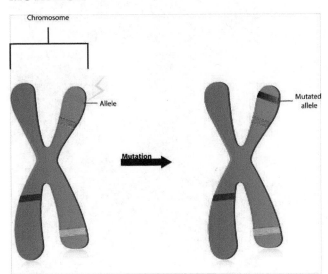

The starting point of Darwin's theory was the variation in traits within each group of organisms—but he didn't know how these traits came about or changed. But in the early 20th century, we discovered that these traits were controlled by genes, segments of twisted coils of DNA (deoxyribonucleic acid) molecules that formed chromosomes in cells. Humans have approximately 20,000 genes and they code for our different heredity traits including eye and hair color, as well as some aspects of behavior and personality. The total number of genes in a population is called a genome, and the Human Genome Project has now been able to analyze the genes that make up the human species.

Chromosomes come in pairs, with one chromosome coming from each parent. Humans have 46 pairs of chromosomes including one pair (either XX or Xy) that determines sex. Sex cells (egg and sperm) have one chromosome from each pair (totaling 23), so that when they join in conception the full number of chromosomes is restored (23 pairs = 46 chromosomes). Other plants and animals have different numbers of chromosomes. Chromosomes consisted of four base chemical pairs (guanine, cytosine, adenine, and thymine) and in cell division, when one of the pairs was not copied exactly, a mutation occurred and a new trait was invented. Most of these trait experiments would probably not be an advantage because the organism was already well-adapted to its environment. But, if the environment changed or the organism migrated to a new area a new trait might come in handy and result in a whole new direction for a portion of the species. Thus, mutation was the source of new variation.

A species does not necessarily get a mutation just when it needs one—it's the luck of the draw. But, if one occurs, especially in a small population, and it provides a reproductive advantage it can rapidly multiply in a group of organisms and take hold. Species tend to have different rates of mutation based on their lifespans and environmental conditions, but it is a process that can give new life to a species when it occurs in the right time and place.

GENE FLOW

Gene flow is the third force in species change. As individuals or populations migrate from one group to another, they bring their genes with them. As they interbreed with others and introduce their characteristics, e.g., blue eyes into the pool of a brown eyed group, the percentages of traits in the gene pool is altered. So the combination of the genes in new ways in populations who encounter each other, is another sources of change in species. Founder effect refers to how a migrating population can affect the traits of the species in the new area.

GENETIC DRIFT

The fourth force in evolution is genetic drift which refers to the chance factor in evolution—a volcano erupts, a river changes its course, or you're visiting the World Trade Center on the morning of 9/11. Your genes will be lost from the gene pool that makes up your population—no rhyme or reason, just chance. Darwin didn't realize that chance factors have probably played a major role in evolution. For example, there have been several major extinction events in earth's history where 75% or more of all life forms disappeared from the fossil record due to climate change or asteroid hitting the earth.

MICRO- & MACROEVOLUTION

The change in variation within a species is called microevolution—it is evolution on a small scale that varies from generation to generation but is not enough to alter breeding patterns enough to create a distinctive species.

Macroevolution is species change on a larger scale so that enough difference in genetic frequencies emerges that a population splits or an isolated population experiences rapid environmental changes or a sudden inflow of neighboring groups. Sometimes species are stable for a long time with only slow gradual change that result in new species, or species are so well adapted that they hardly change at all, e.g., the cockroach. At other times, change can be rapid with massive extinctions and adaptive radiations of new species—a pattern of punctuated equilibrium—stability followed by a big shakeup. If the species cannot cope with environmental change, extinction may occur. Over 90% of life forms on the planet have eventually gone extinct—a sobering thought.

EVOLUTION MISUNDERSTANDINGS

There are a number of common misunderstandings about this species change called evolution by both creationist and evolutionist students, outlined in a study done at the University of Tennessee-Knoxville. First, students and the general population misunderstand that science has proven that evolution is true, or that evolution is "just a theory." Evolution is without question a very well confirmed theory, like gravity (which no one questions) with many lines of evidence such as vestigial organs, laboratory experiments, and the fossil record. But, technically all scientific theories are open for new evidence that might change them in the future.

Another misunderstanding is that creationism can be taught as an alternative to evolution in a science course. But, creationism is not science and it does not follow the scientific method—it is a religious belief and belongs in religious studies. The problem is also whose creation story should be covered: yours, Native America, whoever is in the majority? It sounds fine until you have to learn the other guy's silly belief, not yours. Lastly, some people misunderstand that if you accept evolution you cannot believe in God. There is NO reason you cannot accept both evidence for species change as well as maintain beliefs that go beyond science. Most people in the world do, according to a 2014 MIT study.

EXCAVATION AND DATING METHODS

To explore how human evolution has occurred, archaeologists and biological anthropologists have developed methods to find, date, and analyze fossils and cultural artifacts and better understand how evolution has affected us as a part of nature. First, a survey of a site or locality is conducted to give an overview of what data might be collected and the best way to approach the excavation.

Archaeologists as well as biological anthropologists often work in teams and observe from the air, consult topographic maps, talk with local people for clues, review cultures in the area, identify vegetation patterns, and study what other discoveries were made nearby. Photos, video, satellite imagery and google earth are often used, as well as sonar, metal detectors, ultraviolet, infrared, ground penetrating radar, magnetometers to detect metal, and other technological techniques.

Scientists then take samples from certain areas or dig test pits to find features such as structures, monuments, settlements, midden garbage dumps, trails, surface tools, bones, pottery, or other artifacts that are under the surface. A section is usually left untouched for future generations of anthropologists to use the next century's technology to explore—unless the site is in danger of being destroyed. If the results are promising, plans are made for a larger investigation based on the information obtained.

The excavation, itself, starts with provenience, the precise location of remains and artifacts. These are mapped in order to be able to reconstruct the site later and show the associations or relationships, as well as dating. A site is sectioned off into squares marked by stakes and string in a grid pattern. An arbitrary point in the grid is determined to be the datum point from which all references are made (such as the center of the grid point to by the trowel, shown on right).

A video and/or drawn record shows the context where each piece of evidence was found. Shovels and backhoes may begin a dig, but small trowels, picks, and even dental tools will be used for detailed work. Dirt from the site is sifted for bits of bone, beads, or pottery. Water is then added and the fine material that floats is skimmed off and looked at under a microscope to identify plant pollen to help determine the climate.

All material removed from the site is then cleaned, cataloged with a number, and properly stored. Large items are encased in plaster and will be cleaned off later. Using both quantitative (statistics) and qualitative (interpretation) methods, biological anthropologists and archaeologists put all the pieces together, formulate hypotheses about what was found and create a narrative or "story" of the site. Finally, the results are shared with other scientists through journal articles and conferences, and with the general public through magazines, best sellers, documentary films, and museum displays. The Peabody Museum at Yale or Smithsonian Institution, for example, educated generations about evolution, prehistory, and history.

Finding out the age of these discoveries is critical—it allows us to reconstruct a time sequence that might include migrations of human populations, rise and fall of tribes or civilizations, inventions and borrowing of technology, and climate challenges that cause people to adapt in new ways. By dating artifacts and fossils we can also try to understand the culture that produced them. There are two primary types of methods used by archaeologists and biological anthropologists—relative and chronometric dating.

RELATIVE DATING

Relative dating compares artifacts or rock layers to determine which is the oldest. Sequences of items can be matched with other sequences to fill in the story. Stratigraphy analyzes the layers of earth based on the lowest layers being older and those closer to the surface being the newest.

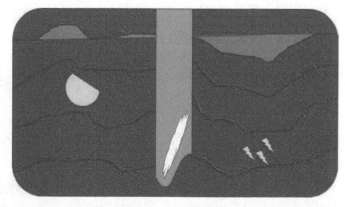

On the right, is depicted a series of rock layers. One contains a pottery bowl, another three projectile points, and a third, a piece of bone.

At first glance, the pottery bowl appears to be the youngest of the artifacts, and the bone and stone points, the oldest because they are lower in the earth. However, by mapping the layers of rock strata it's clear that a pit was dug in the rock layers, and the bone that was deposited in that layer is actually the youngest.

CHRONOMETRIC DATING

Chronometric dating is based on atomic processes and natural decay rates of rocks, bones, and gasses that provide a range of actual dates. Radiocarbon (also called C14) dates organic materials—bone, shell, and teeth—and studies the proportion of C14 and C12 in the material. C14 decays to C12 at a constant rate of 5,730 years which is called the half-life when half of the C14 has turned into C12. If the ratio is 50:50 then the material is about 5,000 years old. This can be calculated up to about 50,000 years before the proportions are so small that they are hard to measure.

Potassium-Argon dating is based on volcanic rock. K40 decays into A40 argon gas which gets trapped in the rock. K40 takes 1.3 billion years for half of the material to be transformed, so this can provide much older dates from about 200,000 years ago to 4 billion years. Fossils or artifacts found in volcanic rock layers can be dated in this manner. There are many other methods of dating used by anthropologists, including ways to understand how DNA changes over time, comparing the species change in animal fossils found near human bones, looking at pollen under a microscope to determine the environment at the time, and comparing patterns on pieces of broken pots to identify a tribe or time period.

ARCHAEOLOGICAL INTERPRETATION

With all this information and dating of materials, anthropologists turn to the task of interpretation. Early archaeology focused on artifacts themselves, e.g., British researchers removed many Egyptian treasures to the British Museum in England—an ethical issue that is still in dispute with Egypt. Today, there is more awareness that these discoveries belong in the land where they were created and the focus is on the people who made the treasures rather than the things themselves.

Anthropologists are also aware of gender and other social issues that can affect interpretation. Joan Gero (1991) pointed out a long-standing male bias in analyzing prehistoric stone tool. Archaeologists over-focused on standardized core tools and assumed that only males used them for hunting and that this male effort drove human progress forward. Small irregular flake tools were ignored even though they were far more numerous and used by women and children. Investigations of Chumash Native American burials or Upper Paleolithic Venus 'fertility' figures showed that gender had been over-emphasized by archaeologists in stereotypic ways that the evidence did not bear out. Archaeologists today also show more respect for indigenous belief systems and, as a result, also gain cooperation which leads to additional discoveries. Even the idea of 'preserving the past' calls into question whose past, and preservation for whom?

CULTURE

Culture is the complex of ideas, behavior and technology that helps people to survive and adapt to new environments. It is the primary way that humans have adapted and it has co-evolved with the development of our brain and bodies. A successful culture meets the physical and psychological needs of individuals in terms of meaning and quality of life, identity, mortality, health, conflict, and resources. Anthropologists strive for cultural relativism, keeping to your own values, but trying not to judge the practices of others recognizing that puzzling behaviors may really be adaptive in other environments. Ethnocentrism results when you think your culture is superior and devalue the ways of others.

SUPERSTRUCTURE
Worldview, Language
Religion, Arts

STRUCTURE
Institution organization
Family, Politics, Economy

Marvin Harris (1968) developed a theory of cultural materialism in which he divided all of culture into three sections of a barrel: an infrastructure, which refers to the life and death matters of subsistence, birth rates, and disease; structure, which is the way a society organizes its institutions; and superstructure, the worldview, language, arts, religion and symbols of a society. Anthropologists vary as to which portion is most influential but all agree that culture form an integrated whole that is structured and patterned, and transmitted to and adapted by the next generation.

CULTURAL MEMES AND RULES

A "culture meme" is an idea or unit of behavior that represents a society such as how you study or how to tune an engine. For example, what are the "rules" of an American "restroom" where no one actually "rests"? Males learned by observation the implicit procedures of how to stand, where to look, what to say or not say. Traffic also follows explicit patterns and laws, but also has some conventions that vary from region to region like how much horn honking or speeding is acceptable. We accumulate thousands of these cultural memes and use them unconsciously as the "right" way to do things.

Many cultures have long instruction in cultural rules and proper practice or ritual, e.g., religious bar mitzvah or becoming an eagle scout. This may involve reciting scripture, saying an oath of values, making faith statements, ordeals or tests of competence, special dress or outfits, or new attitudes and behavior. These explicit and implicit rules and patterns structure culture and give it meaning. You also draw your individual identity from these memes.

ENCULTURATION

Enculturation is how we learn to be human and adopt the specific folkways of our community. Culture is learned and modified through both obvious and obscure means. Each generation is steeped like tea and shaped both directly and indirectly whereby you acquire modified forms of the culture and its memes from the previous generation. Enculturation is sometimes explicit such as table manners or learning to drive a car, but is largely implicit and learned indirectly through our observations, social interactions, and experiences with the world and environment.

For example, a son (above) may just watch how his father starts a fire over and over, and then he learns to do the same. Some things are learned this way in the West, but we are more accustomed to direct instruction that we receive in schools. We give lectures where students are expected to sit passively and "absorb knowledge," although trends are returning to learning by doing and greater student active critical thinking.

Many societies nurture children with hands-on lessons and artfully scaffolded distractions that involve the parents such as games rather than spanking or other punishment. For example, foragers, such as the !Kung Bushmen of the Kalahari in Africa (above), have 70% body contact with babies throughout infancy which regulates breathing and brain wiring and reduces sudden infant death. They also have better cognitive functioning, and less allergies/asthma and ADD. !Kung babies grow up with strong attachments and empathy for others.

This surprises people from cultures like ours that rely heavily on puritanical notions of punishment and "corrections" or just park kids in front of TVs or tablets to entertain themselves. We tend to teach the value of the individual not the group. As a result identity forms in foraging and other societies more rapidly than in the U.S. In contrast, modern industrial and consumerist society creates more anxiety, fear, depression and a less developed sense of self. Medical anthropologists argue that this makes some individuals turn to self-medicating through alcohol, drugs and other addictions. In a sense, our culture makes us ill. Recently, a social movement called *Parenting Without Borders* utilized this information to rethink our school systems and how we raise children, using models from other cultures with greater interpersonal intimacy.

SHARED SYMBOLIC INTEGRATED WHOLE

All human societies share some basic ideas and behaviors while other traits may be very different, e.g., marriage customs or how to make a living. The importance of shared culture becomes clear when someone violates the rules. For example, in the Northeast of the U.S. people talk louder and more energetically, and tease and banter back in forth to establish friendly relationships but this might seem rude in the South where strangers avoid talking about areas that might lead to challenge or conflict.

Culture is also integrated into a whole where one area affects or relates to another. For example, when the automobile was invented it gave more privacy to couples, allowed families to travel longer distances or live further away from work, and created gas refining, gas stations, repair shops, manufacturing companies, logos, etc. Better gas mileage means fewer stops in gas stations and fewer cokes and chips sold as well.

Most people understand that cultures vary but form a kind of integrated whole that is distinctive. But, a challenge develops when trying to understand a ritual or behavior that is radically different and violates Western notions of human rights. For example, some cultures practice female circumcision whereby the female genital clitoris is nicked or removed, and the outer labia may be sewn together only to be painfully opened and reopened each time the woman gives birth. The practice causes suffering during intercourse, menstruation, and bladder and colon functions, and reduces sexual feeling which reinforces patriarchal control of women.

However, anthropologists Boddy (1997) and Abusharaf (2000) point out that the condemned practice also gives a symbolic meaning of a renewal of purity and fertility that helps justify the practice in those cultures. Women are encouraged to focus on being "mothers of men" and giving birth to boys. They are rewarded for starting a new lineage and attaining high status is central because your lineage will be named in tribal genealogies. Anthropologists don't justify this practice, but they show that a practice that abuses women is also part of a cultural whole of values, social roles, and rituals. In fact, many anthropologists practice "advocacy anthropology" in which they actively seek to change cultures and improve the status of women and minorities.

ANTHROPOLOGICAL PERSPECTIVE

ETHNOGRAPHY

Ethnography refers to the description of cultural behavior. Anthropologists do fieldwork, meaning actually experiencing and observing culture, and consider holistically both our biological and cultural nature. Ethnographers make a distinction between the "emic" insider perspective of the people studied and the anthropologist's own "etic" analysis, drawing conclusions from observations and comparisons with other cultures. Fieldwork has changed over time. Early studies of the Trobriand Islands focused mostly on men's activities. But, the emic perspective of the Trobrianders was that women's work with yams was just as important, so now anthropologists often work in gender teams to gain all perspectives.

Interviewing is a key method by which rapport is established and anthropologists carefully listen to both what is said and what is left out or nonverbal. In participant observation, you immerse yourself in the culture and "walk the walk," i.e., do what the people do so you can experience some of the emic perspective. You keep good notes including your own reactions and reflections and use insight to analyze the themes you find. This gives you close intimate knowledge of a culture and even friendship with the people you are studying. What you might lose in objectivity you gain in analysis, novel insights, and ability to observe hidden or rare behaviors. You also see that what people say is often not really what they do.

ETHNOLOGY

Ethnology takes ethnographic information and makes comparisons among societies to understand patterns and develop theories to explain human behavior. Anthropologists have a variety of theories about culture. Cultural idealism holds that humans are mostly shaped by ideas and symbolic concepts. It stresses the need to see the world from the perspective of "the other" and interpret the web of significance that humans create, e.g., designer labels. They focus on key symbols, images, or rituals.

Cultural materialism argues instead that humans are shaped mostly by the environment and economic conditions such as their subsistence form, how they use resources, tools that are available, climate, etc. Symbolic ideas, such as avoiding pork for religious reasons, are ecologically sound and religious ideas are developed to support what is really an adaptation to nature. Evolutionary psychology stresses how humans have been shaped by adaptations to the challenges of their ancestral prehistoric environment. For example, studies show that higher social classes produce more sons, while lower classes have more daughters because each provides an advantage in a specific environment.

CULTURAL FICTIONS

Cultural fictions are ways that societies gloss over problems or inequalities with distractions or out and out deceptions. For example, circumcision, the removal of the foreskin of the penis on men is not widely practiced globally or even recommended except in areas of health concern such as HIV-AIDS areas of Africa. it started in Egypt about 15,000 years ago and originally was designed to emasculate enemies or mark slaves. In the 1800s, doctors made well-intentioned but spectacularly false claims about penis size and avoiding masturbation. But, only about 33% of males worldwide are circumcised.

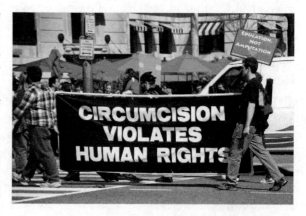

Cross-cultural humor is especially effective at seeing through the cultural fictions we take for granted. Australian comic Jim Jeffries' routine on gun control mentioned earlier, makes a comparison of the low number of murders with guns in developed nations like Australia versus the U.S. which has thousands of gun deaths. For example, in 2011, guns murdered 35 people in Australia, 200 in Canada, but over 9,000 in the U.S. Why is America so violent with mass shootings at epidemic proportions, e.g., the military recruiting attack in Chattanooga, Tennessee in July, 2015.

Anthropologist note that the U.S. is extraordinarily high in what's called structured violence compared with other developed nations. Our society is highly socially and economically unequal resulting in high crime and prisons that incarcerate over two million people. We view crime exclusively as an individual issue deserving punishment, but inequality is caused by social conditions such as drugs and broken families which provoke the violence in the first place. Activist Michael Moore linked this condition with the genocide of destroying Native American tribes, slavery, brutal civil war, high rape and other crimes against women, capital punishment, and lack of functional healthcare for all. This results in a fear-based culture with racism and individualistic me-focused social values. When others respond that people, not guns, kill people, they are also putting the focus on behavior and cultural expectations.

MYSTERY: THE "OTHER"

Tyra Banks is well known as a model and host of reality television series, *America's Next Top Model,* Tyra was the first African-American woman to be on the cover of the magazines *GQ, Sports Illustrated,* and *Victoria's Secret Catalog* and her exotic beauty provoked curiosity about her racial mixture. She had herself and her contestants complete DNA testing with AncestryDNA analysis. The testing showed that she is only 79% African, and also 14% British, and 6% Native American. Like most African-Americans she is of mixed race.

A show model contestant who believed she was 100% African-American discovered she was actually mostly Asian. These DNA clues can also help guide genealogical searches. Singer Mariah Carey who appears to "look white" actually identifies as mixed or black, based on her Venezuelan father. Interestingly, the history of America has been to consider anyone mixed to be non-white, e.g., Tiger Woods is perceived as African-American, although he, himself, identifies also as Thai, Chinese, and Dutch. How has skin color and race become such a defining factor for our identity—or for that matter our gender, ethnicity, disability, or sexual orientation?

Most everyone can recall a time that they felt like the other if only on a vacation, going to a big city, or living with neighbors who are "not like us." Gays, persons with disabilities, minorities of all kinds, and other students have reported bullying, name-calling, and cyber-stalking.

So how and why do we come to define those different from us as "the other?" Even nonconforming people from within a society get defined in a negative way and are rejected or discriminated against. Separation, inequality, and factors such as povery and lack of education, good nutrition, etc., can allow us to cast those we fear or who are different from us as "the other." This is critical in U.S. society today. The U.S. now has the most unequal distribution of income in the industrialized world—the top 1% owns more than all the lower 99% combined. The 400 richest Americans (all billionaires) have the same wealth as the bottom half of all Americans combined! From 1978-2010, top CEO salaries increased by 1,000% while worker wages actually went down in terms of the cost of living!

As the globe moves toward becoming a Type 1 civilization, the haves and have-nots come into conflict. Western materialism spreads provoking a "need" for material goods even in poor countries. This requires natural resources that multi-national corporations seek to control. Nonwestern traditional cultures react against this move toward a Type 1 civilization because of the history of colonialism and exploitation. They form a sense of "self" by creating cultural and religious boundaries resulting in "terrorism" which then serves to reinforce the desire of controlling nations to move against "the evil doers" of the moment.

Social science studies show that common experiences and shared tasks based on equality, shared resources, needing each other, identifying with the other, and common goals all help to reverse this process. On a micro-individual level, it is just getting to know someone from the other group whether in the military, new neighbors, as roommates, through inter-racial relationships, or discovering your brother whom you love, is gay. On a macro-societal scale, it is finding sustainable cooperative ways to live on the planet and reduce social injustice and inequality—while still maintaining incentives for entrepreneurship, growth, adventure, and discovery—the hallmarks of the human species.

Anthropologists show that our society is not alone; most societies define some individuals as the other. However, our particular challenge is that we are pluralistic society with many different ethnic groups, regional differences, political diversity, and social class issues. But, we will also be defined as a society by how we treat those who are considered to be the other. We will have to develop full sustainability in the future in terms of our subsistence within the ecosystem, but we will also have to create a socially sustainable society with a large middle class and social cooperation and mutual respect.

Applied anthropologists work with governmental agencies, nonprofit organizations, and different native and ethnic organizations to foster this goal. The danger is that the information and income gap may become so great that social discord, unrest, or even revolution will erupt, as it has in many societies in the past.

CRITICAL THINKING & WEBSITES

1. Create an imaginary plant or animal and illustrate how each of the four forces of evolution would lead to the creation of a new species.

2. Should the British Museum return mummies, gold artifacts, and parts of pyramids and monuments to Egypt, especially if they can be properly cared for?

3. You are an anthropologist who finds a totally new stone tool shape in a site in Tennessee. How would you investigate and analyze the tool, keeping in mind a focus on the culture and avoidance of gender bias?

4. Research a routine from Jim Jeffries or one of your favorite comics and describe what insight into our culture they provide.

5. Using anthropology concepts and methods, how would you investigate Moore's argument that America is too violent?

6. Many societal cultural fictions have to do with social injustice and they are revealed through a study of computer gaming: see http://crown.ucsc.edu/activities/social-fiction-conference/.

7. Look at some of the youtube best gay wedding speeches ever for how modern families are embracing "the other": https://www.youtube.com/watch?v=W-4hriuVgoc.

8. America's Next Top Model is a surprisingly revealing unintentional anthropological look at what is considered beauty in our society, how media and the fashion industry shape our tastes, and amazing details of facial expressions, body postures, and ways humans convey emotions. Tyra even invented a new word: "smizing" (smiling with your eyes—so often important for actors and models). Check out: the smizing youtube video: https://www.youtube.com/watch?v=IolPTBw6M9M, and also the show's site: http://www.cwtv.com/shows/americas-next-top-model/.

9. Try the Urinal Game for fun: http://www.gamefudge.com/The-Urinal-Game.

REFERENCES

Abusharaf, Rogaia Mustafa. (2000). Female circumcision goes beyond feminism. *Anthropology News* 41 (March), 17-18.

Alpers, Philip & Wilson, Marcus. (2013). Global Impact of Gun Violence: Firearms, public health and safety. *Sydney School of Public Health*, The University of Sydney. GunPolicy.org, 14 August. Retrieved December 13, 2015 from: http://www.gunpolicy.org/firearms/region/.

Arogundade, Ben. (2015). What is singer Mariah Carey's ethnicity? Black, white, mixed race? 65,000 fans ask about her racial heritage. Arongudade. Retrieved from: http://arogundade.com/what-ethnicity-and-nationality-is-mariah-careys-black-white-mixed-race-her-heritage-ethnicity-nationality-parents.html. December 13, 2015.

Arogundade, Ben. (2015). Black History 1997: He's not black, he's Cablinasian—Tiger Woods declares his racial independence. Arongudade. Retrieved from: http://arogundade.com/what-race-and-nationality-is-tiger-woods-black-or-cablinasian-his-heritage-ethnicity-parents-mother-nationality.html, December 13, 2015.

Banks, Tyra. (2015). *America's Next Top Model*. CW Network. Retrieved from: http://www.cwtv.com/shows/americas-next-top-model, December 13, 2015.

Boddy, Janice. (1997). Womb as oasis: *The symbolic context of Paraonic circumcision in rural northern Sudan. In The Gender/Sexuality Reader*. Roger Lancaster & Micaela De Leonardo, eds., 309-324. New York, NY: Routledge.

Chappelle, Dave. (2015). *Dave Chappelle Show: The Black White Supremacist Full Video*. Retrieved on December 2, 2015 from: https://www.youtube.com/watch?v=u_W0Qa8v0k.

Colwell-Chanthaphonh, Chip. (2009). The archaeologist as world citizen: On the morals of heritage preservation and destruction. In *Cosmopolitan Archaeologies*. Lynn Meskell, ed. 140-165. Durham, NC: Duke University Press.

Conkey, Margaret, & Gero, Joan. (1991). Tensions, pluralities, and engendering archaeology: An introduction to women and prehistory. In Engendering Archaeology, 3-30. Oxford, UK: Blackwell.

Darwin, Charles. (1859). *On the Origin of Species by Means of Natural Selection, or the Preservation of Favoured Races in the Struggle for Life*. London, UK: John Murray.

Dawkins, Richard. (1976). *The Selfish Gene*. Oxford, UK: Oxford University Press.

Harris, Marvin. (1968). The Rise of Anthropological Theory. Walnut Creek, CA: AltaMira Press.

Haviland, William, Prins, Harald, Walrath, Dana, McBride, Bunny. (2014). *Anthropology: The Human Challenge*, 14th ed. Boston, MA: Cengage.

Kardashev, Nikolai. (1964). Transmission of information by extraterrestrial civilizations. *Soviet Astronomy* 8: 217.

Levanda, Robert, & Schultz, Emily. (2015). *Anthropology: What Does It Mean To Be Human?* 3rd ed. New York: Oxford University Press.

Lucas, Gavin. (2012). *Understanding the Archaeological Record*. New York, NY: Cambridge University Press.

Miller, J. (2008). "Otherness." *The SAGE Encyclopedia of Qualitative Research Methods*. Thousand Oaks, CA: SAGE Publications, Inc., pp. 588-591.

Moore, Michael. (2012). Open Mic Blog: Celebrating the Prince of Peace in the Land of Guns. *Huffington Post*, December 24, 2012. Retrieved on December 2, 2015 from: http://www.huffingtonpost.com/michael-moore/gun-violence-united-states_b_2358115.html.

Pryor, Richard. (1982). *Richard Pryor Live on the Sunset Strip: The N-word*. Hollywood, CA: Rastar Films (SONY Home Entertainment). Retrieved on December 2, 2015 from: https://www.youtube.com/watch?v=hULhZqhw9yU

Ridley, Mark. (2004). *Evolution*. Malden, MA: Blackwell Science.

Rock, Chris. (1996). *Bring the Pain: Black People Vs. Niggas*. Retrieved on December 2, 2015 from: https://www.youtube.com/watch?v=f3PJF0YE-x4.

Skinner, Michael. (2009). Multi-billion dollar mining boom: The economics of war and empire in Afghanistan. *Global Research*, February, 27, 2009.

Sykes, Bryan. (2001). *The Seven Daughters of Eve: The Science that Reveals Our Genetic Ancestry*. New York, NY: Norton.

Weiss, M. L., & Tackney, J. (2012). *An introduction to genetics*. S. Stinson, B. Bogin, & D. O-Rourke, eds. Human Biology: An Evolutionary and Biocultural Perspective, 2nd ed. Hoboken, NJ: Wiley-Blackwell.

1. Describe a time you felt like "the other" in a situation. What is you thinking now?

2. Choose a setting that is "the other" to you (based on race, religion, social class, sexual orientation, disability, etc.). Be in that setting for 1-2 hours and interact with someone who is the other to you. This could mean attending a very different church, synagogue, or temple; a music event; an ethnic family gathering, etc. Interview the other person about their origins and cultural identity (continue on back).

4 PRIMATES:
Culture and Cognition

Humans are classified as primates, along with monkeys and apes. We sensed how intelligent great apes were, but it was not until we taught them language and studied their own societies in their own environment that we realized they have families and cultures of their own.

LEARNING OBJECTIVES

1. Describe the major characteristics of primates.

2. Describe the Strepsirhini, especially lemurs and tarsiers.

3. Contrast the new and old world monkeys.

4. Describe the four great apes (chimpanzee, gorilla, bonobo, orangutan).

5. Describe great ape culture and language ability, including families, alliances, emotions, and traditions.

6. Explain why great ape culture is a model for the culture of early human ancestors.

PRIMATE CHARACTERISTICS

It's hard to watch monkeys or apes in the zoo or in nature documentaries and not see human traits in their appearance and behavior. These similarities did not go unnoticed by the early explorers who brought these animals back to royal menageries in Europe. By the 17th century, scholars were speculating on how they might be related to us, and Carolus Linnaeus created a major classification of animals based on observable physical traits and placed humans in the same group as monkeys apes and other primates—although he did not challenge special creation.

Primates are highly adaptable and live in a wide range of habitats over several continents, largely in tropical areas. Most are adapted for life in trees and they eat a wide variety of plant and some animal foods. Although primitive forms rely greatly on sense of smell, monkeys and apes overall emphasize vision, some with depth perception and color vision. Their eyes face forward and each provides stereoscopic vision with slightly overlapping images which provides the depth view. They have a great deal of eye-hand coordination and grasping hands and feet. Some have opposable thumbs which allow not only a power hand grip but also a precision one, e.g., ability to pick up a dime.

Primates also invest a great deal of energy into their children and have a strong sense of touch. In fact, primates spend most of their time grooming each other in combinations that reflect their social organization. This prolonged care results in fewer children, but smarter, longer-living, and more socially adept progeny. Parents invest more in children and children have a longer period of learning to become an adult. There is also a tendency toward upright posture and larger brain. This teaching and learning provides primates with important skills for survival. Monkeys have some traditions passed from generation to generation, and great apes clearly show evidence of culture.

PRIMITIVE PRIMATES

LEMUR

The primate story begins with the first primates to evolve. The *Strepsirhini* include lemurs and lorises of Madagascar who emerged about 55 million years ago. They have primitive (meaning "ancestral and basic") traits such as a wet nose, scent glands, and strong sense of smell, as well as a combination of nails and claws on their fingers and toes. Their lower teeth serve as a tooth comb. They live on the ground in extremely seasonal environments and they have adapted and evolved into a large number of species. Female ring-tailed lemurs are dominant while males are submissive although they compete with each other through "stink fights" by rubbing their tails on scent glands on their wrists.

TARSIER

The rest of all primates are classified as *Haplorhini*: tarsiers, new and old world monkeys, apes and humans. Tarsiers are sort of in-between the primitive primates and monkeys, although clearly classified as *Haplorhini*.

They are found in Southeast Asia and are a rather unique primate with specialized large eyes for seeing at night. However, everyone is struck by their tiny hands (not paws) that have fingernails (not claws) and appear very humanlike. Some science fiction creatures have been based on the appearance of tarsiers.

MONKEYS

NEW WORLD MONKEY

New world monkeys have larger brains, fewer teeth, and greater reliance on vision. About 70 species of New World monkeys are found in Latin America and are arboreal, meaning they spend most of their time in the trees using their prehensile tail for balance and to keep their hands free for eating insects, fruits, and leaves. They have broad noses with nostril that face outward.

An intelligent new world monkey is the capuchin (left) who lives in large territorial groups. They are particularly good at catching frogs, and eating crabs and shellfish by cracking them with stones, a kind of tool use. They cleverly select ripe fruit and drink the juice, then discard the fruit until it dries when they crack it open with large stones and grab the nut inside. In laboratory experiments they have also shown a rudimentary understanding of money, even trading sex for money.

OLD WORLD MONKEY

Old world monkeys are the most successful and diverse group of primates and they occupy a large number of habitats in Africa and Asia from tropical rain forests, to savanna woodland and mountains. Probably the best known are baboons and macques, especially the amazing and beautiful snow monkeys of Japan. Old world monkeys range from those who are arboreal and live in trees to those who spend their lives more on the ground. They are medium to large in size and have tails—a good way to distinguish them from apes. Their nose is distinctive and the nostrils face downward. They have the same number of teeth as apes and humans, two incisors, one canine, two premolars, and three molars in one quadrant of their jaw.

Some old world monkeys have fascinating features. The proboscis monkey spends a great deal of time in the water and has a long nose which they float on the surface as they swim and walk under water. Mandrills have a red penis combined with a lilac scrotum, and their face is also brightly colored. Vervet monkeys have been found to have a number of 'words' for predators or alarm. Old world monkey babies cling to their mother's hair and reach maturity in around four to six years. The basic social organization is around the mother with most males leaving the group when they become adolescents. Many species have strong dominance hierarchies and family life.

Baboons (right) form the genus *Papio* and are concentrated in East Africa and to the north and were considered to be sacred by the ancient Egyptians. They have strong dominance hierarchies and spend a great deal of time grooming each other. They are very sexually dimorphic with males being twice the size of females. They have long dog-like muzzles with heavy and powerful jaws and long canine teeth. They are terrestrial and have developed hairless patches of skin on their bottom for sitting on sand and rocks.

Japanese macaque are famous for their behavioral traditions. In 1952, researchers left sweet potatoes out on a beach of a provisioned island and an 18-month female named Imo wash the sand and grit from the potatoes by dipping them in the salt water, at the same time "seasoning" her vegetable. Her family quickly learned the new behavior and it spread—although adult males were the last to learn. Later, the monkeys learned to gather wheat grains, float them on the sea water, and then scoop them up by the handful!

GREAT APES AND THEIR CULTURE

CHIMPANZEE

Chimpanzees live in equatorial Africa, along with gorillas and bonobos. Chimps have long arms as well as long fingers and toes for grasping branches and other objects. They live in the rain forest although some have adapted to drier environments. Chimpanzees are regular knuckle-walkers, having a digit on their middle finger that supports their weight, although they can also engage in bipedal walking for brief periods. They eat a variety of plant foods and insects plus meat, including bushpigs, antelopes, and the red colobus monkey. They hunt and share prey with each other.

Chimpanzees live in large groups of closely bonded males, although some West African groups are more female centered. Chimpanzee social structure is flexible with members moving in and out of the band. Adult females usually forage alone or with their children and about half of them migrate out to other groups. Individuals form lifelong attachments and live to be 40 years of age or older. Chimpanzees have large brains, use stone and stick tools, and select plants with medicinal properties when they are ill.

GORILLA

Gorillas live in central Africa and form eastern and western groups. They are knuckle-walkers also, and are the largest of the primates with some males weighing 400 pounds. Their heads come to a point know as a sagittal crest. Gorillas have a reputation for being terrifying and looking fierce (left), no doubt due to the King Kong books and films, however they are shy intelligent vegetarians eating mostly leaves and some fruit.

Some western lowland gorillas are facing extinction because of loss of habitat and continual human warfare in the area. Mountain gorillas number only around 700 which makes them very endangered, as well. Mountain gorillas live in groups centered on one or two large silverback males, several females and their children. Usually, young gorillas leave their natal group and join other groups.

BONOBO

Bonobos were discovered by scientists only in the 1920s and are found only in an area south of the Zaire River in the Democratic Republic of the Congo where there has been constant warfare making study difficult. They are similar to chimpanzees in appearance, except that their legs are longer and their faces darker. But they are less aggressive and competitive and violence rarely occurs because they are female dominated and use sex to resolve conflicts—sometimes five times a day! They have been dubbed the "make love, not war" primate.

Females primarily bond with their female friends, and two or three females do not hesitate to confront a male. On the other hand, female-male bonding is also important. Bonobo sexual behavior involves female-male genital rubbing and intercourse, but sexual unions also occur female to female, male to male, and adults to children. Sex is separate from reproduction. They also cleverly use sex to diffuse and distract from tense social situations, e.g., competition about food or social relationships. Should a tense situation begin, a bonobo steps in and initiates sex as a peace-making gesture.

ORANGUTAN

Orangutans are perhaps the least well-known or understood of the great apes. They are the only great ape to be found outside of Africa and although they once lived in the Middle East and across Asia, they are now found only on the islands of Borneo and Sumatra. On Borneo, their food sources are dispersed so orangutans are forced to be more solitary; on Sumatra they are able to form small social groups or temporary pair bonds. Males have twice the body size of females and can walk bipedally on the ground carrying a large staff or walking stick. Females are usually found vertically in the trees and vines, holding an infant.

Orangutans have large brains too, and discoveries were made in the last 20 years showing they make and use tools, especially for processing spiny fruit with thick rind in the swamps. They have a very quiet temperament unless disturbed and the name "orang utan" means "wise old person of the forest." They are severely endangered because of habitat loss, primarily due to deforestation and clearing for palm oil production as well as other products. When apes were just objects in a zoo or laboratory they seemed familiar but clownish or puzzling. It was only when we traveled to Africa and Asia and studied their societies in natural settings that we gained insight into the complexity of their social lives and technology. In particular, there is growing evidence of great ape culture, i.e., learned traditions and behavior patterns use to interact with others and solve problems of daily living.

CULTURE AND SOCIAL BEHAVIOR

Great ape social relations are highly fluid with friendships forming and changing as events occur. Great ape social life begins with the mother infant relationship. Apes spend five or six years with their mothers, learning about relationships with others, how to forage for food, and navigate the territory. Most time is spent grooming each other which is not so much for cleanliness as it is for bonding. Great apes also do a degree of sharing, and at times even engage in social deception. One chimpanzee at the Gombe Stream reserve spotted food and in his excitement began to emit food grunts. Not wanting to tip off others, he covered his mouth with his hand and tried to soften the grunts so others would not hear.

TOOL MAKING

All four of the great apes excel in making tools to one degree or another. Orangutans have multiple stick tool kits used to process different kinds of fruit and when living near human settlements have quickly picked up behaviors such as washing clothes at the dock, trying to light a fire, or stealing a canoe and paddling downstream. In addition, Van Schaik and his colleagues (2003) showed that orangutans had at least 19 behaviors that indicated culture, from how they made nests, to using branches as fly-swatters, to making whistles of leaves of grass. Gorillas and

bonobos use leaves in instrumental ways and poke with sticks. Several apes modify sticks into ideal shapes for catching termites in their nest. Different populations have unique ways to process the termites with some using the stick like a popsicle. Female chimpanzees have now been observed to make spears used to capture bush babies and other small prey in the crooks of trees. Breuer et al. (2005) showed that two female lowland gorillas in the Congo used a branch to see how deep the water's edge was, and as a walking stick. So, humans are not the only tool makers.

COMMUNICATION

Great apes have over 20 vocal communications that we now know convey different meanings, such as warning, aerial predator, or food. Even more complex are their facial expressions and hand and body gestures such as a beckoning gesture. Apes even have different learned gestural traditions. Chimpanzees in the Tai forest try to attract females by shaking a branch low and under-handed, while at the Gombe forest the male shakes the branch over his head. Infants observe their mother's communications and then in play with other youngsters try out facial expressions and body postures in their rehearsal for adult roles. These gestures are flexible and carry subtle meanings. While not symbolic like human language, their communication conveys a great deal by expressing emotion and transmitting information.

INTELLIGENCE

Apes are great problem-solvers at least at the level of a five to six year old, perhaps even older, child. They find and process food, navigate a territory with other nearby groups or individuals, and build sleeping nests at night or on the ground. Their tool-making skills are impressive and requires planning and problem solving. Making judgments about size, shape, and function indicates a preconceived idea of what is being made. For example, the chimps making spears for hunting chew off the tips to sharpen them for greater effectiveness and orangutans using stones to crack nuts or selecting tools from their stick kits also show forethought in how they select the size and weight of the stone and how to strike.

POLITICS

The complex political lives of all the great apes is now well documented. They live in rich social worlds where it is important to know who each individual is aligned with and where power opportunities or risks exist. Primatologist Frans de Waal tells a harrowing story of chimps in a zoo who carefully engineered retaliating against a leader who had displaced them as the powerful leaders of the group and essentially executed him. They bit him repeatedly and tore out his testicles. A female friend of his was powerless to intervene but later retaliated herself by driving one of the perpetrators up a tree and keeping him there for hours. Yet, reconciliation is also part of the tradition of apes. Female chimpanzees are known to take the hands of two males in conflict and gently move them near each other toward friendly grooming.

SELF-AWARENESS

A mirror mark test was created with children to see when they first could recognize themselves in a mirror and understand that it was not another child but themselves. All four of the great apes have passed the mirror self-recognition task by rubbing at a spot placed earlier on their forehead while looking at their reflection. This suggests at least some body-visual matching and understanding that the image is not another individual, but themselves. Apes are known to also use mirrors to groom their face and mouth and sometimes to look behind themselves at others in a deceptive manner.

EMOTIONS

Primatologists studying great apes in both laboratory conditions and in their natural habitats have noted the similarity in emotions between humans and great apes. All the great apes appear to laugh, pout, and whimper showing a range of emotions. Although care needs to be taken not to over-anthropomorphize (give human traits without evidence), great apes are seen exhibiting surprise, dismay, frustration, and even grief. At one chimpanzee preserve in Africa, a chimpanzee died and his entire group came to a fence and watched in silence and then slowly moved away, as if in mourning. A chimpanzee in a well-studied family at the Gombe Stream Preserve stayed at the side of his dead mother for weeks, didn't eat, and within a short time appeared to die of grief.

SPIRITUALITY AND WONDER

While it is difficult to get into the mind of an ape, there are occasions when they sit, as we do, gazing at a sunset or sunrise, or looking in awe at a racing waterfall. Orangutans, in particular, seem to be thinking all the time and then just quietly go and solve a problem. Chimpanzee expert Jane Goodall shares a story of when she first began her research and an adult male chimpanzee, David Greybeard, who could have harmed her but instead just slowly reached out and shared a nut with her, lingering and holding her hand. In laboratory settings, gorillas and chimpanzees have taken to painting and seem to have a sense of composition and style. All these observations suggest something deeper in the mind of an ape—perhaps just a glimmer but definitely real.

PERSONHOOD

Because of all these ape-human similarities, some scientists and philosophers have called for all four great apes to be declared to be ape-persons under the law and receive special environmental protections in their natural habitats and also from biomedical and other invasive research. Called the Great Ape Project, it has now been passed in at least two developed nations, Spain and New Zealand, with others soon to follow. It will probably take several decades for this to be a reality in the U.S., but federal research agencies and Congress have already banned breeding of apes for

biomedical experiments and zoos are aware of the need to provide extensive enrichments for apes living under human care.

APE LANGUAGE

Along with standing upright and using tools, language was a huge milestone in human evolution and was considered to be unique to our species. Language was based on arbitrary symbols and allowed humans to talk about the past or things not in view, so you can imagine scientific curiosity about whether or not monkeys or apes have a language of their own or can learn human language and cultural systems.

Early scholars speculated about language ability and wondered if apes might be taught to speak. Experiments didn't begin in earnest until the 1900s. Attempts to teach speech semi-failed; they were able to hoarsely say and understand a few words such as "papa," and "cup" but the process was tedious. Great ape natural gestures such as an outreached hand to beckon to others or request sharing seem more promising.

By the mid-20th century, three research projects began with chimpanzees. Allen and Beatrix Gardner taught sign language to a chimpanzee Washoe, Duane Rumbaugh and colleagues taught a chimpanzee Lana a computer lexigram system of geometric designs that stood for concepts. David and Ann Premack created colored plastic chips for a chimpanzee Sarah that stood for different ideas or concepts such as 'more than.'

All three methods showed that chimpanzees could learn small vocabularies of a couple hundred symbols, use them to communicate, and ask and answer questions through symbols. The signing chimpanzee Washoe was even able to adopt an infant Loulis who observed and learned signs from his mother who even began to deliberately teach signs. For example, Washoe placed a chair in front of Loulis and she signed "sit/chair" several times, carefully watching his behavior. It seemed that the apes were not only learning they were teaching. Later studies by Francine Patterson with gorillas showed that larger vocabularies could be achieved and that apes could invent signs of their own, e.g., "finger bracelet" for a ring.

Sue Savage-Rumbaugh explored categories of words with chimpanzees who learned the computer lexigram system. She showed that two chimpanzees, Sherman and Austin, understood and could use categories for objects, such as food and tools. This was significant because if apes can group people or objects into categories they have some abstract representational ability, i.e., they understand that a symbol is something that stands for something else.

Other researchers went onto to study the remaining three great apes, gorillas, bonobos, and orangutans. Savage-Rumbaugh studied several bonobos, including Kanzi, who learned the computer lexigram system. Kanzi learned to comprehend speech was able to classify objects and understand commands. For example, researchers would say even a nonsensical request, such as "Kanzi, put the leaves in the refrigerator," and Kanzi would carry out the action. It was important that some commands not make much sense to make sure Kanzi wasn't just taking a logical action, but really understanding the researchers.

Perhaps the best known of the great ape language projects is from the Gorilla Foundation's longitudinal study of Koko. Many people recall reading a children's book about Koko's Kitten. Koko learned signs based on American Sign Language and invented words of her own such as "finger bracelet" for a ring. Koko was raised by Francine "Penny" Patterson in California where people were very excited to learn that an ape could use language. Patterson, despite criticism, raised Koko as much like a human child as was possible and celebrated holidays like Valentine's Day and Halloween with Koko. Her goal was to expose Koko to as much symbolic life as possible. Besides adopting a kitten, Koko also painted, named body parts, and called a favorite caregiver "foot." Koko is now an ambassador for the conservation of all great apes and helps the United Nations make everyone aware of the remarkable language abilities of apes at the level of very young children.

CHANTEK

By the end of the 20th century, language research with ape was extended to an orangutan named Chantek raised at the University of Tennessee at Chattanooga by H. Lyn Miles. As an anthropologist, she emphasized human culture equally with language and symbols. A closer look at this project will give a more detailed picture of ape abilities.

A small group of caregivers and students created a family with Chantek, who had normal childhood experiences of going to the lake or mountains, seeing other animals at the circus or zoo, and playing in his yard. He learned names for colors, family members, pronouns, foods, and locations. Interestingly, his largest vocabulary items was for tools; he could sign and use "screwdriver," "wire-cutter," and "hammer," and chain tool tasks for up to 22 steps.

Chantek acquired several hundred signs, for example, "share" for Lyn to break off a piece of a sandwich for him. He began to combine his signs together in novel ways to create new meanings. For example, he called a helicopter a "noisy dog," and the hair on a student's leg a "beard." He referred to things that were present, and also could talk about the past or the future. He was inventive and combined signs for tomato and toothpaste to create a word for "ketchup," and invented a number of different words, including one that seemed to mean, "annoyed."

After five years of age, his language became very symbolic and metaphorical. His drawings were more complex and artistic and he began to make jewelry—in fact, is the only animal in the world to do so. He showed planning, and judgement in the size he cut a cord, how he would string beads and found art objects, and how he would create a clasp for both necklaces and bracelets. He also learned the concept of money by using doughnut shaped metal washers for 'dollars.' He would earn a weekly allowance with household chores and spend his money on candy machines, trips in the car, and tool supplies.

Chantek also was able to tell lies—about three per week as far as researchers could tell. His lies began as simple deceptions such as rearranging cookies so you could not see one was missing or hiding vegetables behind his toilet. As he became older, he showed theory of mind, the ability to know what others can understand, called subjective representation. Chantek also showed understanding of signs as representations. When someone asked him to "sign better," he would deconstruct the components of the sign, illustrate each one, and then turn and illustrate the usage, e.g., enthusiastically say, "chase Chantek!" After years of this culturally-embedded language research,

Chantek ended up living in a zoo which believes that this is too humanizing and should be discouraged. Preventing Chantek from using his encultured abilities, knowledge, and skills raises a number of ethical issues. In fact, 21st century zoos may need to create cultural environments for all great apes, including tool making, navigation, foraging, and hunting. Just looking at a gorilla on a hillside may not be enough.

MODELS FOR HUMAN EVOLUTION

Anthropologists are interested in primates, especially great apes, because genetic studies show that they share 99% of our DNA and are our closest biological relatives. Apes have 48 chromosomes and humans have 46, which seems like a difference. However, one pair of ape chromosomes stuck end to end with another to form human chromosome #2, so we have all 48 chromosomes, two are just stuck together. Living great ape species are NOT our direct ancestor, they are cousins who have undergone their own evolution and have developed their own unique traits. We obviously are not the same species and we know key genes related to language, thinking and problem-solving are different and developed after our split. But, we are much more closely related that certainly people in the ancient world or Darwin's time imagined.

So we look to great apes for models of how to construct what our common ancestor might have looked like and what our earliest culture might have been. We also use fossils, brain studies, genetics, and behavior and anatomy of monkeys, apes, and even wolves, and intelligent dolphins, whales, and elephants for clues for how to reconstruct our beginnings. The task is to identify patterns of anatomy, behavior, and adaptation and extrapolate it to human culture to develop some hypotheses about our early ecology and environmental challenges.

So which ape model should we use? Clearly, we can use gorillas to understand the delicate relationship with the environment and be aware that even a very large primate might have a gentle temperament. Chimpanzees and orangutans with their extensive use of sticks, stones, and leaves, provide a model of the beginnings of technology. Chimpanzees' extensive politics of conflict followed by reconciliation also shows that early human social politics was not likely simple. Bonobo female dominance exhibits a very different social structure than chimpanzees and give us a range of behaviors to model for early human ancestors. How chimpanzees and bonobos are so similar yet have such different social systems is a reminder to view early human social systems in very flexible ways.

Examples of cooperation, altruism, and empathy are especially instructive. Sociologists have stressed how important living in groups has been for human beings, and how society is the fabric that holds us together—we are all really intertwined. Researchers with all the great apes now have a number of observations where apes, like humans, have protected others during attack at some risk to themselves, have helped the young or the elderly along a path, tried to rescue those who have fallen into the water, or remained near ill or dying relatives.

One example with the orangutan Chantek makes this clear. He was painting and making jewelry one summer day when a sudden thunderstorm broke out. Seeing that his human companion had no umbrella or shelter, he quickly looked around at his materials and saw a thick paper cloth. He ripped it in two and pushed it through signing for her to put it on her head. They stood together in the rain and shared the only shelter they could find. This is the empathy also found in great apes in natural settings. When we look at modern foraging human groups today most are cooperative and empathic; if others weren't they did not survive and reproduce.

So we leave this exploration of the apes knowing that our earliest ancestors likely had stick and stone tools, cooperation, complex gestural communication, empathy and other emotions, complex social relations and alliances, deception, insight, and problem-solving skills. Although Darwin suspected it, this is much more than was believed in the "missing link" thinking days of the mid-19th century. But the question is, how did we get from an ape-like culture to a human one?—which we'll see on our next journey.

CRITICAL THINKING & WEBSITES

1. Why do anthropologists study primates, especially great apes? How can information about the behavior and intelligence of apes aid in their conservation or legal rights?

2. What role does a challenging environment play in primates developing adaptations using intelligence?

3. How can anthropologists avoid anthropomorphism when apes and humans share common ancestry?

4. What culture or language ability of great apes seems most notable to you? Why is it possibly unethical to deny the ability of great apes taught to use language and human culture to exercise their skills?

5. See the Living Links website of the Center for the Advanced Study of Ape and Human Evolution: http://www.emory.edu/LIVING_LINKS/.

6. Explore the efforts of Jane Goodall to preserve chimpanzees in Africa at: janegoodall.org., and efforts to preserve orangutans in Asia at: orangutan.org.

7. Check out more about great ape culture at: http://theadvancedapes.com/2013221the-century-of-great-ape-culture/.

REFERENCES

Amundson, Ron. (1985). The hundredth monkey phenomenon. *Skeptical Inquirer*, Summer 1985, 348-356.

Boesch, C. (2003). Is culture a golden barrier between human and chimpanzee? *Evolutionary Anthropology*, 12: 82-91.

Boesch, Christophe. (2012). Culture in primates. In Joan Valsiner, *The Oxford Handbook of Culture and Psychology*. Oxford, UK: Oxford University Press.

Boesch-Achermann, H, & Boesch, C. (1994). Hominization in the rainforest: The chimpanzee's piece of the puzzle. *Evolutionary Anthropology* 3, 1, 9-16.

Breuer, T., Ndoundou-Hockemba, N., & Fishlock, V. (2005). First observations of tool use in gorillas. *FloS Biology* 3, 11, e380. Doi: 10.1371/journal. Pbio.0030380.

Cheney, Dorothy, & Seyfarth, Robert. (1992). *How Monkeys See the World: Inside the Mind of Another Species*. Chicago, IL: University of Chicago Press.

Cheney, Dorothy, & Seyfarth, Robert. (2007). *Baboon Metaphysics*. Chicago, IL: University of Chicago Press.

Cheney, D. L., Seyfarth, R. M, Smuts, B. B., & Wrangham, R. W. (1987). The study of primate societies. In *Primate Societies*, eds. Barbara Smuts, Dorothy Cheney, Robert Seyfarth, Richard Wrangham, & Thomas Struhsaker, 1-10. Chicago, IL: University of Chicago Press.

De Waal, Frans. (1989). *Our Inner Ape: A Leading Primatologist Explains Why We Are Who We Are*. New York, NY: Penguin Group.

Fleagle. (2013). *Primate Adaptations and Evolution*, 3rd edition. Amsterdam & Boston: Elsevier/Academic Press.

Fuentes, Augustine. (2012). Ethnoprimatology and the anthropology of the human-primate interface. *Annual Review of Anthropology* 41, 101-147.

Galef, B. G. 91992). The question of animal culture. *Human Nature* 3, 2, 157-178.

Haraway, Donna. (1989). *Primate Visions*. New York: Routledge.

Hohmann, G. & Fruth, B. (2003). Culture in bonobos? Between-species and within-species variation in behaviour. *Current Anthropology*, 44: 563-571.

Hrubesch, C., Preuschoft, S., & van Schaik, C.P. (2009). Skill mastery inhibits adoption of observed alternative solutions among chimpanzees (*Pan troglodytes*). *Animal Cognition*, 12: 209-216.

Le Gros Clark, W. E. (1963). *The Antecedents*, 2nd ed. New York, NY: Harper & Row.

Miles, H. Lyn White. (1990). The cognitive foundations for reference in a signing orangutan. In *Language and Intelligence in Monkeys and Apes: Comparative Developmental Perspectives*. S. T. Parker & K. R. Gibson, eds., 511-539. New York: NY: Cambridge University Press.

Sanz, C.M. & Morgan, D.B. (2009). Flexible and persistent tool-using strategies in honey-gathering by wild chimpanzees. *International Journal of Primatology*, 30: 411-427.

Tennie, C., Call, J., & Tomasello, M. (2009). Ratcheting up the ratchet: on the evolution of cumulative culture. *Philosophical Trasactions of the Royal Society*. 364: 2405-2415.

van Schaik, C.P., Ancrenaz, M., Borgen, G., Galdikas, B., Knott, C.D., Singleton, I., Suzuki, A., Utami, S.S., Merrill, M. (2003). Orangutan cultures and the evolution of material culture. *Science*, 299: 102-105.

Van Schaik et al. (2003). Orangutan cultures and the evolution of material culture. *Science* 299:102-105.

Visalberghi, E., Addessi, E., Truppa, V., Spagnoletti, N., Ottoni, E., Izar, P. & Fragaszy, D. (2009). Selection of effective stone tools by wild bearded capuchin monkeys. *Current Biology*, 19: 213-217.

Whiten, Andrew, Goodall, Jane, McGrew, W. C., Nishida, T., Reynolds, V., Sugiyama, Y, Tutin, C. E. G., Wrangham, R. W., Boesch, C. (1999). Cultures in chimpanzees. *Nature* 399, 6737, 682-685.

List the evidence below for the cultural abilities of great apes and give the significance of each category.

Ability	Significance

2. What traits seem most humanlike? What argument would you make for conservation of great apes?

5 EARLY BIPEDS:
Lucy and Friends

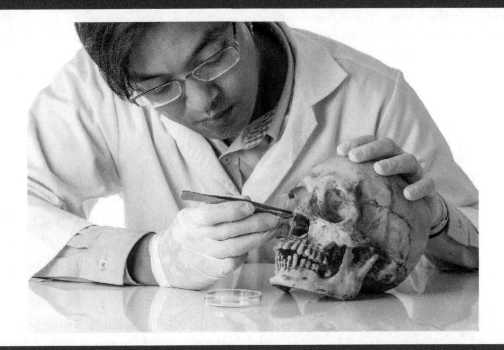

About eight million years ago, the earliest human ancestors lived in the swampy forests and seashores and adapted to their environments by walking on two legs. This freed their hands and led to more tool use, social complexity, and brain growth—and also new hominin species.

LEARNING OBJECTIVES

1. Understand how anthropologist investigate human ancestors and reconstruct their lifestyles.

2. Describe the cosmic event that allowed for the development of the first primates.

3. Know the significance of the emergence of bipedalism and explain the several factors that may have led to it.

4. Describe the size, physical characteristic and likely lifeways of the first bipeds and the challenges of determining who was the first biped.

5. Describe the fossil Lucy, the genus *Australopithecus*, and how early bipeds likely lived.

6. Describe *Gigantopithecus* and relate it and other hypotheses to the folklore about Sasquatch and Bigfoot in Asia and the Northwest Coast.

INVESTIGATING ANCESTORS

RECONSTRUCTING OUR PAST

For the last several centuries, we have attempted to systematically investigate our origins by seeking evidence in the form of fossils, artifacts, and now genetic analysis. We interpret this evidence to create a narrative story of how we became human, understanding that that story changes as we find new fossils and artifacts. So the human journey is not only one of discovery of evidence, it is also one of interpretation, storytelling, and myth making. We are literally like the picture, looking into the mirror of apelike fossils and culture to find our common ancestor. A number of issues emerged over centuries of exploring our origins.

1. Ape or Human: When Europeans became aware of apes in the 1600s, they immediately recognized the anatomical and behavioral similarities between humans and apes, but still assumed humans were separate from animals and had dominion over them. Darwin stressed our continuity with great apes and other life which became more plausible as additional fossils were discovered. However, we still do not follow biological principles in how we classify ourselves within primates—to be consistent, we should be in the same genetic family as apes.

2. Exceptionalism and Perfection: In the Judeo-Christian tradition, the point of creation was the improvement and perfection of imperfect humans who were guided by a divine authority. Early scientists carried this idea forward and imagined that evolution somehow had the goal of making a perfect human species of one sort or another.

3. Gradual Versus Sudden: As the idea of evolution became more accepted, scientists assumed the process was always gradual with change coming in small increments. But, the fossil record showed some big gaps meaning that sometimes sudden change, called punctuated equilibrium, occurred in a big leap, especially in small populations.

4. Lumpers Versus Splitters: Some scientists saw the similarities in fossils, genetics, or behavior while others stressed the differences and gave each fossil a different species name. As more and more fossils were discovered, trying to figure out the actual species boundaries became a challenge. Further, biologists have multiple ways to define a species based on appearance, genetics, geography, or other factors and splitting became the interpretation for animals which has now become the trend for human ancestors. Besides, every discoverer of a new fossil gets to name it as well.

5. Hero Myth: Myths of great heroes are widespread in human societies, and this theme carried over into the investigation of our ancestors. They must have been "masters" of the environment in some way to be so wonderful to have become humans—after all, humans are the greatest! The possibility that early hominins (meaning human ancestor) might be adapting to their environment just like worms or lizards or the 99% of life forms that eventually became extinct was unthinkable. Humans were the heroes of creation.

6. Hoaxes and Brains: A couple of times the scientific inquiry into our development encountered a fraud, e.g., the Piltdown Hoax. In 1912, a fossil emerged from a gravel pit in England associated with people of credibility that fit expectations that humans were brainy apes—but it seemed to go against the grain of the growing scientific evidence. It took decades for scientists finally in 1953 to develop a method to expose the fraud—it was a discolored orangutan lower jaw attached to a prehistoric human skull. Why was the hoax believed? Cognitive dissonance is likely. If we had to be related to apes, people wanted to think human ancestors were the brainy apes so the hoax confirmed their belief.

7. Eurocentric Focus
A strong Europe-centered focus persisted in the search for our origins; after all, most of the early scientists were European themselves and excavated there. They were also affected by the ethnocentric notion that our development either began in Europe or had its greatest complexity there, centered on the Cro-Magnons. As the fossil record was excavated our origins were proposed to be in Asia, then Africa, and now both—not surprising since this is where we find the living great apes. But the overemphasis on evolution culminating in Europe has subtly continued to this day. Continued discovery of more fossils and artifacts in Asia may change that picture in the 21st century.

8. Linear Versus Bush
The earliest notions of our evolution looked for a "missing link" between apes and humans as if species change always occurred in a straight line. But, the fossil picture that emerged looked more like a huge bush, and we realized that five or more hominin species lived at the same time. The "link" had become links.

9. Cladistics and Genetics Versus Systematic Comparisons
Early analyses of fossil were based only their appearance but a new method called cladistics sorted through the traits of a fossil to create groupings based on evolutionary relationships. More recently means to extract DNA from fossils and compare it with living populations was developed, so now we know we are related to the Neandertals because the DNA says so.

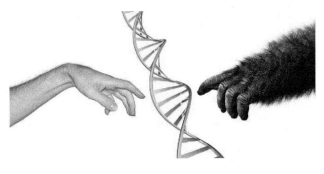

10. Role of the Environment
Gradually, the idea that humans were exceptional has given way to a growing focus on adaptation to the environment and how it resulted in many hominin species. In 1993, Ian Tattersall (2015) proposed a list of 12 hominin species in our ancestry, but twenty years later, there are over 40 hominin species spread out over 7 million years—and no doubt even more to be discovered.

While these issues affect interpretation, the picture of human evolution is still based on solid evidence. But it is clear, that with each hominin and stage of development, our direct and indirect ancestors have engaged in experiments and chance competition for survival that resulted in one lineage becoming food producers, tool makers, and symbol-users with all the challenges we face today. Darwin clearly placed us in nature, but it is a much more diverse and challenging picture than even he ever imagined. It can be frustrating to see the story of human evolution change with each new fossil discovery. This makes some question evolutionary theory itself. But, it is more like someone dropping pieces of a puzzle on the ground. Some get lost, some are buried in the grass—but anthropologists pick up pieces one by one to see the big picture.

PRIMATE EVOLUTION

THE COSMIC CALENDAR

One way to put the human lineage into perspective is to use the Cosmic Calendar suggested by Carl Sagan in *The Dragons of Eden*. Physicists have determined that the universe is 13.8 billion years old, so if we put its starting point on an imaginary year-long calendar, January 1st would begin with the Big Bang and the present time would be on December 31st. Each day would cover about 38 million years. On this scale, life begins on September 21, dinosaurs on December 25, and apes and hominins not until New Year's Eve evening. Modern humans did not appear until an hour before midnight! Put on the scale of the size of a football field—humans don't appear until the last blade of grass just before the goal line!

According to the geologic record, one of earth's three or four extinction events played a role in the development of primates. The K-T Event, 65 mya (million years ago), caused a mass extinction of about 75% of all life on earth. The extinction of most of the dinosaurs opened up adaptive radiation of underground mammals and aquatic animals, while some dinosaurs still survived as birds and small reptiles.

This is supported by a thin rock layer found around the world with high levels of iridium which is rare. But, because it is common in asteroids, scientists hypothesize that an asteroid hit the earth and its catastrophic effects caused the extinctions. The Chicxulub crater in the Gulf of Mexico is dated to the same time and has debris from an asteroid impact, so it is the likely location.

FIRST PRIMATES

The oldest know primate in the fossil record was part of the mammalian radiation following the K-T Event. *Plesiadapis* was a rodent-like mammal from around 55 mya who appears to be closely related to tree shrews and flying squirrels. The earliest primates flourished in Europe and Asia and later Africa. Monkeys began to emerge around 35 mya, and by the Miocene Epoch 5-23 mya, great ape ancestors emerged in the warm areas of East Africa and the Mediterranean. Later, a split occurred between the Asian orangutan and the ancestors of African apes: chimpanzees, gorillas, and bonobos.

By about 6-8 mya, the hominin (human ancestor) line diverged from the ape-human common ancestor with a locomotor pattern of bipedalism, walking on two feet. This required changes in the shoulder, hips, knees and ultimately skull, supported by lines of evidence from anatomy, genetics, and behavior. Hominins included several genera such as *Australopithecus* and our own genus *Homo*. *Homo* in turn can be broadly grouped into three stages: *Homo habilis*, *Homo erectus*, and *Homo sapiens*, although scientist make additional species distinctions within those broad groups. We are classified today as *Homo sapiens sapiens*. What all these hominins had in common was a new way to move about—bipedalism.

BIPEDALISM

We can envision bipedalism taking place through three major stages. The fossil evidence now suggests that the origins of our lineage begins in the rain forest, perhaps at the edges of swamps, rivers, and streams. Two of the great apes, orangutans and bonobos, are still found in these environments today. Most chimpanzees and gorillas live in forests near water sources also. Why would a tendency toward bipedalism as a way of moving around begin in a swampy forest? Humans are not the only bipedal species, birds, kangaroos, some lizards and some primates are occasionally bipedal. We see that all the great apes from time to time stand on two feet to walk short distances, while carrying infants or objects, wading in water, or peering down a forest trail to a clearing.

In Stage 1, hominins begin as swamp bipeds if not in the water, at least near the water. Carrying food, babies, and objects while reaching for branches and berries might have also helped their success. Stage 2 began as the climate changed around 2.5 mya and our ancestors found themselves in drier grasslands where their already developed bipedalism allowed them to travel long distances and brought other advantages such as seeing predators. In Stage 3, hominins migrated to other parts of the world.

Some recent evidence suggests that migrations out of Africa occurred much earlier than previously believed and likely came in waves. Several hypotheses have been put forward to explain the origins of human bipedalism, shown in Table 5.1. Each of these hypotheses have advocates and all could have played a role although some are more likely than others. Another hypothesis, Elaine Morgan's aquatic ape hypothesis, was strongly rejected by American anthropologists as overstated and almost pseudoscience. However, a very modified "swamp ape" hypothesis can also explain some odd similarities between dolphins and humans, e.g., large brain, eating shellfish, loss of hair, fat layers, breath control, and tearing. While human ancestors may not have gone through an entire aquatic stage, living in and near water certainly played a strong role in our species change.

Table 5.1. Bipedalism Hypotheses and Explanations

HYPOTHESIS	EXPLANATION
Berry Picking	Hominins could get more food by reaching higher or just standing and picking berries or other fruit with two hands. On all fours, they would have to sit, get up, move forward, and then sit again, which is more effort. Hominins could also hold onto a branch for steadying while picking.
Object Carrying	*If orangutans have two stick toolkits, hominins may have had more and had to carry them longer distances. Traveling upright would have allowed them to carry tools and other objects.*
Seeing Distances	On the open dry grassland savanna, hominins stood upright to gaze over the tall grasses to watch for predators. Hominins beginning to scavenge meat from the kills of other animals could also sneak up on predators and then hunt prey themselves.
Traveling Efficiently	*Hominins could go from vertical climbing and hanging in one tree, to moving down and across an area to a nearby cluster of trees, without the expense of going on all fours and then vertical again.*
Body Cooling	In hot environments, reducing the body surface facing the sun would result in less skin hair for greater evaporation of perspiration and keep the brain cool. Retaining thick hair on the head would provide additional insulation.
Swamp Wading	*Apes automatically switch to bipedalism in waist deep water and hominins are good swimmers. Humans have voluntary control of breathing, hairlessness, subcutaneous fat, tears, and other traits shared with dolphins and not with apes. Shallow waters would have also provided additional protein from fish and shellfish, as well as omega 3 acids that promote brain growth.*
Carrying Babies	As hominins spent more time on their feet, infants could not cling to their mothers, so the mothers increasingly carried them on their hips which would have additionally fostered face to face communication.
Carrying Provisions	*Early hominins show reduction of male canines so they may have begun carrying provisions to females rather than fight with other males over food. Babies born with feet for walking would be able to cling less and thus both mother and child would be more dependent on males for survival.*
Arboreal Adaptation	The increased hip and knee extension from being vertical in the trees allowed hominins to have a wider feeding range and access to process fruit. A wider foraging area meant more food and greater success.
Perch Steadying	*While feeding in trees, hominins could hold onto higher branches to stabilize themselves while navigating thinner branches. This would have provided additional food sources.*
Sexual Selection	Some animals have bright plumage or colorful faces that have appealed to females. Female hominins may have preferred males who stood upright for some reason, and mated with them more often.
Ape Preadaptation	*The ape-human common ancestor may all have been bipedal to begin with, and over time apes became more specialized for being quadrupedal or knuckle walkers in the forest, while hominins continued on in the ancestral state.*
Threat Displays	Standing upright may have been only one of several adaptations hominins used to back off competitors. The larger, taller, and louder you were, the more intimidating to others.

FIRST HOMININS

If we turn to the fossil record we see some fairly recent discoveries that shed light on the first hominins. In Chad, in central Africa, there is a fossil skull find, *Sahelanthropus tchadensis*. dated at around 7 mya. What is noteworthy about this find is that Central Africa had green forests and wet environments. The skull braincase volume is 380 cm³ (cubic centimeters), about the size of a chimpanzee, but the position of the foramen magnum, the hole at the base of the skull for the entry of the spinal cord, is more centered which is humanlike and suggests bipedalism.

Orrorin tugenensis is another candidate. *Orrorin* was found in Kenya, and dated at 6 mya. It consist of a jaw bone, teeth, parts of a thigh bone, fingers, and thumb bone of five individuals. Details of the teeth are more humanlike and the leg bones suggest *Orrorin* looks bipedal but still spent a great deal of time climbing trees. In some ways, *Orrorin* is more similar to humans than some later hominins and additional evidence might indicate the lineages.

Anthropologists are most confident about a third choice, *Ardipithecus ramidus* which is dated later, around 5.8 mya. "Ardi" was discovered in the 1990s by Tim White, and has a brain about 350 cm³, long arms, and feet with her big toe to the side for climbing trees, including at night for sleeping nests. Her pelvis strongly suggests bipedalism but also sometimes walking on her palms like an orangutan.

Additional supporting evidence for bipedalism comes from a 3.6 mya trail of footprints found at Laetoli, Tanzania, in East Africa. The trail extends for 70 feet and appears to show three individuals: one large, medium, and small, and it is tempting to imagine a family especially since the small footprints veer off to the side and then return to the two others. The amazing footprints were preserved in volcanic ash and the stride indicates that they were perhaps walking away from a volcano.

What we can conclude is that around 5-7 mya some hominins began to diverge away from the ape-human common ancestor and increasingly rely on bipedalism for their locomotion. How apelike their lifestyle might have still been is still unclear although we can presume that they were at least as culture-developed as living apes today.

AUSTRALOPITHECUS: LUCY AND FRIENDS

GRACILE *AUSTRALOPITHECUS*
Australopithecus represents a large group of fossil hominins ranging from 4.4 to 1 mya. They formed two groups: gracile smaller delicate-boned forms, and larger heavier jawed vegetarians.

The first known species *Australopithecus ramidus* was found in Kenya and we now have nearly 100 fossil specimens representing over 20 individuals. The context is woodland surrounding a lake, and the tooth wear suggests that *ramidus* was eating a lot of leaves and other plant cellulous. *Australopithecus anamensis* is dated to 4 million years and had teeth shaped more in the humanlike direction suggesting a wider diet than mostly leaves.

We know a great deal more about the next species, *Australopithecus afarensis* who lived between 3.9 and 2.9 mya. The most famous *A. afarensis* is the fossil "Lucy" who was found in the Afar wetland region of Ethiopia. Lucy is a 40% complete skeleton who stood 3.5 to 5 ft. tall and had a brain size of around 420 cm^3 similar to great apes. Lucy still had slightly curved fingers and toes suggesting climbing in trees. But, her pelvis is very humanlike and her femur (thigh bone) angles in toward the knee suggesting habitual bipedalism. Her teeth show reduced canines, also humanlike, but a U-shaped upper jaw is more apelike.

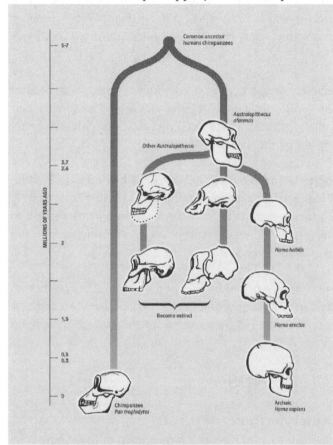

The verdict is that she is small brained and apelike in some features, but clearly a hominin. The Laetoli footprints described above were likely also made by A. afarensis. So by 4 mya, human ancestors were definitely bipedal with a mosaic of ape and hominin traits.

Later *Australopithecus* includes *A. africanus* who lived between 3.8 and 2 mya. The first *Australopithecus* discovered was the Taung Child found in the early 1900s. The skull was discovered in a limestone quarry and was reported to Raymond Dart, a physician in South Africa. He saw the infant primate skull and named it "southern ape from Africa" but noticed the position of the foramen magnum and knew it was a hominin. Taung was about three or four years of age and had a cranial capacity of 400-500 cm^3. Evidence showed that the child would have matured earlier than humans do today and was probably killed by an eagle.

Interestingly, environmental evidence suggested she lived in a drier savanna habitat putting her in Stage 2 of bipedalism development. The claim that Taung was a hominin was angrily criticized by scientists who were shocked at the child's apelike traits. How could something so apelike be our ancestor? It took decades to accept the idea that human ancestors might have had a small-brain and that bipedalism developed first. Other *Australopithecus africanus* fossils were later discovered also with a forward foramen magnum indicating bipedalism and a cranial capacity of 400-500 cm^3. This showed some increase in brain size with a rounded cranium (top of skull).

ROBUST *AUSTRALOPITHECUS*

Later *Australopithcus* species were also found in South and East Africa and some are called *Paranthropus robustus* by anthropologists who see them as a more separate branch from human ancestors. Unlike the gracile *A. africanus*, their skulls are more gorilla-like and they have strong jaws and a sagittal crest that runs the length of the top of the skull. They are dated from 2 to 1 mya and likely had a vegetarian diet. They stood three to four feet tall and had a cranial capacity of 400-500 cm³. They seem too specialized to be a likely candidate for human ancestry.

HUMAN ANCESTOR CANDIDATES

At various periods, one or another of these australopiths were considered as possible direct human ancestor. However, two other fossils emerged recently who seem more likely. In 1999, Tim White made an exciting *Australopithecus* discovery in Ethiopia and named it *Australopithecus garhi* meaning "surprise." *A. garhi* was dated at 2.5 mya and had a brainsize of 450 cm³. But the big news was that *garhi* was found with mammal bones that had cut marks such as those made by stone tools and evidence of bones being pounded to extract the rich fatty marrow.

More recently, it was shown that primitive stone tools were also associated and at a nearby site around 3,000 stone artifacts were found in the same deposits. For several decades, anthropologists assumed that only the *Homo* lineage would have the ability and intelligence to produce shaped stone tools. But, now this technology is being pushed back to another genus living around the same time. It may be that a number of later australopiths went beyond the nut cracking with stones of great apes and began to actually shape the stones in order to extract scavenged meat and marrow.

A second candidate for human ancestry is *Australopithecus sediba* dated to 2 mya. Its name means "wellspring fountain." *A. sediba* was actually found by a nine year old son of paleoanthropologist Lee Berger. We have six skeletons from South Africa including adults, a juvenile and infants. They were found together and may have fell to their death in a cave.

A. sediba has a mosaic mixture of traits suggesting it may be transitional between *Australopithecus* and *Homo*. Its cranial capacity is 420 cm³ within the australopith range and its shoulder, arms and curved fingers all suggest evolution from *A. africanus*. *A. sediba's* teeth suggests their diet was a forest one of fruit, but they also ate wood, bark and grass—more like a chimpanzee. *A. sediba's* hand is surprisingly human which hints at tool-making and their brain also may be reorganized. Whether *sediba*, *garhi*, or other early biped, the tendency to modify stone tools was a growing cultural tradition and means to adapt to a changing environment.

71

Which *Australopithecus* species is our closest ancestor is hard to say yet, and we will need more evidence to make this determination. However, it is clear that by 6 million years ago our distant ancestors began to become more bipedal but remaining otherwise very apelike. By 2 mya their descendants had more specialized teeth, slightly larger brains, human hands, and were walking in the open savanna, with some making stone tools as well as wood and bone tools that have not been preserved.

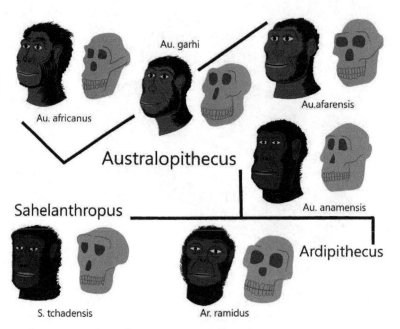

These species seemed to have restricted ranges and we know that evolution can be more rapid in small populations, so this may have fostered hominin development. As they developed more hominin traits, they still retained many apelike characteristics, especially those related to climbing and sleeping in trees. Some began to specialize in rough vegetarian diets of grass while others began to use stone tools to scavenge meat but they all remain pretty apelike in their lifestyle and their brains stay relatively small for almost five million years.

We definitely do not start out as big brained apes. But, at the end of this period we see that there may be a dietary shift and *Australopithecus* or any other hominins may have turned to eating some scavenged meat processed with stone tools which had major dietary consequences for our ancestors. This new technology, built on the nut-cracking stones of ape culture, could have made a big difference around 2.5 mya. Certainly, it is something that caught on, because the first *Homo* hominins are definitely using stone tools.

One final twist--chimpanzee tool-makers are primarily female, e.g., termiting sticks and spears. Twentieth century scenarios mostly imagined that males made the first tools, but 97% of chimp tools are made by females. This blows the old "man the hunter" hero myth that was so popular out of the water, so to speak, and puts the female swamp hominins right back into human evolution. So, we can thank Lucy and her friends and descendants for the culture we have today.

GIGANTOPITHECUS AND SASQUATCH

Gigantopithecus is a puzzling apelike species that lived just before the early bipeds around 9 mya. The genus lasted until about 100,000 years ago when it presumably became extinct in Asia. It is a fascinating primate who had a huge range from India and Pakistan to China and Southeast Asia, and lived at the same time as *Homo* in these areas. In fact, human predation or survival competition may have been the activity of our ancestors that caused *Gigantopithecus'* extinction.

For thousands of years it was the practice in China to crush *Gigantopithecus* fossils and use as a medicine and aphrodisiac. It was discovered in 1935 by Ralph von Koenigswald who noticed that a Chinese pharmacy was grinding up "dragon bone" fossils into a powder used in traditional Chinese medicine, sometimes as an aphrodisiac. He started to collect what fossils he could and out of the collection emerged this new species.

Gigantopithecus includes several species that are the largest apes even known with some estimated to have been 6-9 feet tall and weighing 800 pounds, based on skeletal information—no pelvic bones have been found so other features are used to make this estimate. Another possibility is that they might have been clamberers more like orangutans today especially given their large size. They were highly sexually dimorphic with females half the size of males. Their thick jaws and heavy tooth enamel showed they ate tough foods such as bamboo—much like pandas today, and some of their molar teeth are quite worn from a fiber diet. Today they are classified in a group of smaller apelike ancestors to orangutans.

Tall, probably hairy, and apelike with an armspan of 10-12 feet? Does any of this sound familiar? Can anyone say "Bigfoot"? Mainstream anthropology says no, but several anthropologists, including Grover Krantz, Geoffrey Bourne, Colin Groves, Jeff Meldrum, and a group of interdisciplinary scientists called the Relict Hominoid Inquiry believe it is worth investigating or at least critically keeping an open mind. Even chimpanzee expert Jane Goodall has speculated that *Gigantopithecus* might still exist.

This is because *Gigantopithecus* resembles stories and sightings in oral traditions in India and Tibet about Yeti, or the abominable snowman. China also has stories about Yeren "wild man," Australia provides reports of a large apelike being, Yowie, and Indonesia has tales of Orang Pendek, although Pendek is usually described as smaller. So there is widespread Asian and Australian reports of such a creature.

Across the Bering Land Bridge in the Northwest Coast of North America Coast Salish First Nations tell stories of Sasquatch. Sasquatch is hairy and muscular stands 6 to 10 feet tall, and is covered in dark reddish, brown, or black hair. Some report a pronounced brow ridge and a sagittal crest like that found on gorillas, as well as seeing footprints in the snow. North America as well abounds with similar reports, especially from the Northwest. There is even a Tule Indian Reservation in California that has a "hairy man" pictograph on a rock in Yokut Cave that has been dated to 500 CE.

A pseudoscience claim is that Sasquatch and Bigfoot are real. They place great stock in the many reports, some from trained observers. A number of groups of informal investigators collect accounts and mount expeditions in the forests of northern California, Oregon, Washington, and British Columbia in Canada. Reports usually indicate traits like a pronounced brow ridge and crested cranium with a hairy tall body and often unpleasant body odor. Footprints of Bigfoot have been cast and they can be as large as two feet long. Most believers claim Bigfoot is omnivorous (plant and animal diet) and is mainly nocturnal. This would be unusual because all the great apes and humans are diurnal and Bigfoot reports do not mention the large eyes that true nocturnal primates exhibit.

An artifact often mentioned by pseudoscientists is a film shot in California in 1967. The Patterson film, shot by Roger Patterson and Bob Gimlin, shows a hairy figure walking away from the camera with a bouncing gait and looking over her right shoulder. The film has been in numerous History Channel programs and is highly viewed on youtube.com.

However, critics believe that it does not show the bipedal gait of a large primate and is really someone in a gorilla suit. Most apes walk bipedally with a sway or move rapidly forward on all fours. The Bigfoot figure in the film seems to jaunt, holding her fist at her side, unlike apes. Suspicion is added because one of the filmmakers worked in the film industry in California. Family members themselves have reported it is a hoax and some have even named John Chambers, who appeared in Planet of the Apes.

Another pseudoscience claim is that they are really extra-dimensional beings who come to earth to guide humans. While this is always possible, the question is what is the evidence? An answer might be how elusive Bigfoot appears to be, but a simpler explanation is stick to the power of folklore rather than such an extraordinary claim. Further, why would extra-dimensional beings look like tall apes?

A number of known hoaxes are associated with Bigfoot and Sasquatch. One in Clayton County, Georgia in the 2000s resulted in a major CNN news conference and worldwide coverage. A few weeks later the conclusion was that the discoverers had taken a gorilla suit costume and scattered some animal entrails on it. A close look at the Bigfoot face pretty clearly indicated a gorilla mask with stereotyped scowl, not a naturalistic great ape cadaver.

INTERPRETING THE EVIDENCE

One possibility is that *Gigantopithecus* originated in southwest Asia and crossed the Bering Land Bridge into North America, and ranged to remote mountain and cave areas in Asia as hominins moved east. A second option is that some other later hominin species such as *Homo heidelbergensis* which lasted in China until 12,000 ya might have survived with a toolkit of stone tools, fire, and shelter.

A third possibility is that people are actually seeing shaman of the Coast Salish people who make spiritual pilgrimages for years in the forest, living like an animal and connecting with nature. Their hair and beards grow long and they are covered in animal skins so the mistake is possible. After so much isolation, their behavior may also be strange or in their spiritual quest they may wish to be left alone and largely avoid other humans.

Most recently, geneticist Bryan Sykes analyzed possible Bigfoot samples for DNA and concluded all were various nonprimate animals. This exemplifies the best possibilian approach—be open to evidence, collect and analyze it, and then make a determination. Other evidence for legitimate scientists to examine includes eye witness testimony, collections of footprints, and photos. No bones, feces trails, dead bodies, confirmed hair samples have been identified yet, although Jeff Meldrum believe some footprints may be valid. Further critics need to address interpretations for why folklore about large hairy apelike beings proliferate—that alone is worthy of study.

In the end, all of the sightings maybe hoaxes, misperceptions of bears or other animals, and campfire folklore. But Sasquatch is worthy of anthropological investigation and skeptical but possibilian thinking.

CRITICAL THINKING & WEBSITES

1. Which cause of bipedalism seems most likely?

2. What might it have been like for human ancestors to have five or more other hominins living around them?

3. Visit the Smithsonian Institution site: humanorigins.si.edu.

4. View a scientific site for Sasquatch organized by Dr. Jeff Meldrum: www.isu.edu/rhi/

5. Find out more about fossil videos at National Geographic: nationalgeographic.com.

6. Watch the Patterson film on youtube, especially the slow motion version: https://www.youtube.com/watch?v=Us6jo8bl2lk. What is your critique?

7. Describe one issue that is a challenge in investigating our ancestors. What is your reaction?

8. Describe the genus Australopithecus and the significance of fossils such as Lucy or Taung child.

REFERENCES

Begun, David. (2016). *The Real Planet of the Apes: A New Story of Human Origins.* Princeton, NY: Princeton University Press.

Bridgeman, B. (2003). *Psychology and Evolution: The Origins of Mind.* Thousand Oaks, CA: SAGE Publications.

Brunet, Michel, Guy, F., Pilbeam, D., Mackaye, H. T., Likius, A. et al. (2002). QA new hominid from the Upper Miocene of Chad, Central Africa. *Nature,* 418 (6894), 145-151.

Cunnnane, Stephen. (2005). *Survival of the fattest: The Key to Human Brain Evolution.* Singapore: World Scientific Publishing.

Jurmain, R., Kilgore, L., Trevathan, W., Ciochon, R. (2014). *Introduction to Physical Anthropology,* 2013-2014 edition. Belmont, CA: Cengage.

Kuliukas, A. (2013). Wading hypotheses of the origin of human bipedalism. *Human Evolution,* 28 (3-4), 213-236.

Levanda, Robert, & Schultz, Emily. (2015). *Anthropology: What Does It Mean To Be Human?,* 3rd ed. New York: Oxford University Press.

Morgan, Elain. (1997). The Aquatic Ape Hypothesis. London, U.K.: Souvenir Press.

Pontzer, H., Raichlen, D.A., Rodman, P.S. (2014). Bipedal and quadrupedal locomotion in chimpanzees. *Journal of Human Evolution,* 66, 64-82.

Sykes, Brian, Mullis, Rhettman A., Hagenmuller, Christophe, Melton, terry W, Sartori, Michel. (2014). Genetic analysis of hair samples attributed to Yeti, Bigfoot and other anomalous primates. *Proceedings of the Royal Society,* London, August, 2014.

Tattersal, Ian. (2015). *The Strange Case of the Rickety Cossack: And Other Cautionary Tales From Human Evolution.* New York, NY: Palgrave Macmillan/St. Martin's Press.

Wheeler, P. E. (1984). The evolution of bipedality and loss of functional body hair in hominoids. *Journal of Human Evolution,* 13, 91-98.

Wrangham, R., Cheney, D, Seyfarth, R., Sarmiento, E. (2009). Shallow-water habitats as source of fallback foods for hominins. *American Journal of Physical Anthropology,* 140 (4):630-642.

1. Evaluate the hypotheses about Sasquatch and similar creatures with some measures used to describe the early bipeds:

Hypothesis	Evidence
Sasquatch is a remnant of an apelike hominoid: *Gigantopithecus*	
Sasquatch is a remnant of a fossil human ancestor: *Homo heidelbergensis*	
Sasquatch sightings are due to secret Salish shaman rituals	
Sasquatch is a hoax, misunderstanding, or folklore fantasy	

2. What additional evidence would you like to properly assess the Sasquatch claims?

6 *Homo*:
Tools, Language and Ideas

In two million years, our ancestors went from an apelike episodic culture with sticks and simple stone tools to blades, fire, shelter, and symbols with planning and mental representations. This resulted in the further expansion of the human brain and an exponential explosion of culture.

LEARNING OBJECTIVES

1. Understand the origins of the genus *Homo* and its major species.

2. Describe the physical characteristics and episodic culture of *Homo habilis*.

3. Describe the physical characteristics and mimetic culture of *Homo erectus*.

4. Describe the mosaic physical traits and representational culture of *Homo heidelbergensis*.

5. Describe the assimilation model of the origins of Homo sapiens and the amazing culture of the Upper Paleolithic.

6. Describe the puzzling new discoveries of *Homo naledi*, *Homo neandertalensis*, Denisovans, and *Homo floresiensis* and their implications for understanding our origins.

HUMAN?

Fossil evidence suggests that our own genus, *Homo*, began around 2.5 million years ago. The name implies being human, although not necessarily a modern human. While *Australopithecus* bodies are almost like ours from the neck down, we are not so identified with them because their skulls are still apelike.

But, scientists continued to create more species as they found more fossils, because there is an element of judgment and art in determining species boundaries which can be intersecting in living species. The inevitable competition among the major research teams also led them to name new species with every fossil discovery. As the number of hominin species increased, anthropologists conceived of the early bipeds as further and further away from *Homo* and characterized them as "distant cousins," "proto-human," or just "bipedal apes." In a sense as the number of hominin species increased, the early bipeds were demoted.

LUMPERS AND SPLITTERS

So what should be the criterion for membership in *Homo*? Information about culture and behavior is somewhat indirect, a combination of older and new physical features can be present, structural details can be ambiguous, and technology can be diffused to others.

A great new resource is the ability to identify certain genes associated with one fossil or another and use it to determine species boundaries. However, even here hybrids between two species may confuse the matter and DNA differences may be a population not a species issue. Some paleoanthropologists split fossils into many species, while others lump them together. The trend in recent years in biology has been has been to split, but there can be good reasons to lump.

Brain size is a common factor for classifying fossils in our genus *Homo*. But, there also may be regional or sexual variation. A species may also last a long time with a smaller initial cranial capacity gradually becoming larger—exactly where should the species line be drawn? Species classification is challenging because you don't have all the pieces of that puzzle. A number of recent fossil discoveries in Eastern Europe, Africa, and Asia may be related to us but they provide special challenges and may cause us to rethink size and height when placing species boundaries. What we do know, is that other species of humans existed over the last couple of million years, with some even lasting into near-modern times.

Given all these issues, at the present time, *Homo* is divided into four broad stages each with similar related species that are grouped here: 1) *Homo habilis*, the "handyperson" and stone tool maker; 2) *Homo erectus* who developed fire and better tools; 3) *Homo heidelbergensis* who developed advanced tools and representations; and 4) *Homo sapiens* who had advanced culture, hunting strategies, and cave art. Within these stages many anthropologists include other species that may or may not keep their present names in the future.

HOMO HABILIS

Homo habilis was discovered in the early 1960s by the family team of Louis and Mary Leakey, discoverers of several of the hominins of this period. *H. habilis* is found in East Africa sites at Olduvai, Turkana basin, and Hadar, and also in South Africa at Sterkfontein and Swartkrans — all sites that have yielded many hominins.

The best interpretation is that either *A. garhi* or *A. sediba* were the immediate ancestor to *habilis*, although it is always possible that a yet undiscovered hominin species gave rise to our ancestry. *Homo habilis*, spans from 2.3 or earlier to 1.4 mya. What's fascinating about this tenure is that *habilis* lived side by side on Lake Turkana with several australopith species and even later *Homo*. In fact, the latest evidence suggests that both *habilis* and *Homo ergaster* (an African form we are grouping with *Homo erectus*) may actually be sibling species representing splitting lineages from an earlier australopith ancestor.

H. HABILIS SKULL AND BODY

The post-cranial skeleton (from the neck down) of hominins was already very humanlike in form in *Australopithecus*. *H. habilis* was short and had long arms compared with modern humans but you would recognize its skeleton as human. But, a distinguishing characteristics of *Homo habilis* is a significantly larger brain—presumably as a result of the growing stone tool technology and the diet shift to include more meat.

The *habilis* brain increase is impressive; it is about 20-40% larger than that of the australopiths and early bipeds and about half the size of modern humans. The shape of the cranium, the top of the skull, is also much more rounded and some details of the tooth structure are more humanlike as well. Although there is some variation in the *H. habilis* fossils, one specimen KNM ER 1470 has a stunning cranial capacity of 775 cm³, one of the largest for this species. This is almost twice the size of the brain of the australopiths.

But, because *sediba* and *garhi* are otherwise similar and also used stone tools, some have questioned placing *habilis* in the *Homo* genus at. They consider it to be just an advanced australopith based on cladistic analysis but the large cranial capacity for classification as *Homo* is hard to ignore. Ultimately, classifications will likely be done through a combination of both brain size and cultural complexity since both are hallmarks of our species.

OLDOWAN TOOLS AND EPISODIC CULTURE

Homo habilis is associated with a solid stone tool industry called Oldowan. Many aspects of culture are not preserved in these fossil hominins. We don't know what they thought, how they felt, and how many perishable containers, wipers, sticks, and other objects they made. But, the shape of a tool and its apparent purpose can be circumstantial evidence to determine the type of cultural processes a fossil species might have engaged in.

The teeth of *H. habilis* suggest an increasingly generalized and omnivorous diet, meaning a lot of different types of food including likely scavenged meat. The type of tools associated with *Homo habilis* are called Oldowan, after the Olduvai Gorge where they were first found. They consist of flakes taken from a core chopping stone and were probably used for digging root vegetables, penetrating fruits with tough skin, and scraping scavenged meat off of bones. The core itself was likely used for digging, and surely *habilis* also used digging, scraping, and poking sticks.

Psychologist Merlin Donald characterizes this intellectual stage as episodic, here-and-now thinking with problem-solving for immediate tasks, but still without a great deal of planning or foresight. This addition of increased meat protein to the diet may have also directly affected brain growth as well and opened up whole new ways to expand culture and social complexity. Oldowan tools are a bit more complex than australopith ones, so it's likely that the intelligence and social behavior of *H. habilis* took a step forward.

HOMO NALEDI

Homo naledi is a fascinating new discovery made by Lee Berger who also discovered *Australopithecus sediba*. The new fossil discovery, tentatively dated at 2 mya, was made in 2013 by cavers in Lee Berger's team in the Rising Star Cave system of South Africa. *Naledi* means "star" in the local language.

The discovery startled not only Berger and his team, but all of paleoanthropology. This was because not only are these major discoveries rare, Berger was claiming that the evidence suggested that the *naledi* individuals were deliberately buried in an extremely challenging cave with only tiny openings today.

Berger reported finding over 1,000 hominin specimens deep in the Rising Star cave which represented 15 individuals including men, women, and children. The skeletons were found below a vertical chute 39 ft. long which led to a chamber littered with the fossil bones.

The evidence suggests that *naledi* was bipedal, stood about five feet tall and weighed 100 lbs. Their hands showed better adaptations for grasping than australopiths but still had the curved shape of the australopiths for climbing trees. Their pelvis and shoulders also resembled the australopiths. However, their cranial capacity was 560 cm^3 which just makes the lowest end for the genus *Homo*, but the structure of the braincase is definitely *Homo*. Naledi also had long legs and very humanlike feet.

Most scientists are concluding that their skeletons resemble the australopiths but that they have features like *habilis* and even the next stage of hominins, *Homo erectus*. Berger even speculates that the individuals may have engaged in other social rituals. Further cave exploration in the Rising Star system and finding additional individual will help a great deal.

One possibility is that some South African fossils formed small populations in which major changes could emerge and spread within the group. If so, this is an important part of the world that needs to be explore for better understanding of our origins.

HOMO ERECTUS

DISCOVERY

In 1891, a Dutch anatomist Eugene Dubois, excited about Darwin's evolutionary theory, energetically set out to find the 'missing link' in Indonesia. On the island of Java, he found a skullcap with a cranial capacity of about 600 cm³ and other hominin remains near the Solo River dated at about 1.5 mya. The scientific community was shocked and mocked him, only to return decades later to apologize and beg to see his find. Driven to despondency, Dubois had buried the fossils under the floor of his dining room and written that maybe they were just baboons. They were not and he was exonerated.

Today, the general consensus is that *Homo erectus* originated in Africa. But, the earliest dates of 1.8 mya in Southeastern Europe and 1.6 mya in Indonesia may give equal credit to origins in Europe and Asia with further fossil finds.

SKULL AND BODY

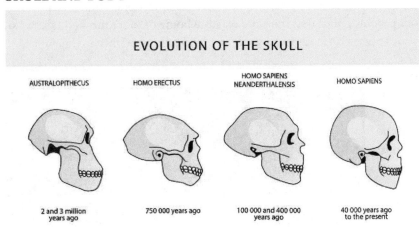

EVOLUTION OF THE SKULL

AUSTRALOPITHECUS	HOMO ERECTUS	HOMO SAPIENS NEANDERTHALENSIS	HOMO SAPIENS
2 and 3 million years ago	750 000 years ago	100 000 and 400 000 years ago	40 000 years ago to the present

Homo erectus likely weighed around 100 lbs. and stood about 5 ft. 6 in. tall. *Erectus* cranial capacity was larger than earlier hominins, from 700 to over 1200 cm³.

The skull also had a distinctive pentagonal shape broader at the base than at the ears. The skull is fairly long and has heavy brow ridges and little forehead. Some skulls also have a distinctive sagittal keel ridge along the top of the skull, probably for robust muscle attachments. The enlargement of the hypoglossal canal opening that connects nerves in the tongue and mouth suggest that speech ability was enhanced at this stage, which would also aid enculturation and culture change.

Nariokotome (also called WT 15000) is an almost complete skeleton of an eight year old boy found at Lake Turkana with a cranial capacity of 880 cm³ dated at 1.6 mya. Developmentally, he was already an adolescent in *erectus* years and his post-cranial skeleton looks very modern. A female *Homo erectus* date at 1.3 mya was found in Gona, Ethiopia and shows her birth canal was already enlarged to deliver bigger brained babies.

Fossils found at Dmanisi in Eastern Europe in the Republic of Georgia are really startling. These individuals are dated at 1.8 mya and are very short although they have the typical *erectus* long skull, low braincase, and pentagonal shape. But, the front of their faces looks more like *Homo habilis* with a brainsize of 600 cm³. Further, Dmanisi Skull 3 was found with Oldowan choppers and scrapers more associated with habilis. Other European evidence shows that *Homo erectus* lived in caves in Atapuerca, Spain, and at Gran Dolina cave where there is even evidence of cannibalism.

Finding very primitive looking Dmanisi *Homo erectus* so early at 1.8 mya undermines the idea that hominins did not leave Africa until they had a large brain and well-developed tools. This has required anthropologists to develop some new ideas.

Three hypotheses have been offered. *Erectus* may have left Africa with small brains and Dmanisi may be a relict leftover local population of that early stage. *Homo erectus* may have also originated in Asia or Eastern Europe—and Africa was not its sole home. Third, *Australopithecus* or *Homo habilis* may have migrated out of Africa much earlier and independently evolved to *erectus*. Asia is so little explored and excavated that paleoanthropology must be open to hominin origins possibly also found there, if future evidence is sought.

HOMO ERECTUS IN ASIA

Later Asian *Homo erectus* includes the famous site of Zhoukoudian, dated at 0.8 mya which provided the remains of 40 adults and children, the largest amount of *erectus* fossils anywhere. Also, more than 100,000 artifacts at the site suggested that it was occupied over thousands of years. In the last century, interpretations from the site claimed that the cave was a dwelling and that *H. erectus* engaged in big game hunting and cooked meat over an open fire. But, more recent re-analysis has questioned this scenario. It is more likely that *erectus* was prey, not predator, and that the cave was the home of sabre toothed tigers, not us. Often, imaginative ideas about our species turn out to be mundane when the evidence is considered.

ACHEULEAN TOOLS AND MIMETIC CULTURE

Homo erectus had a culture of stone tools in Africa, Europe, Indonesia, and mainland Asia. Early tools resembled the Oldowan choppers of *Homo habilis,* but later tools include an Acheulean hand axe, awls, burins, and scrapers. The Acheulean axe was a stone core with flakes removed on two sides to form an axe-head biface, and was likely used for digging and for scavenging meat. A new site in South Africa suggests that *erectus* hominins controlled fire by 1 mya because of the ash and charred bone found with the tools.

Merlin Donald characterizes Acheulean core bifaces and other culture of *H. erectus* as reflective of mimetic culture, the first symbolic stage of human thinking. Mimetic refers to imitation and how the two sides of the biface imitate each other. This means that *erectus* could hold a stone shape in mind and with each blow make it look more like an ideal form, and then replicate that process on the other side.

This mimetic skill may also have extended to other forms of imitation such as rituals, dance, and maybe even instruction with language. Evidence for the addition of grandparents to the cultural mix provided a continuity across at least three generations which also enhanced story-telling, enculturation, social memory, and cultural complexity. *Homo erectus* was an impressive advance in the human journey. Their life ways caused selection for larger brains and a growing mental capacity. With an expanded tool kit, *erectus* became a better scavenger and digger of plant foods. This major change in adaptive strategy set the stage for the next development in the *Homo* line.

HOMO HEIDELBERGENSIS

MIDDLE PLEISTOCENE

The Middle Pleistocene lasted from 780 kya (thousands of years ago) to 125 kya and is also known more popularly as the Ice Age. Glaciers advanced and retreated repeatedly during this period causing extreme ice and cold in Europe and Northern Asia and also more arid conditions in Africa.

In this period, we find descendants of *Homo erectus* in Africa, Asia, and Europe who have changed enough that Middle Pleistocene hominins are called *Homo heidelbergensis* (named after a fossil from Germany). Anthropologists struggle a bit with this stage of hominins and have also called them "premoderns" and "archaic Homo sapiens." Thus, it is more a name for a stage of cultural development between *erectus* and *sapiens* than a sharp species boundary. Further, in remote Southeast Asia and Australia, *Homo erectus* and other puzzling hominins existed side by side with both *heidelbergensis* and later *Homo sapiens*, some until 12 kya! So the emergence of humans is not a simple linear progression.

SKULL AND BODY

H. heidelbergensis lasted for 500,000 years and is characterized by a mix or mosaic of *erectus* and *sapiens* traits. *Erectus* traits included a large face, projecting brow ridges, small forehead, and thick cranium top of the skull. *Sapiens* traits were a larger and rounded braincase, more vertical facial profile, and a less protruding back of the skull. The oldest African *heidelbergensis* is Bodo who showed the heavy brow ridges of his *erectus* heritage at 600 kya. In addition, Bodo had cut marks on his skull indicating that his skull tissue has been scraped away or defleshed which could be due to cannibalism or a ritual burial practice still done today of letting a body decompose and then gathering and cleaning the bones.

Another *Homo heidelbergensis* skull, called Kabwe or Broken Hill 1, was discovered by a miner in the 1920s in Zambia, Africa. He also had a mosaic of *erectus* and *sapiens* traits with a large cranial capacity of 1,300 cm^3, actually typical of modern *sapiens*. *H. heidelbergensis* fossils from China raise a provocative question. They show the same mosaic of traits but have additional features such as flat noses and shovel-shaped incisor front teeth, traits which are found in modern Chinese today. Chinese paleoanthropologists argue that Chinese people evolved directly from *erectus* to *heidelbergensis* to *sapiens* locally, which may suggest a multi-species origin for humans.

LEVALLOIS TOOLS AND REPRESENTATIONAL CULTURE

Merlin Donald characterizes this stage as representational. Toward the end of the Middle Pleistocene period, a new stone tool technique called Levallois appeared that required a whole new thinking ability— mental representations. With each blow, earlier Acheulean tools looked more and more like the final product. But, the Levallois tool required mental representations for three stages. Lateral blows first created a flat striking platform, then downward blows removed thin blades from the core. Finally, the edge of the blades were worked and shaped. Some of these flakes and blades are 10,000 times sharper than surgical steel. *Heidelbergensis* hominins also lived in caves and built structures of bones and stones as well as continued the use of fire. They ate a wide variety of plants and animals and added fish and marine life to their diet. One site at Schoningen, Germany has wooden spears preserved from 400 kya and also horse bones—were they eating them or riding them? With mental representations they could imagine both.

HOMO SAPIENS

ASSIMILATION MODEL

Finally, our journey takes us to our own species, *Homo sapiens* and a controversy regarding our origins. The regional continuity model (also called multi-regional hypothesis) was developed by Milford Wolpoff and held that different groups of hominins evolved from earlier populations right in the local region, and changed at varying rates to become *Homo sapiens*. African hominins crossed the *sapiens* threshold first, while some hominins in Asian never crossed the line and remained *Homo erectus* until they became extinct.

The replacement model was created by Christopher Stringer based on mtDNA studies and held that early *Homo* migrated out of Africa to all parts of the Old World. Around 100-200 kya, later African *Homo sapiens* had a second migration to Europe and Asia and replaced ALL earlier *Homo* forms without interbreeding with them. The claims of this model were over-exaggerated, and denied any interbreeding anywhere which seems unrealistic. It almost took on pseudoscience aspects as it was dubbed the "Eve hypothesis."

Further genetic research which revealed interbreeding between modern *Homo sapiens* and Neanderthals about 80-50 kya required a compromise called "partial replacement." The entire Neanderthal genome has now been determined showing that most Europeans carry 2-6% Neanderthal genes from this interbreeding. This partial replacement idea is also supported by archaeological finds and some other fossil evidence. Interestingly, another paleoanthropologist, Fred Smith, suggested an assimilation model almost 20 years earlier that represented the most reasonable reconciliation of the replacement/regional continuity dispute. But some anthropologists were so busy insisting that they model was absolutely correct, that his suggestion was not fully accepted until recently. It's a lesson in how there can be a culture lag in science in accepting ideas that make the best sense.

SKULL AND BODY

The earliest finds of modern *Homo sapiens* are found in East Africa in Ethiopia and are dated to around 200 kya. Herto, the best preserved modern skull, was discovered by Tim White's team and is dated at 160 kya. These Ethiopian hominins have a very large cranium with a cranial capacity of 1450 cm^3. It is now proposed to be *Homo sapiens idaltu* which means "elder" in the Afar language of Ethiopia. In terms of other areas of Africa, modern humans date in South Africa to 100 kya as and may have migrated there from the north or have evolved there separately.

Homo sapiens is also found in the Near East. Skhul and Qafzeh caves have yielded moderns dated at around 100-120 kya. Zhoukoudian and other caves in China also have modern *H. sapiens* dated later, around 40 kya. In fact, a Jinniushan skeleton dated at 200 kya seems to have modern Chinese features showing extensive continuity with older populations in the area. Modern *sapiens* make their way to Australia by 40 kya and probably used bamboo rafts to make the ocean journey. Fascinating remains at Kow Swamp show receding foreheads, heavy brow ridges, and very thick bones which appear more *erectus* in shape but are dated very late at 9 kya. They lived alongside contemporary aborigines who migrated to Australia around 50-75 kya.

Western European *sapiens* is represented by many sites, e.g., a Cro-Magnon site dated at 28 kya. A child's skeleton found from Abrigo do Lagar Velho in Portugal dated to this general period shows a mixture of modern *sapiens* and Neanderthal traits. Thus, by 25 kya all the areas of the world have evidence of modern *Homo sapiens*, and the genetic evidence shows the assimilation model works best. At the same time, a number of intriguing relict populations remained which are discussed below.

UPPER PALEOLITHIC

The Upper Paleolithic is a dramatic period of exponential culture change and symbolic development that began around 40 kya in Europe, Asia, and Africa. It presents innovations in stone tool and other technology, the development of cave and rock art, and widespread burials, often with grave goods. It began after the Middle Pleistocene Ice Age in a warming period when mammoths, reindeer, bison and horses were plentiful as were fish and waterfowl. *Homo sapiens* lived in caves but also created shelters and structures of bones, wood, and animal skins some of them formed in dramatic circles of bones.

A significant site in Russia, Sungir, shows extensive burials with grave goods, one with thousands of ivory beads, ivory spears, antler tools, engravings, and other jewelry. Tools from this period also include three foot long almost transparent spear heads that may have been used in rituals, as well as bows and arrows and needles for sewing animal skins.

New tools were invented, notably the atlatl, a bone or wood rod in which was inserted a throwing spear so that the thrusting distance was dramatically increased. Fish hooks and harpoons are also found, along with burins for working wood and bone, boring tools, drilling tools, serrated knives, and shells.

Cave paintings found at over 150 sites and dated to around 40 kya include stunning representations of animals and human handprints painted with iron ocher. Some were made with sticks, hair brushes and feathers while others were created with a spit painting technique by mixing ocher with saliva. Small clay animal figures are found along with figures represented an erect phallus or a female figure with large breasts and hips that suggests fertility symbols.

At Lascaux Cave in France numerous wild bulls and other animals are represented in images of red, yellow, and black, some using the natural bumps and curves of the cave wall as part of the image and suggesting hunting themes. Other cave images include dots suggesting entopic phenomenon—image humans see in altered states which may suggest rituals or trances. Africa also has extensive rock and other art. At Pinnacle Point site from South Africa, ocher, shells, and tiny microlith blades are all dated at 165 kya, which is much earlier than in Europe.

Psychologist Merlin Donald characterized *Homo sapiens* culture as complex, mythic, and representational and fostered by the further development of language and symbols based on the earlier mimetic skills of *Homo erectus*. In a relatively short time, *Homo sapiens* developed sophisticated tools, portable art objects, and jewelry, cave and rock paintings done with an artist's tool kit which suggests a definite aesthetic sense. Deliberate burials also suggest rituals about the afterlife and close kinship ties. Once the climate changed again and became warmer, H. sapiens had to adapt again and turn to small game hunting, more fishing, and eventually food production by raising plants and animals.

THE PUZZLING OTHERS

HOMO NEANDERTHALENSIS

Perhaps no fossil has captured the popular imagination more than Neanderthals, a branch of the human family that appeared around 600 kya and became extinct by 40 kya. Because of an early discovery of an old stooped Neanderthal man with arthritis, they were portrayed as brutish cavemen and the butt of undeserved jokes. Neanderthals were shorter and stockier than other *Homo sapiens* with a large brow ridge and nose—but a brain even larger than modern humans today. That fact was ignored in favor of the brutish image.

Although most anthropologists still place Neanderthals as our evolutionary cousins, there is growing DNA evidence that *Homo sapiens* interbred with them because Europeans today carry 2-6% of Neanderthal genes. In Europe and the Middle East, Neanderthals appear to have evolved from *H. heidelbergensis* like *sapiens* but drifted apart as a separate group.

Could their culture be a factor in determining their species assignment? Their culture is called Mousterian and it extended from Europe to central Asia and Africa. Neanderthals had a diversified tool kit and specialized in hunting and skinning and preparing meat based on wear patterns on the tools. They used thrusting spears but apparently did not have long distance weapons such as bow and arrow. This may be related to the high number of serious

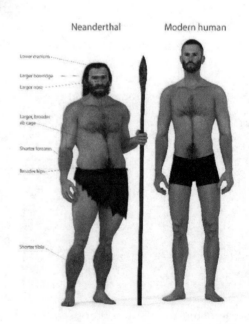

injuries found in their skeletons, most similar to contemporary rodeo riders. Neanderthals also ate shellfish and hunted dolphins and seals. They had body decorations of bird feathers, animal skin clothing and jewelry which indicates a sense of self and how you appear to others. A shell pendant was perforated and even colored with yellow ocher. Neanderthal speech has also been the subject of much analysis and we assume it was similar to that of modern *Homo sapiens*.

Evidence for religion is an interesting marker for humanness. Leaving aside the *Homo naledi* burial issue, human burials begin around 400 kya, and there is clear evidence that Neanderthals buried their dead by placing the body in a flexed position and adding grave goods. For example, Shanidar cave in the Middle East shows burials with flowers, and care of older individuals who were sick or injured.

Enrique Baquedano has described a cave in Spain where Neanderthals gathered around the grave of a toddler with a circle of hearths marked by 30 horns of bison, red deer, and other animals. At another site in Uzbekistan, a child was buried encircled by goat horns, and in France an individual was buried with an arrangement of stone slabs and bear bones. Therefore, anthropologist Barbara King concludes that Neanderthals "contemplated the complexities of life." So, Neanderthals "seem" very human and it may be time to put Neanderthals closer into the human consciousness based on culture if not genetics.

DENISOVANS

Another group that has puzzled paleoanthropologists are the Denisovans. In 2008, researchers working in the Denisova Cave of the Altai Mountains of Siberia discovered a finger bone and two teeth dated at 80 kya. What's so interesting about such fragments? The mtDNA analysis of the finger bone showed that the Denisovans were not *Homo erectus*, Neanderthal, or modern *Homo sapiens*! When the whole genome was plotted (three billion base pairs), the Denisovans were determined to be a separate branch of hominins from Siberia—living side by side with Neanderthals and moderns. Genetic analysis showed that the individual was female, dark skinned with brown eyes. Also found with the woman was a beautiful jade cuff bracelet with a doughnut shaped pendant that might have hung from the bracelet, as well as other artifacts.

Most startling of all is that some contemporary human populations carry up to 5-6% Denisovan genes. These groups are found in Pacific Rim areas of Melanesia and New Guinea in the South Pacific, some Japanese, and even some Northwest Coast Native Americans/First Nations. This suggests a coastal migration route.

Recently, a thigh bone from Spain, originally assumed to be Neanderthal, was tested and it proved to be Denisovan as well, 4,000 miles away from Siberia! This means that the Denisovans may have had a much wider range and may not be a remnant population at all. This is an exciting possibility—a whole new branch of humans. The DNA evidence even showed a yet unknown human ancestor—more hominins are out there for us to find. Additional studies are underway and we may be able to fully trace human migrations all over the world through DNA. Several companies now offer the general public DNA testing to determine genetic origins and these can show immediate geographic ancestry as well as deep ancestry of thousand and millions of years ago.

HOMO FLORESIENSIS

Few shocks in the world of paleoanthropology compare with the discovery in 2004 of a short small-brained hominin in Liang Bua Cave on Flores Island, Indonesia (referred to in Chapter 1). It was an incomplete skeleton of a fossil nicknamed "Flo" (LB1) that seemed similar to the Dmanisi *Homo erectus* finds in Georgia. Her brain was 417 cc.— the size of a chimpanzee! Yet, in other details she was definitely *Homo*.

An immediate response from American anthropologists was that she was microcephalic—a disorder of brain size. Indonesians and other anthropologists disagreed and now it seems that Flo is another sister species classified as *Homo floresiensis*. A leading hypothesis is that she descended from *Homo erectus* on Java and had rafted to tiny Flores Island 1 mya—another surprise. This date is firm because stone tools associated with her are dated to that period. Her small stature suggested that very early *Homo* may have migrated out of Africa to Dmanisi in Asia and onward to Indonesia, and remained fairly primitive. Natural selection may have selected for smaller individuals because of scarce resources on islands.

A number of other arguments were put forth to explain what came to be known as "the hobbits," but, hard to place in the *Homo* line, she was given the title *Homo floresiensis*. Flo's descendants lasted very late on Flores Island and it is tempting to connect this with the local folktales about the "Little People." Some reports state that even the Dutch may have seen Flo remnants as late as the 1500-1600s.

The bottom line is that the human journey is a much more puzzling and branching than linear thinkers of the 19th century ever imagined. Ultimately anthropologists may consolidate these fossils in different ways but the overall story is one of continual cultural invention and adaptation—for six million years.

CRITICAL THINKING & WEBSITES

1. Do paleoanthropologists have too many hominin fossil species, or too few? What principles should be used to organize this explosion of humans and our cousins?
2. What was the purpose of cave art?
3. What sense of self would a *Homo* hominin have if we found they had symbols shown by jewelry, clothing, body decoration, and arrangements of objects?
4. Browse through the fossils listed on the Smithsonian Institution website: si.edu.
5. Check out the website of the discoverer of *Homo naledi*: http://profleeberger.com/.
6. Watch sci-news.com for the latest information on fossil discoveries.
7. Listen to Barbara King's posts on NPR's 13.7 Cosmos & Culture: http://www.npr.org/sections/13.7/.

REFERENCES

Bermudez de Castro et al. (2011). The Gran Dolina-TD6 human fossil remains and the origin of Neanderthals In *Vertebrate Paleobiology and Paleoanthropology*, 67-75.

Ciochon, R., et al. (2009). Rediscovery of the Homo erectus bed at Ngandong: Site formation of a Late Pleistocene hominin site in Asia. *American Journal of Physical Anthropology, Supplement* 48:110.

Falk, Dean. (2012). Hominin brain evolution, 1925-2011: An emerging overview. In *African Genesis: Perspectives on Hominin Evolution*, Sally C. Reynolds & Andrew Gallagher (eds.). Cambridge, UK: Cambridge University Press, pp. 145-162.

Falk, D., et al. (2005). The brain of LB1, *Homo floresiensis*. *Science* 308:242-245.

Feffing, R., et al. (2011). Earliest human occupations at Dmanisi (Georgian Caucasus) dated to 1.85-1.78 Ma. *Proceedings of the National Academy of Science USA* 108(26):10432-10436).

Green, R. E., et al., (2010). A draft sequence of the Neandertal genome. *Science* 328:710-722.

Jurmain, Robert, Kilgore, Lynn, Trevathan, Wenda, & Ciochon, Russell. (2014*). Introduction to Physical Anthropology*. Belmont, CA: Cengage Learning.

King, Barbara. (2016). Were Neanderthals religious? *13.7 Cosmos & Culture*. National Public Radio, December 7, 2016. Retrieved December 15, 2016.

Meyer, M., et al,(2012). A high-coverage genome sequence from an archaic Denisovan Individual. *Science*, 338:222-226.

Smith, F. H. (2002). Migrations, radiations and continuity: Patterns in the evolution of Late Pleistocene humans. In: *The Primate Fossil Record*, W. Hartwig (ed.), pp. 437-456. New York, NY: Cambridge University Press.

Spoor, F., et al. (2007). Implications of new early Homo fossils from Ileret, East of Lake Turkana, Kenya. *Nature* 448:688-691.

Stringer, C. B. & Andrews, P. (1988). Genetic and fossil evidence for the origin of modern humans. *Science* 239:1263-1268.

Walker, A., & Leakey, R. E. (1993). *The Nariokotome Homo erectus Skeleton*. Cambridge, MA: Harvard University Press.

White, T. D. (1986). Cut marks on the Bodo cranium: A case of prehistoric defleshing. *American Journal of Physical Anthropology* 69:503-509.

Wolpoff, M. H., et al (1994). Multiregional evolutions: A world-wide source for modern human populations. In: *Origins of Anatomically Modern Humans*, M. H. Nitecki & D. V. Nitecki (eds.), pp. 175-199. New York: Plenum Press.

Wood, B, & Collard, M. (1999). The human genus. *Science* 284:65-71.

NEANDERTHALS

Dating/Where found	Physical Characteristics	Culture characteristics

Do Neanderthals seem "human" to you based on their traits and culture?

H. FLORESIENSIS "The Hobbit"

Dating/Where found	Physical Characteristics	Culture characteristics

What would you want to know about "Flo" to place her in the proper species?

DENISOVANS

Dating/Where found	Physical Characteristics	Culture characteristics

If some humans carry 5% Denisovan genes, are they fully human? Why or why not?

7 FIRST AMERICANS:
Pacific, Atlantic—Or Both?

Sometimes, long standing ideas are challenged by new evidence and alternative theories. A good example is the old hypothesis that the Bering Land Bridge was the only way people arrived in the Americas. New evidence is challenging this idea—the trick is to sort out the science from the pseudoscience, but also to assess new evidence with a possibilian open mind.

LEARNING OBJECTIVES

1. Analyze how settlers convinced themselves that Native Americans did not build the mounds in their area.

2. Critique the orthodox Bering Land Bridge hypothesis for the peopling of the New World.

3. List the new evidence for a possible Pacific water route to the Americas via boats and rafts.

4. Describe the Solutrean hypothesis and why some archaeologists believe people came to the Americas also from prehistoric Europe.

5. Evaluate the hypothesis that Vikings made contact with North America around the year 1000CE.

6. Describe the possible origins of the Olmec, and how Olmec and Mayan civilization showed that the New World civilizations were as elaborate as those of Europe, Africa, and Asia.

MOUNDBUILDERS

People in the U.S. were either born here or arrived here by some manner. Naturally, there is a curiosity about the first to come to this land, where they came from, and what were they like? Most Americans are accustomed to statements that "Columbus discovered America." But, in that statement is embedded a particular cultural perspective—that of Europeans. Comic Dick Gregory quipped that he'd like to discover a Cadillac the way Columbus "discovered" America. The discovery certainly is not from the African-American or slave point of view, neither is it one from Native Americans, who were already here having discovered it tens of thousands of years earlier.

When 16th century Europeans arrived in the New World they found people who were already here and believed either than Europeans were new friends and trading partners or that they were invaders. An estimated 50-90% of Native Americans were destroyed by warfare, disease, and cultural genocide. Native Americans lacked the immunity to many common infections of Europeans, e.g., the common cold.

Europeans justified colonizing westward by claiming land for European monarchs, arguing that it was God's will, saying that natural resources like gold were free for the picking. Most of them viewed Native Americans as savages worthy only of extermination or conversation to European beliefs and customs. The U.S. Government broke treaties and even gave Indians smallpox infected blankets in deliberate acts of genocide.

East of the Mississippi, the invaders found mounds and other stone and earthworks, now dated to 5500 years ago, e.g., Monk's Mound at Cahokia near St. Louis. This mound is larger than Egypt's pyramids and even Serpent Mound in Ohio. The land was being farmed and settled by people with European ancestry. Some settlers simply plowed over the land to make it their own, and much archaeology was lost. However, many others wondered what the mounds were, who made them, and what they might contain. People dug up bird-shaped stone pipes, copper and antler ornaments, carved shell and mica sheets, spear and projectile points, and stone disks. They were amazed at the skill and beauty of the artifacts.

By the 1800s, the obvious explanation was that the mounds had been made by the indigenous people the Euro-Americans had driven into death, poverty, reservations—or just simply, off. Early explorers had even reported use of the mounds by Natives. But, the settlers had an ethnocentric view that their culture was superior and the best in the world. They could not imagine that the craft, engineering, and artistry was actually the work of "savages" they had driven away.

They developed a convoluted notion to keep from valuing the Native culture. They began to argue that Natives had driven off an earlier civilization who had actually made the mounds. They claimed that everyone from Vikings and Welsh to Egyptians and the Chinese had really made the mounds. They even attributed the mounds to the "survivors" of Atlantis or argued that the mounds were remnants of the Garden of Eden.

They argued that Indians were just hunters even though Native Americans were raising maize when they arrived. While Thomas Jefferson and others recognized this prejudice, it was a Tennessee naturalist, Cyrus Thomas, who gathered the evidence of Native culture across the U.S., including actually interviewing Native Americans, and drew the correct conclusion that local tribes had made the mounds.

You would think the case would then be closed. However, once the mound builder issue was settled, the new distortion was that the existing Native populations and their mounds were only very recent, a convenient way to erode deep Native claims to the land that was stolen. Other scholars suspected that the crude stone tools increasingly found throughout the U.S. were from an early arrival of Native Americans to North America over the Bering Land Bridge from Asia, but the dominant view was a recent Native appearance.

Most people minimized the stone tools and other objects as just pebbles and rejects of stoneworkers and craftspersons. Scholars who suspected the artifacts were Native American and very old figured they needed additional evidence or a fuller connection to the earth. They reasoned about the Pleistocene which had ended about 10,000 years ago. They thought that if they found any projectiles directly associated with bison, mammoths, and other large animals of the Pleistocene, then Native Americans would definitely have the better claim. How could those tools and implements be in mammoth sites with some projectiles even sticking into the bones—unless Natives had been around to shoot the arrows. With persistence, they found those sites and it vindicated the scholarly view and the Native claims.

But, it took several centuries to begin to see the peopling of the New World in more scientific perspective. Now, the primary sources to understand the first Americans comes from archaeology, cultural studies, geology, paleoanthropology, and genetic evidence. Still, some American archaeologists, even with great training and good intentions as well as much better methods, continued to adopt orthodox explanations. They can be less willing to accept new evidence and cling to older views they were taught themselves, while new evidence accumulates.

We now have five major hypotheses, some including pseudoscience explanations, and new evidence is leaning us in a surprising new direction away from orthodoxy, reminding us that it may take a while but science is inherently and ultimately self-correcting.

BERING LAND BRIDGE

The Bering Land Bridge hypothesis was and still is the orthodox explanation for the arrival of people to the New World from Asia. Most Americans learn this in elementary and high school and it has become commonly accepted by most. Proponents point out that around 30,000 years ago, Ice Age glaciation caused the exposure of Beringia, a land area between Russia and Alaska. Beringia fell under water again when glaciers retreated about 10,000 years ago. This gave a window for migrating human populations, perhaps following mammoths and other large game, to flow into the New World after 25,000 years ago. The glacial barrier into interior North America broke up around 13,000 years ago which would have allowed people to move east of the Rockies into the interior of the U.S. and Canada in a second migration wave.

Genetic studies clearly support Siberian and other Asian origins for Native Americans. MtDNA haplogroups or genetic types show groups A, B, C, D, and X are all frequent among both Native Americans and Siberians and Han Chinese. But the picture is complex and other studies described below indicate other origins as well. The first criticism of the Bering Land Bridge hypothesis was that the Bridge was one way of arrival, even the major way, but there might be others.

But, an even more damaging issue was pointed out. The second challenge to the Bering Land Bridge story is that there is a lack of archaeological evidence along the land route. Investigators have looked extensively along the route but with no success. Nobody dropped or lost anything, or was buried with grave goods? Fossilization is a rare event and the population was probably not huge; however, no evidence at all was hard to use to support the Land Bridge hypothesis.

The third criticism was that the proposed ice-free interior corridor did not open up until about 13,000 years ago. This was too late to explain the many earlier sites around North and South America that archaeologists were discovering. So archaeology was left with a big inconsistency: early sites of occupation and a main theory of an ice-free corridor that occurred too late to explain the presence of the early sites.

With each generation moving an estimated 35 miles per lifetime—it takes a while to walk from Asia to the tip of South America. Additionally, the corridor was a wasteland with rocks, silt, and sand and few fish or other wildlife to eat. So, a recent migration likely occurred around 10,000 years ago, but they were not the first Americans, reasoned the critics.

The critics looked more extensively in Central and South America. The early sites in South America are particularly troubling. Monte Verde in southern Chile was a wet peat bog with remarkable preservation of wooden structures, hearths, projectile points, leather straps, mammoth meat, human footprints, etc. It's dated at 1,000 years older than the corridor route. This was further evidence that the ice-free interior corridor could not explain all or even most of the occupation sites in the New World.

To try to speed up the journey, archaeologist proponents of the Land Bridge hypothesis began to propothat once in California and Mexico, early Natives may have taken boats southward. But, the critics responded, why wait until San Diego? Boats could have been taken at any time, including from the start of the journey!

It does seem clear that Native American roots include Asian ancestry, based on DNA, tooth shape, and other features. But, American archaeology holding only to the Bering Land Bridge as the primary means for arrival in the Americas may be much like how 18th century settlers clung to Ancient Egypt or Atlantis as the source of the mounds. In the settler's case it is their own ethnocentrism. In the case of American archaeology, it is more a continuation of an orthodox tradition, and archaeologists will require a very high level of evidence to the contrary to begin to make what is called a paradigm shift to another hypothesis.

Many introductory textbooks stress this scenario and it is the one still taught in schools. However, South American archaeologists, geneticists, and paleoanthropologists are more open to new evidence especially that pointing to Pacific Rim water journeys. This might ultimately require American scientists to acknowledge other scenarios and perhaps as many as three or more migrations by various means will become the new orthodoxy.

What are Native views? Most Native tribes state they have occupied their lands since the beginning of time—an essential statement when broken treaties and threats to their existing lands continue to the 2st century.

PACIFIC WATER ROUTE

In recent years, a new possibility has emerged that is gathering more evidence. This hypothesis argues that humans migrated into the New World along a water route from the Pacific Ocean in boats or rafts. From the South Pacific they may have followed well-known currents directly to Central and South America. A more northern route would have taken them to the Philippines, Japan, and coastal Asia, across the Aleutian Islands and down the Northwest Coast to California, Mexico, and finally Central and South America.

Anecdotally, people have long noticed the similar in physical appearance of Southwest Native Americans and Indian populations in Central and South America. These people often report being mistaken for Polynesians from the South Pacific especially when travelling in other areas of the country. In 1996, a skeleton was found on the banks of the Columbia River in Washington State and became known as Kennewick Man who was dated at 9,000 years ago. Analysis by James Chatters and Douglas Owsley of the Smithsonian suggested Kennewick's features were Polynesian or Southeast Asian, and not like the local Native tribes who presumably migrated to the area later. However, a 2015 genetic study showed that Kennewick did have DNA similarities to contemporary Native Americans, especially the Coville tribe in northeast Washington, so he may be a mix of early Polynesian and later Siberian migrations.

Luzia is a 11,500 year old skeleton of a Paleoindian young woman from Lapa Vermelha, Brazil. Her skull is narrow with a projecting face and chin unlike most contemporary Native Americans and more like Australian aborigines and Melanesians of the South Pacific. Walter Neves who studied Luzia proposed that her ancestors were originally from Africa and had migrated over thousands of years to Southeast Asia, arriving in the New World around 15,000 years ago. There are a number of similar examples of early New World peoples sharing resemblances with South Pacific peoples.

There are also many cultural similarities. For example, designs in paintings by the Coast Salish of British Columbia showing oral history of their ocean journey following their ancestor the orca whale, also echoes the South Pacific physical similarity. The designs on their canoes as well as their structure also resemble boats seen in coastal Japan, Solomon Islands, and Indonesia. They also wear woven cedar strip hats that look identical to those used by rice planters in coastal South Asia.

Northwest Coast First Nations also celebrate with potlatch wealth distribution similar to wealth distribution systems found in Papua New Guinea shown in the Disappearing World documentary Ongka's Big Moka. A Moka is an economic exchange in which the giver accumulates a large nmber of pigs and food items and presents them to another tribe in friendship, but to also build prestige and status for the giver, much like philanthropy. The Moka that was the subject of the film consisted of 600 pigs, thousands of dollars, 8 cows, a truck, and other material wealth. Likewise, a potlatch although dealing with other forms of wealth from the area such as blankets and dried fish, similarly involves a prominent individual redistributing wealth to others. In turn, the recipients will themselves hold potlatches, so eventually goods circular around the community while building prestige for individuals.

The Coast Salish also create totem poles of animal and human images that resemble Maori and other South Pacific objects and wood statues. Chickens and sweet potatoes are also common to both areas. Interestingly, the Chumash tribe of California has Tomolo boats that are similar to Polynesian vessels—how their planks are sewn are found only in Polynesia and Chile. Finally, the Salish carry high percentages of Denisovan genes. The Denisovans were the mysterious Neanderthal-like population of Spain to Siberia who created a beautiful jade bracelet described in the last chapter. The other high percentage of Denisovan genes is found in New Guinea and throughout Micronesia in the South Pacific.

Additional genetic evidence includes a virus usually transmitted from mother to baby through breast feeding. Antibodies to a virus HTLV-1 found in Japan, especially among an indigenous northern population, the Ainu, was recently found among Coast Salish and other First Nations in coastal British Columbia as well as in coastal Ecuador mummies. So there is growing support for the Pacific Rim water route hypothesis, even in the U.S. The question remains what proportion of contribution to Native people comes from the Pacific route vs. the Land Bridge.

SOLUTREAN HYPOTHESIS

Yet another hypothesis comes not from the Pacific but from the Atlantic. But the story starts with projectile points found in the Southwest called Clovis. In the 1930s, scientists found a projectile point in Clovis, New Mexico in association with mammoth bones dated at about 13,000 years ago. An infant boy buried at another site confirmed that Native American ancestors were associated with the Clovis culture. Other Clovis sites were also found in eastern North America so scholars concluded that they represented the first arrivals to the New World and it was assumed they came across the Bering Land Bridge.

Researchers sought to find more evidence of the Clovis culture. Discoveries suggested that Clovis people hunted mammoths and ate over 125 species of plants and animals based on bone remains and pollen found by sifting earth at Clovis sites. This is a much richer diet than eaten by many Americans today, especially in terms of minerals in which we are deficient. However, when the big herds disappeared so did the Clovis culture, with some arguing that Clovis people may have overkilled the large animals they hunted and had to turn to other subsistence activities.

Later populations made shorter Folsom points but with a longer flute in the center for hafting spears. These were discovered in 1908, following a flood in New Mexico that exposed them—sometime archaeology just lucks out and artifacts are exposed by natural processes such as erosion, floods, and melting ice, or by construction projects. These Folsom points are dated to about 9,500 years ago and show a degree of culture change or migration.

The first challenges to the Clovis hypothesis came from other sites in the U.S. that appeared to be older. These included Virginia's Cactus Hill, two caves in Oregon, South Carolina Topper site, Meadowcroft rock shelter in Pennsylvania, and others. Even older sites were found in South America, e.g., Pedra Furada in Brazil dated to over 40 kya. Further, it is odd that no projectile points before Clovis have been found anywhere—maybe Pacific migrations went directly to South America, and then some groups migrated north?

The second challenge came from a brand new hypothesis born in the Smithsonian Institution in Washington, D.D. Called the Solutrean hypothesis, it was put forth in 1998 by Dennis Stanford and Bruce Bradley. Solutrean tools are found in the Mediterranean in Europe and are dated to 22,000 years ago. They are made by taking large flakes from a stone biface and then pressuring around the edges.

Stanford noticed that Clovis and Solutrean traditions had striking similarities. He began to construct an hypothesis that European populations may have migrated westward by boat along the edge of glaciers in the North Atlantic Ocean to North America with Solutrean technology. He and his collaborators pointed out that tools found at Meadowcroft and Cactus Hill actually show a transition between Solutrean and Clovis forms with intermediate forms.

Also, some of the bone needles of this period in France and Spain look like needles still used by Inuit in the New World. Further, a bone with a mammoth drawing that looked very European was found in Florida and dated at 20,000 years ago. Sanford explained that the Solutreans didn't bring all their culture with them, e.g., cave art, because they were just a small maritime group. But they did bring the essential—their fluted points.

Genetic studies gave a mixed but provocative picture. Geneticists classify humans into a number of different haplogroups based on MtDNA coming only from the mother. Haplogroup X is found mostly in Europe and the Middle East. The only other area in the world is Northeast U.S. and Canada—nowhere else. This suggested two possibilities.

First, an early route from Europe could have gone straight across Asia, or possibly through the Middle East by boat. The Solutreans could have boated around India to Indonesia and finally to the Pacific and across Canada. A second possibility is that they could have followed the glaciers westward past Greenland to the Northeast coast of North America. A 2014 report showed that a 24,000 year old skeleton from Siberia possessed haplogroup U which is also found in Europe, which might support the eastern route. In addition, another common European haplogroup, haplogroup R, is frequent among Ojibwe and Chipewyan Native Americans of Canada. Despite similarities in the artifacts and some DNA evidence, American archaeologists are very skeptical about the Solutrean hypothesis, however. They will require more evidence before the matter is settled.

VIKINGS AND EUROPEANS

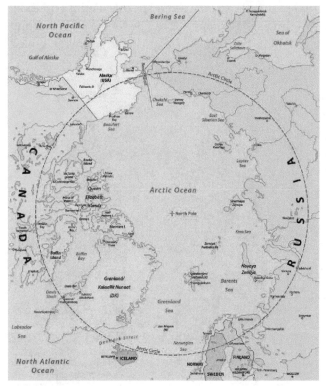

Many other investigators claim a more recent European or Middle Eastern route to the New World, one that is only 1-2,000 years old. These center on Phoenicians, Irish Druids, Vikings, the Welsh, lost tribes of Israel and the Bible. Of these suggestions, the Viking hypothesis has received the greatest attention.

Vikings were impressive seafarers and raiders in northern Europe. They were fierce with a great warrior, trading, and oral literary tradition. They invaded other European areas, Great Britain, and Russia around 1,000 years ago and colonized Greenland. They had powerful Knaar long ships 80 ft. long that could travel about 13 knots and sail across tough seas.

Leif Erikson, a Greenland chief, encountered a merchant Bjarni Herjolfsson who claimed to have seen land when he traveled west of Greenland. Erikson purchased Herjolfsson's ships, according to historical reports and took a crew of 35 men to find the land. It's suggested that he may have reached Labrador and Newfoundland. There is actual evidence that Erikson set up settlements in L'Anse aux Meadows in Newfoundland, and used it as a ship repair point.

Erikson also reported visiting a land called "Vinland" so there has been speculation about where this might have been located, including southeast Canada or even New England. Some believe that this may have been around the Gulf of St. Lawrence. A glance at a polar view of the earth (above) shows the plausibility of these voyage. Later Norse explorers continued to trade and sail to Vinland. Besides some actual settlements found in these areas, there is some cultural and genetic evidence. Butternut squash native to southeast Canada was also found in Newfoundland prior to modern times. In Spirit Pond, Maine, a Viking coin was found, and a number of amateur investigators point to the famous Kensington Ruin Stone, although most investigators consider this to be a fake.

Interestingly, the Norse had a word for Native Americans, "skraeling," whom they found to be unattractive. Nevertheless, the Native American Wabanaki Confederacy in New England and Northeast Canada have oral history that they are part Viking and their regalia shows European influences.

For example, the Micmac flag of Newfoundland has a European design that was constructed before later European contact in the 1500s. We know for a fact that when the pilgrims landed in Massachusetts, they encountered Natives with red hair and blue eyes who spoke English, so clearly English sailing ships had ventured there before Columbus.

In terms of genetics, there is even more Haplogroup X in Europe than Asia, so it is possible that these genes may have also arrived relatively recently from Vikings and the English. Most surprising is that there is also evidence of Native American mtDNA in Iceland. There are 80 Icelanders who carry genetic markers found in Native Americans and also East Asians but not the Inuit who also live in Greenland and arrived in the New World more recently.

Additional evidence of Vikings in the New World may help sort legend from reality. In the meantime, more and more Americans are having their own DNA tested and are making fascinating discoveries as presented in a number of commercials for DNA testing and television programs. Harry Connick, Jr discovered that he had some African-American ancestry, while African-Americans find that they may be half or more of European ancestry. Archaeologists and geneticists are now able to trace deep movements of human populations over the centuries, identify Jewish heritage from the mtDNA and Y chromosome, and show that most Americans are of greater mixed heritage than their family oral history may indicate.

OLMEC AND MAYA

OLMEC

Another New World hypothesis concerns the Olmec, a mysterious culture found in tropical lowlands along Mexico's Gulf Coast and dated around 3,000 years ago. Although most archaeologists are convinced that the Olmec culture had its origins in Mesoamerica, a few are not so sure.

The best known Olmec sites are San Lorenzo Tenochtitlan and the La Venta pyramid, and this culture is known mostly through their architecture, art, and huge stone sculptures. They created colossal stone heads 10 ft. tall.

One example is the San Lorenzo Tenochtitlan Colossal Head 6 which has surprising South Pacific facial features. They also made statues, figurines, glyphic writing, and cave paintings, many fashioned from jade, obsidian, and magnetite. Many clay figures appear to represent babies some stylized with others appearing realistic. This suggests strong artisan specialists as well as extensive trading networks.

The Olmec appears to be the first great Mesoamerican culture, and the first to produce small cities which served as impressive centers for politics, religion, and culture. The cities were focused on an elite family or chieftain and had numerous surrounding villages. Indications are that they had a priestly class, well-defined myths about the stars and cosmos, sacred places, deities, and extensive rituals and ceremonies. They also practiced ritual bloodletting and played a distinctive Mesoamerican ballgame.

Because of the nature of this art, there has been considerable speculation about African or Asian origins for the Olmec. Archaeologists have strongly objected, stating that such claims invite ethnocentric racism, once again taking merit away from Native Americans by claiming their culture is derivative.

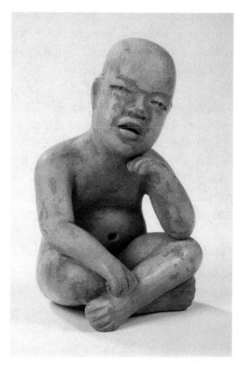

However, Betty Meggers of the Smithsonian Institution is not so sure. She noted that the Olmec civilization originated around the time of the Shang dynasty in China whose art the Olmec culture resembled. She hypothesizes that the Olmec may have been influenced by refugees from that area who made it to the New World.

Smithsonian scholars note a number of possible cultural connections. There are some writing similarities, markings on pottery similar to Chinese oracle bone writings. It's also interesting that jade was important to both the Chinese and the Olmec. Both cultures also had knowledge of the position of true North—not known to all societies in the ancient world.

But what is most striking is the Pacific/Asian facial features of the colossal heads and baby figures with epicanthic eye fold, goldfish statues that look identical to Chinese ones, and striking jade mask that are also very Chinese looking. This raises the issue of diffusion and independent invention but also takes on a hint of plausibility given the growing acceptance of a Pacific water route to the Americas.

Contact from China has been a long standing debate by those interested in first Americans. The Chinese were great sailors and some may have ventured east across the Pacific to the New World. Chinese maps show a distant land of Fusang supposedly visited by monks 1,500 years ago. We know that Chinese sailor Zeng He may have done so centuries later. He led a fleet of ships on several expeditions all over the Chinese coast and westward along Indonesia and even India and Africa.

Seven of his voyages are recorded from 1405 to 1433—before Columbus. In addition, there were a number of maps circulating in Europe that seemed to show the New World. In fact, Columbus was aware of these maps in putting together his own expeditions. If the Chinese were a source for these maps it would indicate that Zeng He or others might have circumnavigated the globe before Magellan.

In 2002, Gavin Mendes popularized this idea *in 1421: The Year China Discovered the World.* There was a brief glimmer of support for the Chinese in the Americas when anchor stones were found off the coast of California that strongly resembled those used by Chinese ships. However, geological analysis showed they were made of shale found in California and were used by Chinese-American fishing boats locally in the 19th century.

MAYA

The Olmec culture was in decline by 400 BCE, probably related to environmental changes that forced a change in their subsistence pattern. However, there may have been a link to the later Maya civilization. For example, a possible relationship between Olmec and Maya has been proposed for the Mask Temple wall at a later Mayan site of Lamanai in Belize where the Olmec-like face resembles the colossal heads of the earlier Olmec society.

The Maya civilization was developed 4,000 years ago in southeast Mexico, Guatemala and Belize as well as other regions of Central America. The Maya were an agricultural society that developed cities with massive monumental architecture including large temple pyramids such as the great El Castillo temple pyramid at Chichen Itza. Other major cities were Tikal and Teotihuacan. By 1,000 years ago there was a political collapse resulting in warfare, abandonment of cities, and a shift northward by the population.

This is also likely due to climate change as the area became drier and this affected groups in the American Southwest as well. For example, the Anasazi culture of Chaco Canyon in New Mexico was also abandoned when the climate became drier.

The Mayan writing system is sophisticated and well-developed and dates to 300 BCE and is different from the Olmec writing system. Unfortunately, out of thousands of books in which their culture, learning, ideas and rituals were recorded, only four have survived. Writing on stelae, vessels, facades, and cave walls as well as small objects helps rescue the situation somewhat with some additional information. The writing system combines phonetic signs representing syllables with logograms representing entire words, for a total of about 500 glyphs. Scholars can now read the majority of texts which are organized into glyph blocks read in two columns from left to right.

Mayan mathematics also stands out and is based on a bar and dot counting system commonly used around 1000 BCE. The Mayan invention of "0" may been at the same time as the Babylonian system, or even earlier. The numbers 1, 2, 3, and 4 are represented by dots; 5 is a bar, 6 is a bar with a dot above, and so forth until two bars for number 10. The Mayan calendar is also famous and is based on a solar year, roughly 360 days. In addition, they used interlocking cycles of time which they employed for prophecy.

The point is that both the Olmec and Mayan civilizations were sophisticated and complex and served to remind Europeans that the world was not Euro-centric. Other civilizations on other continents were elaborate, had dramatic architecture, social classes, ruling elites, literature, religion—all the elements of what Europeans would call 'refinement.'

There are many more hypotheses about the first Americans, e.g., Africans in the Americas, Irish monks and Welsh royalty, and of course, ancient aliens from the pseudoscience community. While many of these notions do not have support they do serve to provoke interest in our origins. As we gather more evidence, we will likely see other migrations, genetic evidence, or even examples of contact. But, it is important to recognize that whether the first Americans were from the South Pacific or northern Asia, culture in the New World became well developed and impressive in its own right. The attempts to devalue Native American culture and attribute its achievements elsewhere, failed.

While some Native claims may be more a matter of belief than evidence, such claims are understandable given the efforts of the settlers from the East to break treaties, take lands, and remove them to reservations. Today, many Native tribes suffer from this oppression which has resulted in poverty and health issues. However, Native groups look to the future for vibrant new ways to interpret their traditions. Many have become partners with archaeologists, seeking out their origins and a better understanding of the past.

CRITICAL THINKING & WEBSITES

1. Why is it plausible that *H. erectus* boated to Australia but not that Upper Paleolithic Solutrean people boated to North America, a hundred thousand years later?

2. What other evidence of Asian or South Pacific migrations would you like to see?

3. Is pseudoscience useful in that it provokes public interest in the first Americans?

4. What arguments were given to claim Native Americans had not built great mounds the size of pyramids?

5. Describe the Pacific Water Route.

6. What additional evidence would you like to see to indicate Vikings visited America before Columbus?

7. An interesting animation of the Bering Land Bridge is at:

   instar.colorado.edu/QGISL/bering_land_bridge/.

8. For the latest American archaeology perspective on the first Americans try: csfa.tamu.edu.

REFERENCES

Diehl, Richard. (2004). *The Olmecs: America's First Civilization*. London, UK: Thames and Hudson.

Coe, Michael, and Koontz, Rex. (2008). *Mexico: From the Olmecs to the Aztecs*, 6th edition. New York, NY: Thames and Hudson.

Dillehay, Thomas D. (2000). *The Settlement of the Americas*. New York, NY: Basic Books.

Fagan, Brian. (1990). *The Journey From Eden*. London, UK: Thames & Hudson.

Feder, Kenneth. (2013/1990). *Frauds, Myths, and Mysteries: Science and Pseudoscience in Archaeology, 8th edition*. Colombus, OH: McGraw Hill Education.

Jones, Martin. (2001). The Molecular Hunt: *Archaeology and the Search for Ancient DNA*. New York, NY: Arcade Publishing.

Klein, Richard G. (2009). *The Human Career: Human Biological and Cultural Origins*, 3rd edition. Chicago, IL: University of Chicago Press.

Levanda, Robert, & Schultz, Emily. (2015). *Anthropology: What Does It Mean to Be Human?*, 3rd edition. Oxford, UK: Oxford University Press.

Stringer, Chris & Andrews, Peter. (2005). The Complete World of Human Evolution. London, UK: Thames & Hudson.

Thomas, Cyrus. (1984). *Report on the Mound Explorations of the Bureau of Ethnology*. Washington, DC: Smithsonian Institution.

Wang, Sijia, Lewis, C. M. Jr, Jakobsson, M., Ramachandran, S, Ray, N., et al. (2007). Genetic variation and population structure in Native Americans. *Genetics* 3(11):185.

Young, Biloine, & Fowler, Melvin. (2000). *Cahokia: The Great Native American Metropolis*. Champaign, IL: University of Illinois Press.

Neves, W. A., Powell, J. F., Prous, E. G., Ozolins, M. B. (1999). Lapa Vermelha IV Hominid I: Morphological affinities of the earliest known American. *Genetics and Molecular Biology* 22(4):461-469.

Stanford, Dennis, & Bradley, Bruce. (2002). Ocean trails and prarie paths? Thoughts about Clovis origins. In *The First Americans: The Pleistocene Colonization of the New World*, Nina Jablonski (ed.), pp. 255-271. San Francisco, CA: Memoirs of the California Academy of Sciences, No. 27.

Brown, M.D., et al. (1998). MtDNA haplogroup X: An ancient link between Europe/Western Asia and North America? *American Journal of Human Genetics*, 63(6):1852-61.

1. Give a percentage likelihood for each of these hypotheses for the First Americans candidates based on evidence:

Evidence	%	
Solutrean hypothesis		
North/South Pacific waters hypothesis		
Bering Land Bridge Clovis hypothesis		
Norse Vikings		

2. Did the Olmec come from China? Why or why not?

8 SUBSISTENCE:
From Kula to Cola

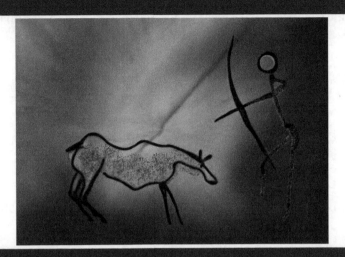

How a society makes a living plays a big role in shaping a culture. Our ancestors went from hunting and gathering, to raising plants and animals and producing food ourselves. While some risked their lives to trade in reciprocal partnerships, others developed a surplus with social inequality and injustice. Some say this was the worst mistake our species ever made.

LEARNING OBJECTIVES

1. Compare and contrast the foraging subsistence pattern of the Ju/'hoansi with other subsistence patterns.

2. Describe the Neolithic Revolution, how plants and animals were domesticated, and why some think it was the worst mistake in the history of the human race.

3. Describe horticulture, pastoralism, and agriculture as food production systems.

4. Explain how early civilization began and developed social complexity and inequality.

5. Understand the varieties of economic exchange including the three forms of reciprocity.

6. Describe the Kula Trade of the Trobriand Islands and determine how they acquire prestige.

FORAGING

How a society makes its living is called the infrastructure of culture—its means of production and reproduction. Many anthropologists view the infrastructure as the driving force of a culture because of the need to adapt to the environment and how subsistence shapes other aspects of culture. Anthropologists group human societies into five basic subsistence patterns shown in Table 8.1, with the basic division being between those who collect vs. produce food.

Table 8.1 Subsistence Types

Type	Description
Foraging	Making your living by scavenging, hunting, and gathering plant foods
Horticulture	Creating gardens with simple tools often using slash and burn techniques
Pastoralism	Domesticating and herding animals often moving seasonally
Agriculture	Using a plow, irrigation, work animals, and fertilizer to create large fields
Complex Society	Large pluralistic societies using agriculture and industry to create markets

The oldest form of subsistence is food foraging which is based on gathering plants supplemented with some hunting. Foragers lived in rich environments such as Northwest Coastal North America, with an abundance of forest animals, fish, and shellfish. Some developed enough wealth to have social classes and a surplus, while others lived in harsh deserts and cold climates around the world where life was more challenging.

Anthropologists focus on foraging societies because humans have spent 95% of our existence as hunter-gatherers. Our bodies and brains as well as language and culture all developed as foragers and if there is anything basic about us, it stems from a foraging way of life. In fact, the other subsistence patterns are so relatively new that we haven't yet resolved many of the problems that have resulted from culture change such as distribution of wealth, disease, and social inequality.

Foragers number less than 75 societies today and have been pushed to marginal areas by later food production subsistence patterns. As a result, most tend to be small and nomadic with several base camps so that they stay far below the carrying capacity of the land. We have a distorted view of these cultures and presume that most nonwestern peoples are inherently marginal, starving, or worse. In fact, foragers are the original affluent society!

The Ju/'hoansi of Namibia in the Kalahari Desert of South Africa are an example of a foraging culture that lived until recently in a challenging but sustaining environment (Lee, 1992). They found expansive food sources and ate more than 100 species of plants along with mungogo nuts, and 30% of their diet consisting of meat for protein. This is a much wider range of nutrients than most of us eat today with our small worlds of lettuce and tomato on a hamburger. The Ju/'hoansi had to adjust to some seasonal foods, but they were far from starvation (Sahlins, 1972).

Remarkably, foragers work less than we do today. Foragers put in an average of only 2.4 working days a week—about 20 hours. Compare that with many students today who take 15 course hours, study an additional 5-6 hours a week, and work at a mall or restaurant for 20-25 hours resulting in an over 40-hour work week. Foragers spent more time with family, relaxing, teasing, and telling stories.

Note that the Ju/'hoansi sharing of resources was also supported by the development of superstructure idea of cooperation, not greed, as a primary value. Watering holes are shared with other groups and possessions are circulated to minimize jealousy and maximize cooperation and social bonds. Their society is egalitarian meaning that they had relatively equal relationships and no formal chief. The status of women was also higher than it is for most today suggesting that for most of human prehistory women had high social status. If there were prehistoric foraging societies who promoted greed and competition, they were less likely to survive.

However, although stable for thousands of years, the Ju/'hoansi have been nearly destroyed by colonialism and domination by western complex society. They have had to "acculturate," meaning adjust to a dominant culture, often to their detriment. Poverty, disease, exploitation, social injustice, and other problems have resulted. Many foraging groups are also struggling with post-colonial governments which are meeting the needs of multinational corporate interests especially in export industries of agriculture or oil production. Most may be extinct by the end of the 21st century unless policies change.

NEOLITHIC REVOLUTION

By 10,000 years ago, when the glaciers retreated and the Pleistocene came to an end, humans had dispersed around the globe from the tropics to the arctic. The climate then became warmer and drier and the big game herds disappeared to the north. Once again, organisms had to adapt to these changing conditions. In several parts of the world humans began to adapt through culture by producing food in response to the environmental stress.

Rather than adjust to an econiche change, our ancestors began to create their own. By doing so humans directly interfered with the genetics and adaptation of other lifeforms to create domesticated species. Humans were not the first organisms to do so—ants and a few other species raise organisms for their own benefit. But, the global impact of human modification of the environment and domestication is still unfolding and we face the serious challenge of solving the resulting problems, if we are to avoid extinction as a species.

PLANT AND ANIMAL DOMESTICATION
The domestication of plants and animals likely occurred in four stages. First, humans simply foraged and harvested wild plants where they were found. Then, humans began to process wild foods and monitor their range and life stages. Third, humans collected and brought seeds to another location and deliberately

cultivated them. Fourth, humans actually farmed plants on a larger agricultural scale by adding irrigation, use of a plow, animal assistance, and resulting fertilizer.

Through artificial selective breeding, humans altered the genes of plants to have them conform to human needs. A wheat-like plant, teocinte began 5 kya with just a few rows of kernels. Farmers selected those with larger stronger kernels and took advantage of any mutations that increased the number of kernel rows, creating what we now know as corn. The same process of artificial selection occurred with wheat, barley, rice and other grains throughout the world. With agribusiness and genetic engineering today, huge ears of uniform rows of tight kernels are created but at a price.

Neolithic peoples ate over 100 varieties of plants. Interestingly, corporate farming today focuses only on only on a few. This drastically reduces the nutrients we get, especially minerals, and puts the species at risk if a fungus or other blight develops. Food today is designed for corporate profit and wide distribution, not global health. The Slow Foods Movement seeks to decentralize food production and draw food from only a 100-mile radius to support local providers and grow more varied varieties. This improves nutrition and provides income for the community.

The earliest domesticated animal was the dog based on evidence from a cave site in Spain from 16 kya. A touching burial at Mallaha, Israel at 12 kya is a puppy that is under the arm of the individual buried. Around 11 kya, goat herding comes from Mesopotamia and sheep from Turkey, and cattle while pigs and cattle were widely domesticated after 11 kya. Humans started with controlled hunting, then followed herds, next control the movements of herds or actively breed them, and ultimately, humans created pens and farms. Traits to determine if the animal fossils found indicate domestication include the number and diversity of species, changes over time to reduce horn size, and gender ratios.

NEOLITHIC CENTERS

The Neolithic began with foraging societies that formed small villages, had abundant resources, and developed social classes. As they turned to cultivation and herding when the climate changed, they created surplus food. Family lineages began to differ in how much food production they achieved. This led to ranked lineages with higher prestige, power, and resources. Eventually, full social classes were created which allowed some people to become fulltime craftspersons, leaders, or military or religious functionaries. This occurred earliest in the Middle East around 12 kya, followed by the Indus Valley in India, China, and Mesoamerica. African and European centers came later around 6 kya. Population grew but the overall quality of life went down.

Natufian culture which began 12.5 kya was structured as a chiefdom with 50-150 people living in houses of stone and mud, with storage areas for grain. Their herding and gardening allowed them to develop crafts and become sedentary. Burials were initially group ones and eventually became individual and showed different status and social class levels. But, settling down brought disadvantages. As the climate continued becoming warmer and drier, lakes in the area dried up and half the woods disappeared. The Natufians had to return to foraging or struggled to still raise cereal crops in poor soil. One of the world's first towns, Jericho, had about 300 residents and was settled by 9.3 kya. It was surrounded by a wall to protect the area from flooding and showed evidence of extensive long-distance trade of obsidian, shells, and ornaments. Cultivation led to population expansion and also a concern about the land, the success of crops, and the weather. Human communities developed spiritual ideas of how to control the environment and ensure food supplies. They also grappled with human mortality.

114

FOOD PRODUCTION

HORTICULTURE

Horticulture is the cultivation of crops in gardens using simple hand tools. A common practice is slash and burn cultivation where vegetation is cut and burned to enrich the soil, and new crops are planted. Horticultural groups have some conflict and violence because they must move their gardens regularly and do not use fertilizer or irrigation. As the population grows groups bump into each other and tension results. The Siona in the Cuyabeno area of the Ecuadorian Amazon harvest cassava (also called manioc and tapioca) by digging up the roots, washing them, and preparing them in a variety of ways.

Harvesting wild cassava led to creating small gardens in forest areas.

The Siona and other Amazon peoples preserved their culture by wise utilization of resources. They also had to maintain their identity through centuries of conquest by the Inca, then the Spanish, and ultimately now by foreign multinational oil companies. Oil extraction has contaminated much of their lands, fresh water is scarce, and the people have developed petroleum-related health issues. Foreign extractive industry of first rubber and now oil has brought forced religious and cultural conversion, slavery, torture, mass murder, and has significantly reduced their population. As a result, their culture is rapidly disappearing.

PASTORALISM

Pastoralism developed at about the same time as horticulture and involved herding animals, frequently forming cooperative trading relationships with the groups that raise plants. Pastoralists manage cattle, sheep, horses, or goats, and usually have to move the herds seasonally, often in long and dangerous journeys for pasture and water.

The Maasai are a semi-nomadic people living in southern Kenya near the Amboseli National Park. They have shown remarkable ability to herd cattle, sheep, goats, and donkeys under difficult conditions in deserts with frequent sandstorms. They move to the green pasture in the rainy season, carrying their possessions by donkey, and in the dry season return to swamps and woodlands, making them among the most successful herders in Africa. Their diet consists of mainly raw meat, raw milk, and raw blood. They are relatively disease-free and have almost no signs of heart disease, diabetes, or cancer—typical Western illnesses. The Maasai are famous for their extensive beaded jewelry and for the "adumu" competitive dance in which males rhythmically jump on their toes to great heights straight in the air. But, the Maasai are under pressure currently to become more sedentary and to engage in some farming, so they too feel the pressure to be less nomadic and abandon traditional ways.

AGRICULTURE

When horticulture becomes more complex, it turns into agriculture. Agriculture adds irrigation, use of plows, animals to pull the plows, and resulting fertilizer. This requires more investment in the land, so human groups settled down in permanent communities, and developed new technologies. This change also shifted the division of labor more toward male control.

Tay farmers are an example of an agricultural society that has lived in northeast Vietnam for over 2,500 years. They have a long tradition of wet rice cultivation although they grow other fruit trees, maize, sweet potato, and animals as well. Their social organization resembles a feudal system with both hereditary aristocrats and peasants, much like medieval Europe. Rulers have a right to control all who live on the land and exploit others through forced labor, taxes, and other forms of tribute.

MONUMENTS AND CITIES

STONEHENGE

Throughout the Neolithic period, humans built structures of earth and stone as well as wooden circles. Stonehenge is a prehistoric stone circle monument in England built around 5 kya. Evidence from the Stonehenge Riverside Project suggested that it was a burial grounds for the dead in association with a nearby wood circle community area for the living. Cremated remains found at Stonehenge date from the earliest phase and continued for at least another 500 years.

Stonehenge began with a circular earth bank and ditch probably with a wood structure, and by 2.5 kya huge bluestones were carved and transported 250 miles from Wales. Next, a circle of sarsen stones were added as well as a long avenue that extended to the River Avon. A number of the bodies found near Stonehenge show blunt force trauma suggesting conflict or ritual violence or sacrifice. One grave contained an older man with a badly damaged leg and a boy buried with gold jewelry, copper knives, stone tools and two

archer's wrist guards as well as tools for pottery making. Surprisingly, the boy was local but the older man came from the Alps.

Two miles northeast of Stonehenge are the Durrington Walls which are associated with three timber circles, hidden by various screens and posts. Numerous houses with oval hearths and furniture are also in the area and along the flint paved avenue. There is evidence of of feasting with broken pottery and animal bones at the Walls and along the Avenue, which suggests seasonal ritual processions along the route to Stonehenge. Cremated remains of the dead may have been deposited in the river or at Stonehenge itself. Thus, the village was the land of the living and Stonehenge the land of the dead.

Astronomical alignments are associated with both sites. Stonehenge is aligned to the summer solstice sunrise and the winter solstice sunset. The wood Southern Circle at Durrington Walls is aligned to the winter solstice sunrise—the beginning of longer light and new life of the season. More alignments may emerge with ongoing research at the site. A number of other stone circles in Europe also show astronomical alignments. Stonehenge represents the transition from the Neolithic to the Bronze Age, and fell out of use around 2.5 kya. It was a way our ancestors tried to make sense of the planet, the seasons, celestial events, and the cycle of life and death.

ÇATALHÖYÜK

Çatalhöyük, dated at 9-7 kya is the largest late Neolithic site found to date and consists of an early civilization settlement of 5,000 to 7,000 people in Turkey. The site shows 18 layers of maze-like apartment residences, some painted with ornate murals, but no temples or public buildings. The structures have rooftop streets, channels for refuse and sewage, and units that were entered through a hole in the ceiling and a ladder.

All the rooms were kept incredibly clean and sparse and had beautiful mural paintings of erect phalluses, hunting, and animal figures. The Çatalhöyük burial practice seemed to be to expose bodies to the elements for decomposition and then bury the bones in pits under the floors. A dramatic female statue seated on a throne with two lions shows a skeleton on the rear which could be a fertility figure or perhaps one associated with ancestors or death. Çatalhöyük shows no evidence of social classes, elites, royalty or chiefs, which suggests that social hierarchies came later, at least in this area.

MESOPOTAMIA

By 7-6 kya, Mesopotamian cities in the Middle East, Mohenjo-Daro in India, and Teotihuacan in Mexico, ushered in city-states. These civilizations concentrated power and were based on agricultural innovation with water control and even redirecting rivers around cities; diversification of labor adding metal workers, and silk trade and other job specializations. They had a central government by elites with armies and fortifications, and growing social stratification of five classes: royalty and priests, managers and professionals, artisans and merchants, military and workers, and servants and slaves. City planning included great avenues leading to temples and monuments, while taxes funded wars of defense and conquest. Laws were codified, and a full-time priesthood emerges to support the status quo. Writing was invented for business accounts and recording the achievements of the ruling classes.

The Standard of Ur, a decorated box dated at 4.5 kya illustrates this social diversity. Sargon of Akkad united warring city-states of Mesopotamia 4.3 kya and created

the first multi-ethnic centrally ruled empire. A later ruler, Sargon II, took his name meaning, "the god made firm the king" and built a palace, Cour Khorsabad/Dur-Sharrukin. On the façade of Sargon II's throne room were two lion-taming spirits who face the observer and symbolized magical deity-king Gilgamesh of Uruk who lived 4.5 kya. He is the main character of the Epic of Gilgamesh, the first great work of literature from Mesopotamia. By 3.7 kya Hammurabi of Babylon created the first known organized government code of laws.

A geographer, Jared Diamond, suggested that the Neolithic revolution and the rise of civilization brought some benefits but was really the worst mistake in the history of the human race. Food production was a response to the stress of a changing environment and it provided more food, population growth, new crafts and technology, and emergence of centralized leadership, which was necessary for creating large scale agriculture, wide trade, civilization, and monuments.

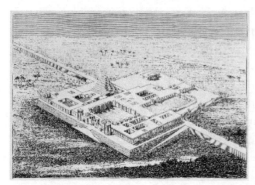

However, its shift from the very diverse high protein diet of foragers to eating limited foods and more cereal grains provided poorer nutrition and quality of life. It provided more workers for the farm, but led to dramatic population increases and greater maternal risk. Foragers work about 20 hours per week, farmers work long hours every day and must tend animals and fields in good weather and bad. Hygiene and sanitation became problems and overall health declined as disease increased. One of the most insidious consequences was the development of social inequality and exploitation of the mass peasant classes who were required to build monuments to their own oppression.

COMPLEX INDUSTRIAL SOCIETY

Today, big landowners in cooperation with multinational agribusiness have edged out small family farmers and landless peasants all over the world. Farming is now characterized by large corporate control over what gets planted or raised, giant slaughter houses, and genetically modified crops. Advocates of corporate farming point out individual investment opportunities, stable use of lands, and efficiency of operations. Critics have pointed out that much damage has been done to the land through corporate practices, and that individuals owning small investment shares in companies in which the CEO's earn hundreds of millions in salaries and holdings is not the same thing as syndicalism—an economic system in which individual workers in the company actually own the corporation. Critics also raise issues about the diversity of food we consume, ethical issues in the treatment of animals, and health concerns about the effects of genetic modification.

The Industrial Revolution began about 200 years ago with the invention of the steam engine. It introduced machines for processing food and making goods for market. This resulted in large scale business operations and mass food production. Machines replaced human labor, animal power, and hand tools which resulted in massive cultural change. The invention of automobiles and other transportation and electronic communication further revolutionized society. Today's industrial food production and global marketing complex involves a network of interlinked distribution centers

aided by electronic and digital inventions that began in the late 20th century. Unfortunately, the control of resources, production, and marketing by multi-national corporations and the location of jobs overseas for cheaper labor has removed control of the economy from individual communities and governments to these corporations. This is a major shift in economic and sociopolitical control. Rather than a blend of individual integrity, social relationships, plus a healthy right to make some profit, the whole system became based only on profit and the human factor was reduced or eliminated as in the housing and Wall Street crisis of 2008. We move from a Kula Trade system described below that fosters close social ties to a Cola system that devalues human relationships and places profit as the highest value. For example, manufacturing corporations have taken jobs overseas leaving high unemployment rates, e.g., Detroit, MI. The world's largest employer, Wal-Mart, moves into a community and provides low prices on lower quality goods—but as a result displaces the family hardware store or retail clothes shop that has higher quality goods and knowledgeable service. When communities object, Wal-Mart crushes the opposition.

Wal-Mart established a store in Acworth, GA and wanted another one just three miles away. When the town objected, Wal-Mart threatened to bankrupt the town, yet Wal-Mart showed TV ads celebrating "small town America." Faced with destruction, the town gave in. The low prices may be a tempting distraction but as a result, wealth becomes more centralized, the U.S. loses the middle class, and the overall quality of life declines. We are motivated by advertisements to crave material goods often with designer labels—Prada handbags, prized golf club, or latest Nike shoe, but it may be an illusion of wealth as we end up empty handed, returning to near-peasant status with very little control over the economy.

ECONOMIC SYSTEMS

An economic system is an organized societal arrangement in which people produce, distribute, and consume goods. Each society allocates natural resources such as land, water, fuel, and technology and labor in various ways. In the European feudal system, allocation of goods and services was based on status with elites automatically obtaining an unequal portion. Under capitalism, distribution is negotiated between buyers and sellers based on a cash system. It has been labeled "free enterprise," and it encourages inventions, but it also sweeps away traditional protections and social relations that can serve as implicit regulatory factors. This has been made clear to rust belt workers who have watched their factories disappear to other nations with lower wage structures.

RECIPROCITY

Reciprocity is an economic system in which there is exchange of goods and services of roughly equal value. It originated with foragers and is characteristic of egalitarian societies such as the Ju/'hoansi. But all societies use some forms of reciprocity on a folk level and in human interactions in business.

In generalized reciprocity, the value of the exchange is not calculated nor is there a time of repayment. An example would be the exchanges between parents and children. People just give things or volunteer, and while it could be reciprocated, no one explicitly keeps count.

In balanced reciprocity, there is a definite obligation to reciprocate promptly in a "you scratch my back, I'll scratch yours" arrangement. For example, a Tanzania woman might raise bananas and give them to a relative with the unspoken understanding that the family member will provide meat or grain to her family. Anger and disappointment can result when the exchange becomes too one-sided and this hurts social relationships and can be the stuff of much gossip.

Negative reciprocity is based on the goal of getting something for as little as possible. It may involve friendship but also a sense of getting a "good deal." It may also include "midnight requisitions," taking some pens from the workplace, wearing your sister's dress without her permission, or rustling cattle.

Gift giving is complex. Everyone know an awkward personal situation in which a gift that was received was less than expected, or a gift was expected but none was received. Sometimes this is a cultural misunderstanding. For example, the term "Indian giver" was a misunderstanding by Euro-Americans about Native economy and culture. When Natives "sold" the island of Manhattan, they were really just extending hunting rights to new friends for a certain period, with reciprocity expected in return.

Europeans did not realize that from a Native point of view the focus is not on the item itself, but on the creation of a friendly relationship that would be maintained through trade and mutual exchanges which would circulate goods around. In fact, throughout the world the relationship is the focus, not the literal gift, even to the point of belittling a gift so as to properly assess the return obligation. Gift giving can even serve as a substitute for war. The Siuai of the Solomon Islands refer to their feast guest as "attacker", and host as "defender," and the competition symbolizes the conflict of warfare.

Other misunderstandings can occur between cultures. The Hopi are a Native American group in U.S. Southwest. The Hopi have a concept of a symbolic spiritual gift is important. It even extends to women's work of gardening and men's spiritual and ritual activities being seen as gifts each gender give to each other. In fact, close kinship ties underlie all the Hopi do.

Peter Whiteley (2004) described the attempt by the Hopi to give a gift to the U.S. President in 1852. The Hopi believed they were creating a symbolic connection between themselves and the President almost 3,000 miles away. They gave gifts of two prayer sticks (representing the Hopi and the President) connected by a cord with feathers representing the two cultures possibly meeting in the middle. They also gave an offering of a cornstalk cigarette and honey-soaked cornmeal representing clouds and rain to provide a magical power to assure the President that good rains would come. The U.S. President understood none of these and the gifts were ignored. Such cultural misunderstandings can have strong consequences.

Redistribution

A trade transaction is an exchange of something for something else but there is a specific calculation of the value of these items as well as a negotiation. This would include shopping online, buying a knife at a swap meet, or selling your house. Barter is a form of trade in which no money is involved and the parties negotiate a direct exchange which can be more balanced or more negative. Barter is becoming an increasingly frequent exchange among Americans, especially in the Far West.

Redistribution requires a strong centralized political organization which has the power to encourage or enforce movement of money, goods, or services. For example, a government assesses a tax or a tribute on each member of the society to support its activities. The authorities then redistribute the resources usually in the form of public services. Tax collection is a form of redistribution with elites often having means to reduce their tax assessment not available to poorer classes.

An example of a redistribution system is a Moka, a highly ritualized exchange where a "Big Man" or "Big Woman" gives a party in New Guinea "with interest." The Big Man struggles over several months and even years to accumulate pigs and other valued items to redistribute to others and up the effort of the last Moka. While giving away his accumulated wealth is highly generous, it is also a way to build status, prestige, and attention to his generosity. It constantly renews the debt of the relationship, keeping social relations alive and energized.

An American example might be Warren Buffet and Bill Gates 2010 creation of the "The Giving Pledge," an effort for the wealthiest people in the world to commit to giving most of their wealth away to charity. As of August 2015, 127 billionaires from the U.S., Africa, Asia, Australia, Europe, have agreed to give at least half their wealth to philanthropic causes. While not necessarily the motivation for the gifts, these actions result in gaining of social status, admiration, gratitude, and respect in return.

Northwest Coast Potlatch

A classic puzzle of economic exchange is the potlatch ceremony of the Native Americans/First Nations of the Northwest Coast of U.S. and Canada. In ranked societies where substantial surpluses of goods are produced, social classes arise and wealth distribution becomes an issue. The solution for Pacific Northwest Coast tribes such as the Salish, Tlingit and Kwakwaka'wakw is a potlatch, a gift ceremonial event in which a village chief publicly gives away food and goods that have been stockpiled for months or years and signify wealth.

Traditionally, the village would store up sea otter furs, dried salmon, blankets, and other valuables while making boasting speeches about generosity, greatness, and glorious ancestors. In cases of extreme abundance, the chief would even destroy the food and goods in a grand display. Other villages would become indebted and throw a potlatch to provide food and goods, later.

The potlatch forms a kind of leveling mechanism so that no one accumulates wealth permanently or risks deadly jealousy. There are many such mechanisms that cultures employ, e.g., verbally knocking down someone a peg or two just to keep them from getting a big head.

MARKET EXCHANGE

In nonindustrial societies, the market place is a space set aside for farmers and craft persons to present their produce, livestock, and material items that they have made. For example, women in Kolcata, India make and trade their baskets at an annual fair— one of the largest in Asia. They learn techniques from each other, display and sell their products, and develop reputations as skilled basket makers. It also becomes a social center where you get news and gossip. Now, women have organized banks to trade and loan money to each other creating almost a separate economic system.

Not just in India, but around the world women are seeking to enter the marketplace as producers and providers on their own terms. Anthropologists note that lifting poverty alone will be a major factor in improving the health and welfare of women and children around the world.

KULA TRADE

Anthropologist Bronislaw Malinowski was fascinated when he visited the Trobriand Islanders of Papua New Guinea and studied their ceremonial Kula Trade. He puzzled about why the Trobrianders would risk their lives to travel hundreds of miles over dangerous open ocean waters—all to give away what appears to others to be worthless shell trinkets.

The Kula Trade is a balanced reciprocity exchange system that includes 18 island communities and has been going on for perhaps millennia. Thousands of seafarers canoe hundreds of miles in difficult seas to establish good trade relations through the exchange of prestige items of jewelry. Their 25 ft. canoes are elaborately decorated through months of great effort and religious rituals and they may be gone for weeks or months—with some lost at sea and never to return. The Trobrianders bring with them red shell necklaces (*soulava*) that are traded around the islands north and clockwise, and white shell armbands (*mwali*) that are traded south and counter-clockwise. After greetings a trader might offer a red necklace, always with the right hand, and in return, a white armband with the left hand will be offered by the trading partner. If a white armband is first offered, it must be with the left hand, and a red necklace would be the correct response in return.

Kula necklaces and armbands are only symbolic, and are rated higher or lower depending on the style and complexity and their histories. Participants trade other goods as well as the system serves to smooth and foster relationship, partners, economic exchange, and a feeling of worth or connectedness with other island communities. The overall goal is lifelong trading relationships as well as a personal display of generosity that brings prestige—although the giver is required to express modesty. The objects do not remain with the partner; they must be passed to other trading partners until they eventually circulate around the ring of islands. A trader is only a steward of the Kula jewelry, and anyone who tries to take a necklace or armband out of circulation invites criticism and scorn, and risks feuds and sorcery magic for unraveling the social fabric that holds the islands together. Trobrianders believe it is more prestigious to give than to receive and well-respected traders become important figures who are admired in their gift-giving.

Traders first participate in lower exchanges where the giver has the higher prestige and slowly works their way up to more important trades. The hereditary chiefs of the islands possess the most important necklaces and armbands and they have the prestige and influence to organize the trading voyages. So, although the shell jewelry is exchanged, its real value is in the social relationships it forges, especially in ranked societies such as the Trobriand Islands. Malinowski virtually ignored another exchange system in the islands, the accumulation and exchange of incised banana leaves made and used by women as highly prized skirts, studied later by Annette Weiner (1980). The Trobrianders are matrilineal, meaning that they determine their relatives only through their mothers. Men within the family work for their mothers' and their sisters' gardens and after a harvest of yams, men must provide large gifts of yams to his brother-in-law, his sister's husband. When a family member dies, relatives "buy back" yams the dead person gave away by an exchange of the grass skirts with the quality and quantity symbolizing the importance of the relationship. A woman's husband is expected to provide the skirts, and a woman's prestige is determined by the degree of wealth provided by her husband. Thus, Kula rights are not automatic.

CRITICAL THINKING & WEBSITES

1. Should a society maintain itself forever or be considered a failure if it changes dramatically?
2. What effect would the introduction of a monetary system have on the Kula Trade, i.e., would the exchanges lose their symbolic and social functions?
3. How do Donald Trump, Bill Gates, and Warren Buffett compare with the Big Man system?
4. Describe one subsistence pattern. Learn what the Bill and Melinda Gates Foundation is promoting at their website: www.gatesfoundation.org.

REFERENCES

Blau, Max. (2013). Lawsuit filed to halt Suburban Plaza Walmart construction. *Creative Loafing*, March 18, 2013. Retrieved on December 8, 2015 from: clatl.com/freshloaf/archives/2013/303/18/lawsuit-filed-to-halt-suburban-plaza-walmart-construction.

Boas, Franz. (1975). Kwakiutl Ethnography. Chicago, IL: University of Chicago Press.

Crunk, Lee. (1989). Strings attached. *The Sciences*, 3, 2-4, (May-June 1989).

Diamond, Jared. (2005). *Collapse: How Societies Choose to Fail or Succeed*. New York, NY: Viking.

Diamond, Jared. (1998). *Guns, Germs and Steel*. London: Vintage.

Granada Television. (1976). *Onka's Big Moka*. London: BBC Television.

Harris, Marvin. (1968). The Rise of Anthropological Theory. Walnut Creek, CA: AltaMira Press.

Heider, Karl G. (1970). *The Dugum Dani: A Papuan Culture in the Highlands of West New Guinea*. Chicago, IL: Aldine Publishing.

Lavenda, Robert & Schultz, Emily. (2015). *Anthropology: What Does It Mean to be Human?*. Oxford, UK: Oxford University Press.

Lee, Richard. (1992). The Dobe Ju/'hoansi, 2nd ed. New York, NY: Holt, Rinehart and Winston.

Loomis, Carol. (2006). Warren Buffett gives away his fortune. *Fortune* 2006. Retrieved December 8, 2015.

Malinowski, Bronislaw. (1922/1984). *Argonauts of the Western Pacific*. Long Grove, IL: Waveland Press.

Marcus, Label. (2006). Walmart, Critics Slam Each Other on Web. *The Washington Post*, July 18, 2006.

McAnany, Patricia & Yoffee, Norman, eds. (2010). *Questioning Collapse: Human Resilience, Ecological Vulnerability, and the Aftermath of Empire*. Cambridge, UK & New York, NY: Cambridge University Press.

McLeod, Mark W., & Dieu, Nguyen Thi. (2001). Culture and Customs of Vietnam. Westport, CT: Greenwood Publishing Group.

No author. (2012). Warren Buffett, Bill Gates Giving Pledge Gets 12 More Billionaires to Commit Over Half of Their Fortunes. Huffington Post, April 20, 2012.

Sahlins, Marshall. (1972). Stone Age Economics. New York, NY: Aldine.

Saitoti, Tepilit Ole & Beckwith, Carol. (1990). Maasai. New York, NY: Harry N. Abrams.

Whiteley, Peter. (2004). Ties that bind. *Natural History*, November 2004, p. 26-31.

Weiner, Annette. (1980). Stability in banana leaves: Colonization and women in Kiriwina, Trobriand Islands. In *Women and Colonization: Anthropological Perspectives*, Mona Etienne & Eleanor Leacock, Eds., 270-293. New York, NY: Praeger.

1. Describe the exact rules of the Kula Trade, e.g., what is done before the trade, what is traded in what direction, how it is presented, and what strategies are used.

2. Why do Trobriand Islanders risk their lives in long ocean voyages?

3. Make or design some necklaces and armbands to simulate the Kula Trade. What strategies would you suggest for success in the trade?

9 SEX AND GENDER: GLBTQIA...XYZ

Sex is shaped by biology while culture shapes gender and identity. Anthropology takes a biocultural approach to understanding sex, marriage, and family and emphasizes the cultural construction of gender, as well as many societies who have created more than two genders.

LEARNING OBJECTIVES

1. Understand how sex is formed biologically and can create intersex individuals.

2. Explain how gender is culturally created and adaptive, and is separate from biological sex.

3. Describe societies with more than two genders.

4. Explain what anthropologists know about attraction and love.

5. Show how societies are organized into families and lineages, solidified by marriage.

6. Understand the GLBTQIA alternatives as well as the trans posing experiments with identity that younger generations are exploring.

BIOLOGICAL SEX

There is no topic of greater individual interest than sex and gender. It involves everyone and our society has become very away of variable sex and gender issues, as well as same sex marriage, and variations in sexual orientation.

Until recently, western society assumed that sex and gender were the same thing and did not change, and that there were only two alternatives: male and female, in a binary system. We now know that sex is more a biological process, while gender is totally culturally constructed.

The sex formation process starts with chromosomes, the DNA messages in the sex cells that code for our traits. One of the 23 chromosome pairs of humans codes for sex and starts a series of eight stages of development of biological sex.

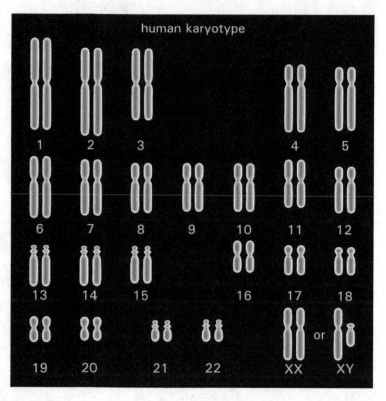

If the individual possesses an XX pair she develops as a female, an Xy, he becomes a male. Other chromosomal combinations are possible such as a single X, XXX, or Xyy but these result in alterations of the process and other biological issues. Geneticists have studied these other variations extensively and have been able to link them with various chromosomal issues. Hospitals now offer conseling centers on genetic matters in most major cities.

The eight stages of sexual development are shown in Table 9.1.

Table 9.1. Eight Stages of Sexual Development.

STAGE	MALE	FEMALE
Chromosome	Xy	XX
Gonads	Testes, sperm	Ovaries, ovum
Hormones	Androgen, profestin	Estrogen
Internal organs	Prostate, vas deferens, seminal vesicles	Uterus, Fallopian tubes
External organs	Penis, scrotum	Clitoris, labia, vagina
Assigned sex	"It's a boy!"	"It's a girl!"
Identity & behavior	I'm a boy	I'm a girl
Social response	"He's a boy"	"She's a girl"

Interestingly, the basic human model is female, and the genital tissues form a labia and clitoris. But by around six weeks hormonal factors begin to transform Xy individuals in a male direction with a flood of hormones which affect genital tissues. The outer laabia folds swell and fuse to form a scrotum while the center clitoris tissue becomes a penis. Therefore, the clitoris and penis are homologous tissues, i.e., coming from the same structures.

That the basic human model is female means that all humans are female for the first weeks of their life. The addition of hormones converts about half of us into males—but sometimes the process goes differently. As we will see societies have very different reactions and solutions for biological sex diversity. Our society in comparison has historically been much more restrictive. The term anthropologists use for this variability is "intersex."

INTERSEX

On occasion, the hormones may be minimal or out of proportion, or the internal or external tissues may be unresponsive, so a genetic Xy males can remain feminized or a genetic XX female may become masculinized. For example, an individual may test genetically as an Xy male, but have the internal structures or external appearance of a female. About 1% of live births show some sexual ambiguity and 1 in 3,000 individuals are intersexes, possessing the genetilia and secondary sexual characteristics of both sexes or some combination of the two in underdeveloped form. There are 46 different types of intersex conditions presenting various combinations of sexual tissues.

For example, Caster Semenya, who was the world 800 meter champion was subject to genetic and other tests that showed she was an intersex individual with external female genetilia but no ovaries or uterus—just undescended testicles. There was no world athletic standard for determining sex, so Semenya was allowed to continue to compete as a female. She stated, "God made me the way I am and I accept myself" (Spaulding, 2009).

But, a troubling case is that of David Reimer who was an Xy male but lost his penis through a surgical mistake and was reassigned at 18 months to be a girl called "Brenda" (Colapinto, 2006). This was based on the belief that gender is binary and it would be better to be considered to be female than to be a male without a penis. As he got older, his testes were removed, he was given estrogen, and another opening was created for urination. Reimer reported being ostracized and bullied and chose to return to being male in his teens. He objected strongly to his "genital mutilation" and inherent male-bias in the surgery. Although he married a female and had stepchildren, he commited suicide at age 38, linked to his sex and gender issues.

By the 1990s, forced sex reassignment in the U.S. was questioned. Johns Hopkins and other hospitals stopped doing sex assignment surgery on children. As an alternative, a growing number of intersexes and others with male/female issues proposed intersex as a third legal gender. Other institutions argued for delaying reassignment until late adolescence when a more informed decision might be made. Psychologists also changed the term "gender identity disorder" to "gender incongruence." In recent years, the United Nations proposed child protection mechanisms to prevent imposition of medical procedures to achieve an ideal gender identity based on culturally-created gender categories.

As the biological evidence accumulates, it becomes clearer that we are all *born this way." Many sexual orientations that have been considered in our society to be a choice, may have a strong biological base. However, culture guides the direction and expression of those choices through the range of genders offered.

SOCIAL GENDER

When anthropology first began in the Victorian era of the 1870s, the view was that women are 'naturally' subjugated in the home and that culture has benefited more from the activities of men, thus creating the "man the hunter" myth. Early ethnographic descriptions of cultures were about men, by men, and for men. In the early 20th century, biological determinism was in favor and people believed anatomy was destiny and that sex and gender were the same.

But, by the 1930s, Ruth Benedict (1934) stressed that western norms of culture and behavior should not be the measure of human nature, and that psychological health was compromised only when individuals internalized their culture's condemnation. Margaret Mead (1928) and other anthropologists learned how flexible gender and attitudes toward sexual behavior really were in human cultures. For example, Mead (1935) ventured to New Guinea and found that the Arapesh believed that both men and women were 'naturally' gentle and nonagressive. Men helped with birthing and even cuddled with their wives during nursing.

In contrast, the Mundugumor believed both men and women were violent and aggressive. Mothers held their infants harshly, gave little nurturing care, and dominated their daughters-in-law. Even sexual behavior included a lot of biting and scratching and brief encounters. Finally, the Tchambuli had role reversal where the men were artistic and fearful, curled each other's hair, and cooked their own meals. The women were confident, dominant, and dismissive of the 'emotional' men the way that women are dismissed in patriarchy. These unexpected reversals suggested that gender was highly flexible.

By the 1960s, field studies of primate behavior showed that female great apes were breadwinners and had more power than many human females! Studies of subsistence revealed that females in human foraging societies had relatively high social status. There are even some female hunting cultures such as the Agta of the Phillippines. Further, forager fathers could be very nurturing, e.g., the egalitarian Aka of the Congo where fathers are playful and loving with their children. Evidence shows that they hold their infants 50% more than do U.S. fathers, and they are gentle with frequent cuddling and kissing.

Field studies also showed that female status declined with food producing societies as females did more work but had less control over production and became relegated to domestic duties. The horticultural Yanomamo of Venezuela females had no resources, kin support, or leadership roles, and were captured from neighboring groups and beaten regularly by their husbands who created an artificial female shortage through infanticide. This shortage then justified more warfare as they took wives from other groups.

The animal herding Nuer of East Africa named women after cattle and had few rights themselves. However, there were some exceptions. The Iroquois in the Northeast traditionally had high female status because males were the leaders, but they served the female clan mothers who selected them and held the ultimate power.

In the last 50 years, anthropology has focused more on a balance of male and female activities, doing longer and more intensive fieldwork, and engaging in empathic participant observation of both women and men. The idea that culture comes only from "man the hunter" has given way to including "woman the gatherer," and an analysis of the patterns of male dominance showing that female status is lowest where women do not have independent income or subsistence activities.

But, even where women are dominated, they can use indirect power and influence, or create outlets for their yearnings through stories and ritual poetry (Abu-Lughod, 1986), objecting to female circumcision, or creating banks by women for women's economic activities. Some women even look to bonobo society in which females cleverly bond together, or human foraging societies with higher status for women.

SOCIETIES WITH MORE GENDERS

CHUKCHI OF SIBERIA

Anthropologists also discovered that cultures can have more than two genders (masculine, feminine). For example the Chukchi of Siberia are reindeer herders to roam the tundra. They have six different genders, each with different roles, dress, hair styles, manner of speaking, rights and responsibilities, and rules for who they can marry. The Chukchi believe that everything is assigned a spirit. When crises occur, negative spirits are to blame, and by switching to another gender spirits might be fooled. Individuals might switch among six genders throughout their lifetime.

BUGIS OF INDONESIA

The Bugis of Indonesia have five genders: masculine, feminine, bissu, calabai, and calalai. Bissu are considered to be gender transcendent and include intersex and transgendered individuals. They enter female parts of dwellings and serve as religious functionaries whose advice and special spiritual powers are sought on holy pilgrimates.

Calabai are "false women" who are almost hyper-feminine and serve as wedding planners and fashion workers who wear feminine clothing. They are regarded as quite beautiful and special. They take a feminine heterosexual role, including many people who are seen as gay in the West. Calalai are similarly "false men" who are biologically female but adopt masculine roles and dress and take feminine gender in marriage. Thus, the Bugis provide a flexible gender system which allow for societal functions as well as individual expression.

HIJRA OF INDIA

The Hijra of India are traveling troups of dancers and entertainers who are important as religious functionaries at birth and marriage ceremonies and who give blessings and entertain guests and visitors. They have a deep history in the religious and scriptual heritage of the area which has themes of andrygyny and gender flexibility. They are considered to be intersex or also transgendered individuals and they form a separate caste with worship of transgendered deities.

The status of the Hijra is fairly low with frequent human rights issues. Poor village boys are sometimes sold into the troop and raised as feminine. Some even serve, especially in cities as sex workers or beg for a living in the streets. Violence against the Hijras is unfortunately common, especially in cities where they can be beaten in public. They also face discrimination in housing, education, and employment.

However, the Hijra challenge Western ideas of sexuality. The male sexual partners of Hijra are not considered to be homosexual, because they play an active role in penetration during anal intercourse. Neither can the Hijra be considered to be homosexual because they are a separate gender entirely with different roles, dress, etc. In recent years there has been pressure to consider all Hijra to be transgendered with a legal third gender status which was granted by India in 2014. Human rights advocates hope to increase their social status and living conditions in the future.

132

AZANDI AND NANDI OF AFRICA

Africa also has examples of societies with more than two genders. For example, Nandi wealthy older widows with children of their own may become a "husband." They take a young "wife" who gets conviently and discreetly pregnant by the widow's male relatives while the widow becomes a father to the new family. It is a clever solution that allows important roles for women throughout their lives and puts the emphasis on nurturing more children.

Perhaps most interesting of all, are the Azande of the Democratic Republic of the Congo (DRC). All Azande males are warriors who take boy wives to cook and make camp for them who become their sexual partners. When the warrior accumulates enough wealth, he may pay a bride price for a female wife for procreation purposes, although some still retain their boy wives. The boy wives mature and become warriors themselves, so the cycle continues. Thus, for the first half of their lives, the Azande males are in Western terms "homosexual" and in the latter half "heterosexual" or "bisexual." This suggests a degree of flexibility in sexual expression in addition to one's biologically-based orientation.

NAVAJO OF THE SOUTHWEST

Native American cultures, including the Navajo, Mohave, Blackfoot, Apache, Sioux, and Maya to name a few, are noted for having a third or fourth gender which include intersex individuals and/or feminine males and masculine females. The Navajo of the Southwest have a gender called "nadle" which has two identities in one body. Nadle actually have higher status and social power than either male or female roles.

In recent decades, some Native Americans have adopted the term "two spirit" to include both additional traditional genders as well as those who identify as gay or lesbian in more Western terms. So anthropologists conclude that heteronormative perspectives are only one alternative and a more accurate view is that gender is a culturally-determined spectrum of identities and social roles that is highly flexible and changeable.

ATTRACTION AND LOVE

Whatever our sexual orientation or gender, flirting is a major way we convey attraction. Some scientists are convinced that humans as well as other animals are affected by pheromones, ordorless chemical messages that affect our social relationships. Androstenol is a female pheromone that has been shown to cause women living together for long periods to develop synchronized menstrual cycles, known as the McClintock effect. Males excrete androstadienone which has other powerful affects over behavior.

Hormones also play a strong role in attraction. Anthropologist Helen Fisher (2004) has linked different hormones and brain chemical to the choices we make in our relationships. She argued that there are three ways we connect: 1) the pure lust of our sex drive, 2) feelings of romance and attraction, and 3) deep loving attachment. On a simple level, lust promotes mating, attraction promotes relationship, and attachment promotes caring, loyalty, and family of choice.

Of the three, Fisher concluded that romantic love is the strongest because the effects of loss are so great that people in many cultures become depressed and even commit suicide or homicide. She used an evolutionary argument that males are more visual in selecting females because prehistorically they were looking for

females who were healthy and would bear children. Females on the other hand focused on a companion and nurturer so she selected a male based on knowledge about his behavior and reactions over time to judge his competence and fitness.

Another factor that affects attraction is personality. Fisher argued that there are four basic personality types that are associated with four different neurotransmitters in the brain. Although we have all these transmitters, we have them in different proportions. Knowing your type can aid in your relationships and workplace. These neurochemical types are shown in Table 9.2.

Table 9.2. Helen Fisher's Four Personality Types That Affect Attraction.

PERSONALITY	NEUROCHEMICAL	BEHAVIOR
Explorer	Dopamine	Creative, artistic, adventurous, risk-taking, enthusiastic
Builder	Serotonin	Practical, sensible, guardian, conventional, calm, very social
Director	Testosterone	Rational, logical, analytical, direct, decisive, competitive
Negotiator	Estrogen/Oxytocin	Intuitive, idealist, wholistic, expressive, emotional, empathic

Fisher explained that knowing your dominant personality type (and its underlying biology) can help you make a better mate choice beyond the fact that most of us choose someone of a similar background, education level, ethnic group, etc. She studied how people on chemistry.com dating website matched up with each other and found that relationships worked better if both partners were of similar primary or secondary types—even if their backgrounds were very different.

She also suggests that male provisioning has a deep cultural history but that with more equal gender roles today couples could share equally in paying for dates, supplying a household, or providing for a family. Other anthropologists note that more equal relationships result when each partner has an independent economic resource or assets are held jointly. Thus, many couples today who choose not to marry still choose to create cohabitation agreements to facilitate division of property should the relationship change.

MARRIAGE AND FAMILY

MARRIAGE

However people are attracted to each other, they form several types of marriages and family systems. Marriage is a relationship between two or more people that requires social, behavioral, and economic obligations. Anthropologists divide marriage into endogamy, marrying someone within your defined social group, versus exogamy, marrying someone outside your group. Most Americans marry within their race, social class, religion, etc., but there is increase in exogamy, marrying outside your group today.

In some societies, marriages are arranged. Families in India consult with each other and begin negotiations to make the best match for their children. Parents are believed to be able to best select potential mates for their children because they will not be overly influenced by strong emotions. There may be caste, social class, occupational, religious, and physical factors that all play a role. Cultures with arranged marriage see the relationship as an extension of kinship, so the marriage is between two families, not two individuals.

About 80% of human societies adopt polygamy in which a man marries more than one wife (polygyny), or woman has more than one husband (polyandry). However, additional spouses require more resources, so most marriages in the world are monogamous, having just one spouse at a time.

The Nuer of East Africa have an interesting form of ghost marriage. When a man dies without sons, his brother or nephew would take a wife in his name and act as a stand-in for him in order to continue his male lineage. The bride gets pregnant by the brother or someone else in the lineage, and all her children are considered to be the sons and daughters of the dead man. The twist comes when the brother or nephew desires marrying and having children considered to be his own, because he is already ghost married with ghost children. When he dies without children viewed as his, the people believe his spirit will be angry, so a male relative of his takes a wife who bears his ghost children, and so the pattern continues. For many societies, such as the Nuer, the social father (not the biological father) is the "real" father recognized.

Polyandry, marrying more than one husband, often brothers, is fairly rare and occurs mostly in Asia. The Nyinba of Nepal typically have a group of brothers marry one wife together with whom they have children. The Nyinba value family harmony so the children may share all the brothers as fathers or may be assigned to each brother sequentially starting with the oldest. The whole system serves as a means to keep a group of brothers together and cooperating with each other in order to keep corporate family farmland ownership intact. In addition, if each brother had a wife, the population might exceed the carrying capacity. This subsistence pattern is reinforced by superstructure religious myths where deities have many husbands and live harmoniously as a model for good family life.

Monogamous marriage, the present form in the West, is changing in our society (Fisher, 2010). Foraging societies were permissive regarding sexuality and had relatively high status for women because they worked outside the home and could forage for themselves. When agriculture was introduced, men became more dominant in subsistence and were seen as the sole breadwinners. Although women were still nurturning children, preparing meals, and maintaining a household, this was not defined or appreciated as "work." Women were relegated to the home, had to be virgins until marriage, could not engage in extra-marital sex like their husbands, and were increasingly stuck with arranged marriages. Separate spheres of male and female activities developed as well.

However, agriculture is dying out as a contemporary subsistence pattern and less that a few percent of Americans live that way. The creation of dual-income households and office jobs where both men and women sit at computers all day are returning us back to foraging lifestyles and to marrying later and having fewer children. Women are regaining more of the economic power they had thousands of years ago and can provide for themselves or live as single mothers raising a family in a matriline. Men may also choose to be nurturers and stay at home dads. Most importantly, marriage is becoming more companionate and peer-based with greater flexibility in roles and division of labor.

FAMILY AND KINSHIP

Various marriage systems create families and other ties of kinship or your relatedness with others. Societies vary greatly in how kin are determined and families come in a wide variety of forms. In a bilateral kinship system with a nuclear family, relatives are recognized on both the mother's and father's side and may consist of same-sex individuals as parents.

A patrilineal family, the most common lineage system, is one where a husband and wife may live together with their children, but both male and female children are considered to be the relatives of only the father's lineage through a common male ancestor. A matrilineal family is the opposite and the children will be closer to mother's brother as a father figure than their own biological father who will play the father role to his sister's children. A matrilineal example is the Navajo where a female head of household is identified with the homestead, land, herds, and gardens and farmland and is sort of the chairperson. The family relates to relatives through her bloodline. The male leader of the household may speak for the family but the head woman is primarily in control. Other family systems exist as well and some households are based on other factors than kinship.

Family groups go on to form larger associations such as clans. A clan is a descent group of families who believe they have a common ancestor, even if that ancestor is unknown or mythical. A clan ancestor may even be a natural force or an animal. For example, for the Coast Salish of Vancouver, the clan ancestor is the orca whale, and members have special spiritual relations and obligations as a result.

136

GLBTQIA AND TRANS POSING

GLBTQIA

GLBTQIA refers to "gay, lesbian, bisexual, queer or questioning, intersex, and asexual or advocate." Other letters may be added in the future, or a new term may emerge. The rather remarkable development of the last 25 years or so in the U.S. is the rapid social change involving openness about homosexuality and other sexual identities, and new federal laws allowing same sex marriage. Prominent celebrities have "come out" and some social scientists argue that gays, lesbians, and transgenders may even be inventing some new quasi-genders based on fashion, mannerism, occupations, slang, etc.

Cisgender refers to individuals whose assigned gender, gender identity, and physical appearance are consistent. Transgender or transsexual individuals are those whose gender identity is at variance with their assigned sex or physical appearance. A medical diagnosis of gender dysphoria is possible and an individual can undergo hormone replacement and other therapies and surgeries to complete the transition.

Openly transgender/transsexual individuals may experience prejudice and discrimination in employment, housing, and other aspects of their lives. Science doesn't fully know what "causes" heterosexuality or homosexuality, or asexuality or any other sexual expression. Some studies have been done on individuals who have already begun hormone treatments, but neuroplasticity, changes in brain structures, may be confounding because the brain is a much more dynamic organ than had been assumed.

On the other hand, some research shows strong biological and genetic factors in sexuality. A 2009 study showied increased fecundity (ability to be fertile) in females who have homosexual individuals in their maternal line. This suggests a possible connection to the X chromosome, e.g., highly fertile females with large number of children would benefit from non-reproducing relatives who served as helpers or culture creators (this would also include heterosexual individuals who choose not to have children, a growing demographic group today).

In addition, social science research has generally shown that gay and lesbian parents are as capable as heterosexual parents and their children are equally psychologically healthy and no more likely to become gay or lesbian themselves. If the evidence is leaning in any direction, it would be that there are biological factors that affect one's internal and external sexual apparatus and secondary sexual characteristics and sexual orientation. Sexual orientation and identity may be a biocultural spectrum upon which some individuals remain consistent throughout their lives, while others move more fluidly within the spectrum or from one end to the other.

Cultures may adapt and choose among many alternatives as to how gender is defined and regulated. But, although there may be degrees of freedom among individuals for the decisions they make in their lifetimes, heterosexuality cannot remain the norm by which all other positions are judged. Likewise, nonheterosexual options cannot be simply dismissed as "choice" as if no biological factors exist. Clearly, we need much more research about the nature of human sexuality and gender and its expressions in a variety of human contexts.

TRANS POSING

What does the future hold? A gender binary system such as the present one in the U.S. is a response to a particular subsistence adaptation and can be challenged by different circumstances. As jobs become more similar and technological there may be less reason for gender distinctions at all. With the addition of other options our society is adding gender neutral bathrooms, using generic pronouns such as "they," and more and more families are seeing members announce a variety of sexual orientations.

One interesting recent phenomenon in the U.S. and Japan is trans-posing (Graham, 2013) which may be the wave of the future. High school and college students, the future generation of the 21st century, are exploring gender and sexuality in new more flexible ways that may become "gender fluid." A biological male students wakes up one morning and wants to wear a dress so he adopts a female nickname and asks for female pronouns or gender neutral pronouns such as "zee," "zim," or "zer." A female wears workclothes and wishes to be called "Tractor," on Monday, but on Wednesday wears makeup and sweater with a heart design and is called "Jennifer."

Stephen Ira (formerly known as Kathlyn Beatty, daughter of actor Warren Beatty) created a video in 2012, "We Happy Trans." His website which promotes a positive perspectives on being transgender went viral. Even those who are cisgender (their biology matches their identity and how they are perceived) may support gender fluidity given the fact that transgender and gay youth are targeted with bullying and violence. But gender is still complicated. Stephen Ira decided at 20 years of age not to complete a transition to male, likes makeup and frilly clothes again, and has a straight male boyfriend. Was she just a confused teen exploring her gender, or is she a partial trans male who back-cross-dresses to female with a nongay nontrans male boyfriend? It can be confusing. However, gender may be becoming a flexible persona not a life-long designation and gender non-conforming may become the rule, rather than the exception. In fact, in 50 to 75 years, which constitutes just two to three generations, dating, marriage and family in the U.S. may be starkly different than it is today as culture adapts to new social conditions.

138

CRITICAL THINKING & WEBSITES

1. Describe how a change in one of the eight stages of sexual development could create an intersex.

2. If dress, hairstyles, occupations, speech, etc., mark a gender, do you think that gays and lesbians, etc. should be considered separate genders in our society today?

3. Choose a marriage you know from among family and friends and compare/contrast it with an agricultural or foraging marriage. Think of who makes the money, the decisions, who sits where, and who has dominance and freedom.

4. Should athletes in the Olympics be able to choose their sex or gender for competition?

5. If female primates make most of the tools, what might this tell us about interpretations of human technological development?

6. Is Stephen Ira feminine, masculine, lesbian, gay, trans, or what? Why is gender so complex? Visit Stephen Ira's website wehappytrans.org and explore gender diversity.

7. Is wearing pheromones (check out pheromones for sale, e.g., love-scent.com) a good idea?

8. See helenfisher.com, and take your dating/marriage personality test at: https://theanatomyoflove.com/helen-fishers-personality-test/personality-test-1/. Take a Myers-Briggs identity test at: http://www.humanmetrics.com/cgi-win/jtypes2.asp. Compare the results.

REFERENCES

Abu-Lughod, Lila. (1986). *Veiled Sentiments: Honor and Poetry in a Bedouin Society*. Oakland, CA: University of California Press.

Altmann, Jeanne. (1980). Baboon Mothers and Infants. Chicago, IL: University of Chicago Press.

Benedict, Ruth. (1934/2006). *Patterns of Culture*. New York: Mariner Books/Harcourt.

Brettell, C., & Sargent, C., eds. Gender in Cross-Cultural Perspective, 3rd ed. Upper Saddle River, NJ: Prentice Hall.

Brown, Lucy, Acevedo, Blanca, & Fisher, Helen. (2013). *Neural correlates of four broad temperament dimensions: Testing predictions for a novel construct of personality*. PLoS ONE 8(11): e78734. doi:10.1371/journal.pone.0078734.

Colapinto, John. (2006). *As Nature Made Him: The Boy Who Was Raised as a Girl*. New York, NY: Harper.

Daily Mail Reporter. (2012). Warren Beatty's transgender son Stephen 'having seconde thoughts about taking final step in sex change.' Retrieved on December 17, 2015 from: http://www.dailymail.co.uk/tvshowbiz/article-2149081/Warren-Beattys-transgender-son-Stephen-having-second-thoughts-taking-final-step-sex-change.html.

De Waal, Frans. (2006). *Our Inner Ape: A Leading Primatologist Explains Why We Are Who We Are*. New York, NY: Riverhead Books/Penguin.

Evans-Pritchard, E. E. (1951/1969). *The Nuer: A Description of the Modes of Livelihood and Political Institutions of a Nilotic People*. Oxford, UK: Oxford University Press.

Fisher, Helen. (2004). *Why We Love—the Nature and Chemistry of Romantic Love*. New York, NY: Henry Holt and Company.

Fisher, Helen. (2010). The new monogamy: Forward to the past: An author and anthropologist looks at the future of love. *The Futurist*, 44, 6, 26-28.

Goodale, Jane. (1994). Tiwi Wives: A Study of the Women of Melville Island, North Australia. Seattle, WA: University of Washington Press.

Graham, Tim. (2013). Trans posing: NPR explores the need to 'loosen the reins of gender expression.' Retrieved on March 1, 2014 from: http://newsbusters.org/blogs/tim-graham/2013/07/17/trans-posing-npr-explores-need-loosen-reins-gender-expression#ixzz2a6AMtGRM.

Hwelett, B. S. (2001). The cultural nexus of Aka father-infant bonding. In C. Brettell & C. Sargent, eds. *Gender in Cross-Cultural Perspective*, 3rd ed, 45-46. Upper Saddle River, NJ: Prentice Hall.

Ira, Stephen. (2012). *We Happy Trans*. Retrieved December 14, 2015 from:
https://www.youtube.com/watch?v=gnZ1pcQIqkQ.

Lancaster, Jane. *Primate Behavior and the Emergence of Human Culture*. New York: Holt Rinehart & Winston.

Lavenda, Robert & Schultz, Emily. (2015). *Anthropology: What Does It Mean To Be Human?* Oxford, UK: Oxford University Press.

Leacock, Elanor. (1983). Interpreting the origins of gender inequality: Conceptual and historical problems. *Dialectical Anthropology* 7, 4, 263-284.

Levine, Nancy. (1980). Nyinba polyandry and the allocation of paternity. *Journal of Comparative Family Studies*, 11, 3, 283-288.

Martin, Emily. (1997). The egg and the sperm: How science has constructed a romance based on stereotypical male-female roles. *Signs: Journal of Women in Culture and Society*, 16, 485-501.

Martin, M. Kay, & Moorhies, Barbara. (1975). *Female of the Species*. New York, NY: Columbia University Press.

Mead, Margaret. (1928/2001). *Coming of Age in Samoa: A Psychological Study of Primitive Youth for Western Civilisation*. New York, NY: William Morrow/Harper Collins.

Mead, Margaret. (1935/2001). *Sex and Temperament: In Three Primitive Societies*. New York, NY: Harper Perennial.

Nanda, Serena. (1998). *Neither Man Nor Woman: The Hijras of India*. Independence, MO: Wadsworth/Cengage.

No author. (2009). Wow, look at Caster Now! *You*, 144, September 10, 2009. (South Africa). Retrieved December 14, 2015 from: http://www.dailymail.co.uk/news/article-1212036/Sex-test-runners-makeover--Caster-Semenya-shows-shes-woman-YOU-magazine-photo-shoot-gender-row-Berlin-championships.html.

Rosaldo, Michelle, & Lamphere, Louise. (1974). *Women, Culture, and Society*. Stanford, CA: Stanford University Press.

Slocum, Sally. (1975). Woman the gatherer: Male bias in Anthropology. In Rayna R. Reiter, ed. *Toward an Anthropology of Women*. New York, NY: Monthly Review Press.

Small, Meredith. (1992). What's love got to do with it: Sex among our closest relatives is a rather open affair. *Discover*, June 1992.

Spaulding, Pamela. (2009). Runner Caster Semenya takes gender test—she is intersexed; MSM reporting is offensive. Retrieved on September 15, 2009 from: https://shadowproof.com/2009/09/10/runner-caster-semenya-takes-gender-test-she-is-intersexed-msm-reporting-is-offensive/

Tannen, Deborah. (2007). *You Just Don't Understand*. New York: NY: William Morrow.

Tylor, Edward Burnett. (1871/2010). *Primitive Culture: Researches Into the Development of Mythology, Philosophy, Religion, Language, Art, and Custom*. Charleston, SC: Nabu Press.

Tanner, Nancy. (1981). *On Becoming Human*. New York, NY: Cambridge University Press.

1. Why do anthropologists argue that gender is culturally constructed?

2. Describe one example of gender diversity in different cultures today?

3. Take the Helen Fisher dating personality test and Myers-Briggs adapted identity test listed under Critical Thinking and Websites. Compare the results and give your own reaction.

10 COMMUNICATION:
Language and Culture

Tiny wedge marks made with a stick on a clay tablet—shared meanings allow humans to keep track of accounts, record victories, send messages, and tell stories. The externalization of knowledge so others distant in time and space can see our thoughts changed the world.

LEARNING OBJECTIVES

1. Describe the three stages of the evolution of human communication.

2. Explain the sources for understanding the origins of human language.

3. Explain why the externalization of knowledge is so important to our species development.

4. Describe the design features of language and how it is structured into phonemes, morphemes, syntax and grammar.

5. Show how society affects culture and culture affects society.

6. Know the types of stories humans tell and why storytelling is so useful for humans.

COMMUNICATION

Two men negotiating a price at a camel sale or getting ready for a caravan? What they have to say to each other is conveyed in their body positions, posture, angle of orientation, eye gaze, head position, gestures, facial expressions, and finally words, grammar, and tone of voice. Communication is a way that organisms connect, transmit information, and affect each other's behavior through meanings. Communication can occur through a number of modalities: visual, auditory, touch, smell—any of the senses that organisms possess. Even bacteria communicate with each other through chemical and behavioral messages. Further, it is hard to imagine how an intelligent species could develop culture, commerce, and technology without using communication based on language and other symbolic systems such as writing and mathematics.

Most anthropologists take a continuity approach to language origins, focusing on its evolution from earlier pre-linguistic apelike forms of cognition and communication. Human ancestors probably started with a basic call system of vocalizations and gestures inherited from our common ancestor. As cultural complexity grew, humans added a second layer consisting of symbols where something stood for something else. These systems were open, so they encouraged new meanings and innovation.

In the third stage, we externalized communication through written symbols so we could communicate with permanent messages across the generations. Our ancestors wrote on cave walls, clay tablets, stones, paper, and now we also communicate digitally. What a powerful tool it proved to be! Today we utilize all three stages in our daily lives and technological activities. And like many human characteristics, language and communication are biocultural phenomena.

LANGUAGE ORIGINS

GREAT APE COMMUNICATION

Anthropologists have several sources for trying to reconstruct the origins and development of language. Great ape natural communication systems are studied such as the begging gesture (left) which can convey a demand, a pleading request, or even humor. Apes have 20-30 vocalizations, which expresses emotional states or has referential meanings, e.g., "snake," or "danger. Several monkey species and other intelligent animals such as elephants and dolphins show this also. Great apes even laugh when they are tickled.

Ape gestures are richer and more flexible than their vocalizations, and can carry subtle variations of meaning. Apes use a range of facial expressions to show emotional meanings, e.g., a pout or threat face. They have a variety of body postures with meanings such as turning your back or kissing your hand. We also see dialects in ape gesturing. For example, chimps hold a branch over their heads to attract females in one forest, and underhanded with shaking in another.

This suggests that the first languages might have been open and flexible gestural systems like a sign language. As we split off from the common ancestor we probably retained the basic ape "gesture + call system" but enhanced the complexity, openness, and flexibility of the signals and their meanings. We have also taught language to all four of the great apes to see what features they can acquire and whether it is homologous, i.e., emerges at the same stages as language in human children.

LANGUAGE ACQUISITION

The cognitive and linguistic stages children go through as they learn a language may parallel the development of language in prehistory. Scientists disagree on the level of innateness of language, but certain patterns are clear. As a child learns the sounds or signs of their language and how to organize them, comprehension precedes production. Children's errors show that they unconsciously discern the complex structural rules of their language, e.g., with irregular verbs such as 'to give' they will say "gived" instead of "gave" for past tense.

Andrew Locke referred to the guided reinvention of language whereby family and child together reinvent symbolic communication and coin unique family terms. They develop ways to anticipate and interpret each other's behavior and invent conventions. Using a socio-cognitive model, Lev Vygotsky and Jerome Bruner showed that much of a child's language development stems from modeling interaction with parents and other adults. Dean Falk (2009) argued that 'motherese'—the modified language that adults use with babies—could be a model for human proto-language. Thus, culture may have been a driving force creating "self-domesticated apes" meaning that hominins began with apelike brains but enculturation, itself, transformed our species.

The creativity by which families and communities reinvent meanings is illustrated by an analysis of the many terms for flatulence, which is excessive gas from digesting food that passes through the anus with which all cultures are familiar. Table 10.1 lists many colorful terms and phrases that have been developed in English for what is commonly called "farts," compiled by Ben Applebaum and Dan DiSorbo (2013):

Table 10.1 Some English Slang Terms to Refer to Flatulence.

Air biscuit	Air tulip	Anal audio	Anal exhale
Anal salute	Answering burrito	Anus applause	Ass acoustics
Barn burner	Blurt	Break wind	Bust ass
Backend blowout	Back blast	Baking brownies	Barking spider
Beep your horn	Belching clown	Benchwarmer	Blast
Bomber	Boom boom	Booty bomb	Bottom burp
Brown cloud	Brown thunder	Bubbler	Bull snort
Butt bazooka	But bongos	Butt tuba	Cheek squeak
Cheeser	Crack concert	Crap call	Cut one
Colon bowlin'	Duck Call	Free speech	Floater
Fanny beep	Fire in the hole	Flatus	Fart
Go walk Donald	Gas	Honker	Heinie hiccup
Hot wind	Lay an egg	Nasty cough	One male salute
Panty burp	Poof	Putt putt	Rear roar
Rump ripper	Slider	Sphincter siren	Squeaker
Stinker	Stinky	Step on a duck	Tear ass
Toot	Tootsie	Trunk bunk	Tushy tickler
Wallop	Whiff	Taint tickle	Thunder

BRAIN CHANGES

A third source of information is an analysis of the differences in ape and human brain anatomy. Ape brains are one-third human size and they lack development in two areas, Broca's area and Wernike's area, that are linked to language and process words and sentences. Scientists recently found a brain-related language gene, Foxp2 which apes also lack.

In addition, a gene mutation arose about a half millions years ago that makes some actions automatic and routine without having to think about it. The gene was discovered by studying a human family with a mutated version of the gene who had language and speech difficulties. When the gene was implanted in mice, the mice became more intelligent! Mirror neurons are another recent discovery which allow sounds and behaviors to be immediately copied and associated which facilitated the connection among sounds/gestures and meanings.

NONVERBAL COMMUNICATION

An estimated 50-60% of human communication is nonverbal. This includes a glance, touch, gesture, facial expression, body posture, or dress and manner. For example, in the 2016 presidential campaign debates, Donald Trump used a pout face also seen in chimpanzees to scoff at his opponents, Carly Fiorina glared at Trump for a remark about her attractiveness not mentioned about male candidates, and Hillary Clinton smiled with a confident body posture to show leadership even though Bernie Sanders was drawing larger crowds at the time. These gestural communications received more coverage than the political content each candidate made. Thus, emotion, body postures and facial expressions can still triumph over reason. This "chimp band" type of social communication is very powerful and deeply affects human relations.

ARTIFACTS

The material remains of our ancestors is a fourth possible source for reconstructing language origins. The complexity and mental processes required for a stone tool would suggest how their thinking was structured. The first stone tools of *A. sediba* and *Homo habilis*, reveals a simple procedure of a few blows and perhaps some planning with the transport of some materials as apes do today. The mimetic culture of *Homo erectus* added learning by observation and possibly teaching and enculturation. With *Homo sapiens*, a two-step structure emerged where an intermediate step was created that did not look like the final product. This requires mental representations to envision the blade tool locked inside the stone. The intermediate step was a representation of what was to come—the final product.

Fossils

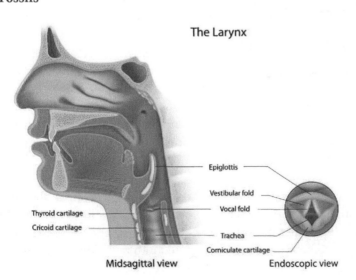

The Larynx

Epiglottis

Vestibular fold

Vocal fold

Thyroid cartilage

Cricoid cartilage

Trachea

Corniculate cartilage

Midsagittal view

Endoscopic view

A fifth source for understanding language origins are the fossils of human ancestors and whether their vocal tract shape and skull braincase are more apelike or humanlike. The vocal tract includes the tongue, nasal passages, and upper and lower parts of the mouth. The larynx is consists of the vocal cords that vibrate as air is pushed out from the lungs. The pharynx is above the larynx which moves about during speech to help form the vowels. Consonants are made by constricting the airflow in various ways such as bringing the lips together to make an "mmm" sound.

Apes have a longer palate and tongue, their larynx is higher in the throat, and they lack the human moveable pharynx. As the early bipeds evolved into the genus *Homo*, our face became flatter, and the back of our tongue moved lower in the throat to become the pharynx, and the larynx also dropped lower. This allowed us to voice a vowel triangle of /a/, /e/, and /u/, the three extreme points of the pharynx. It gave us a wider range of sounds to express speech.

Fossils show that the apparatus began to change around 2 MYA, continued to change through *Homo erectus*, and by around half a million years it was taking closer to modern form. *Homo erectus* fossils also show that their skulls had larger hypoglossal canal openings for nerves and blood flow to the tongue which also suggests developments for articulation of speech. So we conclude that early bipeds probably were similar to great apes in the sounds and gestures they made, but by *Homo habilis* and *erecuts* brain and anatomical changes led to more complex communication. Many processes became automatic and grammar was structured to go from gestures, sounds, and words to sentences.

Robin Dunbar (1999) suggested that most physical grooming, the social glue of the apes, was replaced by vocal grooming—conversation and gossip. We even describe smooth flattery as "stroking" each other. The earliest human languages were also probably gestural. Sign languages used by the hearing impaired and deaf community have all the elements and complexity of speech—just with the hands instead. Clearly language origins is not likely just one thing but a combination of cognitive and communicative abilities based on symbolic culture.

LANGUAGE FAMILIES

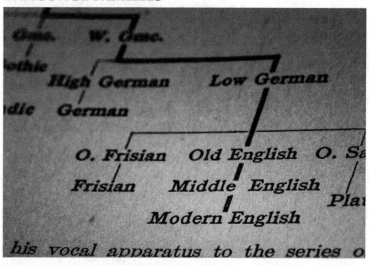

Once in place, a common ancestor language or languages gave rise to a number of descendants just as a common biological ancestor divided into many different species. Using comparative linguistics, scholars pointed to the cognate words of English and German languages, French and Spanish, and Finnish and Hungarian to show they both came from an earlier languages.

All the Celtic, Germanic, Slavic, Romance, and Indo-Iranian language families are in turn branches of a larger Indo-European super family of languages. In fact, there are about 14 major language families today—most all being sibling languages going back to a common ancestor. A few fascinating languages such as Basque, spoken in the Pyrenees Mountains between France and Spain, are linguistic isolates because no other living languages resemble Basque. Their sibling languages apparently died out.

Languages change over time and historical linguistics investigates relationships between earlier and later forms of the same language. We can use markers as ways to determine how long two languages might have diverged from one another and separated, for example, Spanish and Italian. Languages also borrow words from each other and this can be a clue as to how populations migrated into new areas. Technology also becomes a means to create new words, e.g., computer, internet, flash drive, etc.

A major cause of language change is the domination of one society over another, which in the last 500 years has unfortunately led to the disappearance of more than half of the world's 12,000 languages. Also lost is the rich culture and meanings of these languages. English now dominates and other cultures struggle to preserve their own language and traditions. Many of the world's languages have become extinct because of warfare, epidemics, and forced assimilation brought on by colonialism, although revitalization of Cherokee, Ute, and other languages is underway.

EXTERNALIZATION OF KNOWLEDGE

By about 5,000 years ago, our ancestors began to make notations, count with markings, and ultimately develop signs and script symbols for narratives. There are systematic cuttings on a Bilzingsleben bone from Germany dated 350,000, but, it is not until the last 100,000 years, in the Upper Paleolithic that we begin to see more explicit externalization of knowledge. For example, the Blanshard bone depicts possible inscriptions of phases of the moon showing counting or tracking and Levallois tools show representational culture.

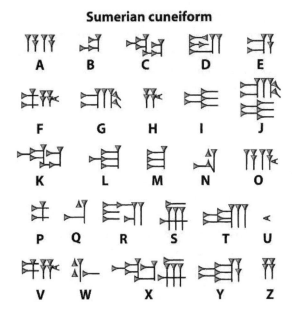

Sumerian cuneiform

PROTO-WRITING

The first writing system were found in the Neolithic period in China around 8,600 years ago. Symbols were carved into tortoise shells (above) from 24 Neolithic graves at Jiahu, Henan province in northern China, as ideographic writing, although we do not yet know their meaning. One symbol might mean a person, another the sun, etc. Chinese is probably an independent invention because it is so different from Mesopotamian representations. Later Chinese inscriptions developed vertical columns of symbols that seem more like text.

By the Bronze Age, starting about 5,000 years ago a number of cultures developed writing: cuneiform (above) in Sumer in Mesopotamia, hieroglyphs in Egypt, logographs in China, and a unique script in Mesoamerica by the Olmec. Cuneiform consists of wedges made with a reed stick. It began as pictographs and by a thousand years later it became more abstract with fewer symbols. Ultimately, it added alphabet letters and syllables, but was gradually replaced by the Phoenician alphabet, the basis of our alphabet today. Wedge indentations were also put on clay balls and tablets.

In Egypt, people developed hieroglyphics around 6,000 years ago which, like cuneiform, consisted of pictures that first stood for words and then became an alphabet. Luckily, a stone stele was found to help with translating the hieroglyphs. The Rosetta Stone, dated around 200 BCE had three languages incised on it: Egyptian hieroglyphs, Demotic script, and ancient Greek, that all said the same thing. Gradually, over many decades scholars were able to understand hieroglyphics.

The advantages of writing are clear—it allowed human minds and cultures to connect across the decades, it preserved cultural history, and it gave the current generation a foundation from the past. Things could be officially written down, and trade and business records could be kept for years. It gave an enormous advantage to our species and it fostered both culture preservation and adaptive change.

LANGUAGE STRUCTURE

There are about 3,000 languages still being used today. Language is an organized structured system using symbols organized by a set of rules to communicate experience. It has a number of design features including:

1. **Semanticity** - symbols have meanings associated with them, such as "hot" or "cold"
2. **Openness** – flexibility so that new meanings can be created
3. **Displacement** – allows you to talk about the past, future, or things not present
4. **Arbitrariness** - symbols don't resemble meanings, e.g., "cat" could mean dog in another language
5. **Duality of patterning** – language has a two-level organizing system of sound/gesture units and a way to organize them through grammatical rules and sentence structure

Meaningful sounds in a language are called phonemes. For example, /p/ in "pat" versus /c/ in "cat." The different sounds change the meanings of the words. These sounds are organized into morphemes, which change the meanings of words. /Go/ is a free morpheme—it can't be broken down into smaller meanings. When you add /-ne/ ending to make "gone" you change the meaning so this is called a bound morpheme because the past tense marker cannot stand alone.

English relies heavily on word order or syntax—other languages accomplish the same task by adding morpheme endings or beginnings onto words to show the part of speech (agent, action) they might be. Grammar can be quite complex—much more so than in English. All the complexity of speech and rules of grammar also apply to sign languages which are fully developed languages, not just simple hand movements.

The Navajo Code Talkers of World War II used complexity to their advantage. Navajo grammar is very complicated. For example, there are 270,000 ways to say "to go." Navajo also requires information about where you are going, what direction, in what manner, with what intention, etc. Analysts agree that Navajos who served in the military as special communication units saved the day because their Navajo language was never decoded.

Most importantly, anthropologists learned that foraging or pastoral societies with less technology did NOT have less complex languages—in fact, the opposite was the case. Languages of simpler societies may have fewer technological words, but may have 200 words for leaves expressing subtle differences in species, color, texture, scent, or size. In short, there are NO primitive languages.

CULTURE AND SOCIETY

LANGUAGE AND CULTURE

Cultures also vary in how individuals use personal space. Edward T. Hall (1959) observed that there are four zones in the U.S.: an intimate zone (6 in.) reserved for only close friends and family members; a personal zone (1-4 ft.) for daily interactions; a stranger zone (4-12 ft.) for acquaintances; and a public zone (12-25 ft.) for speeches and very large groups. People feel uncomfortable when the rules learned by observation are violated. Hall then compared U.S. space zones with those from other cultures. He showed that Americans doing business in South America would do an odd dance down the hall. South American businessmen would try to get closer in the intimate and personal zones, while the Americans would discretely back away inch by inch. It was a dance of intercultural misunderstanding.

Anthropologists investigate the relationship between language and culture—both how language shapes peoples' thinking and how society itself shapes the worldview of the language. The Sapir-Whorf hypothesis explores how the terms we use for things affects our thinking. This was discovered at an insurance company in Hartford, Connecticut where there were a high number of claims because the way flammable materials were labeled "inflammable." People thought it meant things couldn't burn, so they threw lit cigarettes into the container!

Some cross-cultural evidence supports the Sapir-Whorf hypothesis. In English, causality is important and you might say, "Jacob broke the vase." However, Japanese does not emphasize causality (although it can express it) and the sentence would be more like: "The vase broke itself." As a result, English speakers are better at analyzing the agents of accidental events because the issue of causality is more emphasized. The Piraha of Africa count, one, two, many, and thus are worse at keeping track of exact quantities, because that is not important to them. English speakers are worse at distinguishing shades of blue than Russians because their language has many more words for shades of blue.

Interestingly, English speakers use terms like left and right, and visualize the past to the left, present in the middle, and future to the right. Like many other cultures, Pormpuraaw does not use left vs. right, but puts everything in terms of cardinal directions: north, south, east, and west. So when researchers asked people to sort time sequences such as pictures of males at various life stages they placed them in absolute cardinal directions. Regardless of what direction they were facing the baby picture was always at the eastern horizon. In Aymara indian culture of South America, the future is always behind your body and the past is in front, and in China, the future is below and the past is above (Chinese writing is vertical).

LANGUAGE AND SOCIETY

Sociolinguistics examines how social categories such as age, gender, ethnicity, religion, occupation, social class, race, region, etc., influence styles of communication and speech. There are regional dialect variations within the U.S. that include accents but also conversation styles. Northerners playfully bantering and challenge in loud voices while Southerners with a different history are more subdued and indirect saying, "well, bless his heart."

These social meanings change over time. The taboo slang word "fuck," had no sexual meaning originally. Its meaning today was originally conveyed with the word "occupy" which has no direct sexual meaning now.

Another social aspect of language is the context and addressee of your communications. Code switching refers to how you learn to talk one way with your grandparents and another to your closest friends. When a language comes into contact with another, often in a colonial situation, a pidgin language is created which is a mix between the two. An example is the African words "okay" "guy", "banjo" and bozo" which were introduced to English through slavery. When a pidgin language becomes established and you learn it as your main language, it becomes a creole.

AAVE

Anthropologists debate whether African-American Vernacular English (AAVE), also called Black English, is a dialect of American English or an actual creole, but it certainly illustrates the interface between society and language. It is found in urban working class areas and popularized in films, rap, and hip hop music. When it was formalized by the Oakland School Board and used in classes to teach inner city youth it was

called Ebonics. There is a misperception that AAVE is sloppy slang "street talk" that is inferior in some way. Some consider it to have a lower status socially, and many African-American parents do not want their children to use it for fear they will not do well in school, get good jobs, or be treated fairly by police. However, from a linguistic perspective it has NO inferiority because it has all the elements of a true language form including many grammatical rules. For example, AAVE has a distinctive vocabulary, verb tenses, aspect, and use of double-negatives such as "I didn't go nowhere." Its grammar resembles British dialects more than American ones which is probably due to both the slave trade as well as working side by side with British indentured servants. It systematically drops off /b/, /d/, and /g/ on word endings, diphthongs like "boil" are changed to "ball," /g/ is dropped in multiple-syllable words, and final consonant clusters have reduced voicing, e.g., "tes" for "test." It has different verb tenses, e.g., "he be goin," "he been done goin'" and "he be a-goin" where be or been indicates habitual action. In the past tense, be is often dropped, just as it is in Russian, Hebrew, or Arabic. If this were just bad English the differences would be random, but instead AAVE is as rule-governed as English—it just has different rules.

An interesting African-American discourse form is called 'signifying." One way to gain power in a system of oppression is to use language in a contrary way. This takes place in verbal duels called "playing the dozens" in which ritual insults about "yo'mamma" are exchanged in contests of verbal skill. These traditions are then morphed into rap duels and rivalries where verbal intelligence and creativity is highly prized by the community.

STORYTELLING

For hundreds of thousands of years, our ancestors conveyed information about their culture and themselves through storytelling and myth. Stories are narrative spoken or written reports of real or imagined events. A myth is a story strongly based on symbols that conveys an important worldview usually involving deities or explaining the origin of the world. An example would be a society's creation myth of the first person, or deities coming from the sky or up from the ground or sea to create humans and the earth.

Storytelling can take other forms as well. Folklore reflects the ideas and values of a community through a speech, song, chant, or narrative. Elements can be changed over time with different versions that reflect the adaptations of the culture. Forms include folk art, folk songs, ballads, joking tales, proverbs, and sayings. For example, the Dogon of Africa use many stories in the work songs they sing and clap to as they complete their tasks. Another example is quilting, where rural communities in the central Southeast U.S., and also Hawaii and Asia, sew together patterns of fabric in layers to make images. These images may celebrate an event such as a wedding or birth of a child, or represent symbols important to the people. Tattoos have a long history and each generation chooses images important to them: anchors and the word "mother" in a heart for 1940s sailors off to war, black roses and peace symbols for the 1960s, and Asian words and

Walking Dead symbols for the 2000s. Some families choose emblems of their life passages, or all the females in the family tattoo a seahorse on their torso to symbolize their solidarity.

Folktales are stories that are part of an oral tradition passed down through the generations that are expanded and reshaped. Folktales often teach character. The Hungry Little Boy tale from Ghana promotes respect for the elderly and the Banyan Deer tale from Asia shows the importance of concern for others. A legend is a folktale that describes human actions in history and is a combination of both believable and magical events often with an element of awe or uncertainty.

Legends are stories of embellishments about real people and are usually told as if in a conversation or sitting around a campfire. They reflect in some way the collective experiences of the group or they convey commonly held values and traditions. Examples include the legend of Atlantis, Robin Hood who stole from the rich and gave to the poor; King Arthur and the Knights of the Round Table; Shangri-La, an earthly paradise in the Himalayan mountains; and Shango, the god of thunder celebrated as the founder of the Yoruba people of West Africa and the Caribbean. Animal tales are particularly common. A subgroup of folktales is a fable in which anthropomorphic animals who act like people illustrate a moral.

The trickster figure is simultaneously both a helper and nemesis to humans. The trickster shows extensive secret knowledge which allows them to reverse the conventional roles or play tricks on humans. By crossing boundaries, they break society's rules and disrupt life, usually to reorganize it in a new way. The trickster uses craft and cunning, openly mocks authority, and questions the status quo. In Native American culture the trickster is often a coyote or raven. In Africa, the trickster is a rabbit or spider. Native American trickster figures are interesting because they present a different worldview than that of Euro-Americans. Tricksters in European traditions were usually roguish low-status individuals who live by wits in a controlled and corrupt society or jokers in the royal court who said what everybody was thinking but humor masked the reveal. It's about morality and correct social order.

Instead, Native Americans see coyote or raven as an essential and integrated aspect of the spiritual world. Danger, upset, and surprise are all a part of the sacred universe and tricksters are necessary to remind others of that fact. Tricksters are essential to creation itself. For example, among the Salish of the Pacific Northwest, raven is creator of the world as well as trickster. Raven stole fire from the stars, moon and sun — and since fire is essential to human life the raven mediates the balance of life and death. The story is that the Great Spirit made all things in the world in cedar boxes and gifted them to the animal beings who came before humans.

The animals opened various boxes containing mountains, water, seeds, etc. But, Seagull hoarded the box containing light. Raven tried to persuade Seagull to release the light for the world to no avail. Raven then stuck Seagull with a thorn to his foot, the box was dropped, and out came the sun, moon and stars. This allowed the first day to begin. So Raven, even in contrary action, is necessary to the creation process itself. Tales like these are rich and dramatic and served to convey important cultural values and meanings across the generations. Our religious, ceremonial, secret, and family stories continue today to play a strong role in our lives.

CRITICAL THINKING & WEBSITES

1. Should some college courses be taught in AAVE?

2. How has Google Books and other online services affected externalization of knowledge?

3. Describe the three stages of human communication.

4. What is the advantage of writing?

5. Explain one way culture and society affect language or vice versa.

6. Find examples of dialects and linguistics at the National Science Foundation website: http://www.nsf.gov/news/special_reports/linguistics/dialects.jsp.

7. Check out urban legends and folklore at: snopes.com.

REFERENCES

Applebaum, Ben, & DiSorbo, Dan. (2013). The Fart Tootorial: Farting Fundamentals, Master Blaster Techniques, and the Complete Toot Taxonomy. San Francisco, CA: Chronicle Books.

Armstrong, David, Stokoe, William, Wilcox, Sherman. (1995). *Gesture and the Nature of Language*. Cambridge: Cambridge University Press.

Bassler, Bonnie. (2011). *How bacteria talk to each other*. Retrieved December 1, 2015 from: http://online.kitp.ucsb.edu/plecture/bbassler11/.

Boroditsky, Lera. (2010). Lost in translation. *The Wall Street Journal*, July 23, 2010. Retrieved December 1, 2015 from: http://www.wsj.com/articles/SB10001424052748703467304575383131592767868.

Brooks-Pollock, Tom. (2014). *The 66 Gestures Which Show How Chimpanzees Communicate*. Retrieved December 1, 2016 from: http://www.telegraph.co.uk/news/science/10945811/The-66-gestures-which-show-how-chimpanzees-communicate.html.

Bruner, Jerome. (1983). *Child's Talk: Learning to Use Language*. New York, NY: W. W. Norton & Company.

Corballis, Michael. (2002). *From Hand To Mouth: The Origins of Language*. Princeton, NY: Princeton University.

Dehaene, Stanislas & Brannon, Elizabeth. (2011*). Space, Time and Number in the Brain: Searching for the Foundations of Mathematical Thought*. London: Academic Press.

Dunbar, Robin. (1999). *The evolution of Culture: An Interdisciplinary View*. Edinburgh: Edinburgh University Press.

Falk, Dean. (2009). Evolution of Language. In M. Ruse & J. Travis (eds.). *Evolution: The First Four Billion Years*. Cambridge, MA: Cambridge University Press.

Goodenough, Ursula. (2010). *Did we start out as self-domesticated apes?* Retrieved on December 1, 2016 from: http://www.npr.org/sections/13.7/2010/02/did_we_start_out_as_selfdomest.html.

Hall, Edward T. (1959). *The Silent Language*. New York, NY: Anchor Books/Random House.

Hobaiter, C., & Byrne, R. W. (2014). The meanings of chimpanzee gestures. *Current Biology*, 24, 1596-1600.

Kolb, Joseph. (2014). *Last of Navajo 'code talkers' dies in New Mexico*. Reuters. Retrieved on December 1, 2015 from: http://www.reuters.com/article/us-usa-newmexico-navajo-idUSKBN0EF1Z920140605.

Labov, William. (1969). *Language in the Inner City: Studies in Black English Vernacular*. Philadelphia, PA: University of Pennsylvania Press.

Lieberman, Philip. (2006). *Toward an Evolutionary Biology of Language*. Cambridge, MA: Cambridge University.

Ottenheimer, H. J. (2009). *The Anthropology of Language*. Belmont, CA: Wadsworth/Cengage Learning.

Rizzolatti, Giacomo, Fabbri-Destro, Maddalena, & Cattanco, Luigi. (2009). Mirror neurons and their clinical relevance. *Nature Clinical Practice Neurology*, 5, 24-34.

Schreiweis, C., U. Bornschein, E. Burguiere, C. Kerimoglu, S. Schreiter, M. Dannemann, S. Goyal, et al. (2014). Humanized Foxp2 Accelerates Learning by Enhancing Transitions from Declarative to Procedural Performance. *Proceedings of the National Academy of Sciences* 111, 39 (September 15, 2014), 14253–14258.

1. Take the language dialect test at the website listed under Critical Thinking and Websites. How well did it locate your dialect? What is your reaction and critical thinking?

Chapter 11
Spirituality:
Myth and Meaning

There is a special part of the human brain that links our emotions with meaning and the sense that there is something bigger than us. It might be values, ideas, social causes, or the supernatural. We call this phenomenon spirituality and it plays a major role in human life.

LEARNING OBJECTIVES

1. Understand the nature of spirituality and the many forms it takes in human cultures.

2. Know the functions of religion and some examples from other cultures.

3. Review the origin of religion and its development in different subsistence patterns.

4. Explain how religion is closely involved with social control in both positive and negative ways.

5. Explain the basics of the hero myth and how the ancients used the solstice to define spirit beings.

6. Describe the foraging megalithic site Göbekli Tepe and why it is so significant.

SPIRITUALITY

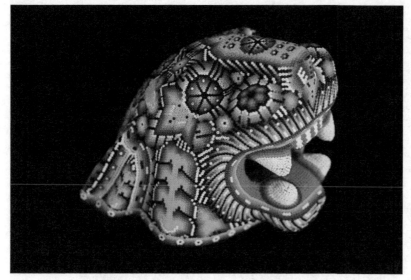

What causes good things and bad things to happen? Ghosts, ancestors, extra-terrestrials, divine beings, and things that go bump in the night? The way that tiger looked before the attack, the old woman at the edge of the village who caused your child to die, and all the bad luck you had recently—they must all be due to evil forces.

The good things that happen to you? It's because you are favored by the gods, are among the chosen people, did the magic perfectly, or are "saved." What is your reward for all this uncertainty and confusion? You will be with the community of believers eternally in the afterlife, sitting on a cloud, not coming back as a bird but as an enlightened one, or enjoying heaven with 21 virgins. How do we deal with good and bad events in our lives and the unknown? Through externalized blame, scapegoating, tit for tat magic, altered states, rites, rituals, and prayer offerings—all the many thoughts, emotions, and behaviors of humanity humans answers that can test the edge of reason and everyday logic.

HUICHOL OF MEXICO

For example, the Huichol people of the Sierra Madre Mountains of Mexico see all of existence as part of a hidden web of spiritual connections which they can access through altered states. They have a communion sacrament of peyote "our elder brother deer" and engage in a ritual "our grandfather fire" where they become hawks and eagles for healing and religious enlightenment. They make stunningly beautiful beaded masks that depict what they see.

TAIKO DRUMMING

On the other side of the world in Japan, a unification of mind, body and nature is sought through drumming. Taiko has deep roots in Korea, China, and India, going back to at least the 6th century. In fact, drumming may be one of the first forms of musical expression—even chimpanzees drum during their rain dance.

160

In ritual Taiko drumming, players are musicians, athletes, and martial artists becoming one with the drum. They train for years and play for communication, military action, theatrical accompaniment, and religious ceremony at festivals. Taiko drummers usually perform as an ensemble with each individual playing on different drums to exhibit their versatility and unity.

One mythological story about the origins of Taiko involves the goddess of sunlight and her brother the god of the sea and storms. The god became angry and created a storm which threatened the land. The goddess fled into a cave and sealed it with a boulder, refusing to come out until another spirit being stomped on a barrel with percussive rhythms and brought the sunlight goddess back into the light.

LADY GAGA PHENOMENON

Surprisingly, spirituality may include popular culture with entertainers and artists who have cult-like followings. Contemporary musician Lady Gaga (real name, Stephanie Germanotta) is one of the best-selling musicians of all time with millions of global fans. She incorporates intense religious and spiritual symbolism in her performances in concerts and videos, with beliefs, rituals, secret symbols, and even scripture.

For example, her music video "Applause" contains both Judeo-Christian and world religious symbolism. She calls her deeply committed followers, "Little Monsters" symbolized with a monster claw arm gesture which Gaga displays. Gaga shows her solidarity by tattooing the initials "LM" on her arm and validates them with songs of individuality, self-empowerment, and being "born this way." She presents a commandment-like "Manifesto" which is recited like a prayer or anthem at concerts.

She even provides a scripture, "Gagapedia," and uses a religious call and response vocal routine for audience participation. She undergoes almost supernatural transformation from female to male, angel, goddess ascending to heaven, much like Kali or Shiva in Hinduism. Finally, she engages in symbolic communion with her audience by calling one of them on a cell phone from the stage, so they literally make contact with the goddess. On a deeper level it uses all the types of cultural memes of religious experience.

RELIGION

Spirituality is a broad sense of feeling connected to something larger than yourself and of finding meaning or sense of how to live based on personal subjective experience. It may involve goals for personal growth, blissful experience, or just moments of transcendence. More and more people in our society are describing themselves as "spiritual but not religious" and emphasizing humanistic ideas about love, moral character, compassion and forgiveness.

Religion is the encoding of that broad spirituality in an organized collection of rules, rituals, or practices to achieve goals. Religion also has a strong sense of right and wrong, definite ideas about the number and personalities of divinities, and precise ways in which members should behave. For example, the five Pillars of Islam provide a framework for worship: 1) creed; 2) daily prayers; 3) charity; 4) fasting; and 5) pilgrimage. Buddhism has the Eightfold Path with the right: 1) view; 2) intention; 3) speech; 4) action; 5) livelihood; 6) effort; 7) mindfulness; and 8) concentration. Other Abrahamic religions also have the Ten Commandments.

Religious practioners may be part-time spiritual specialists called shaman, or a full-time hierarchy of priestly figures who may be abbots, priests, ministers, mullahs, imans, rabbis, etc. Some religions are quite rigid, but most change over time such as Catholicism condemning Galileo and then asking for forgiveness centuries later. A few have exploration as a main commponent. For example, the Tibetan Dalai Lama stated that Buddhist beliefs should be abandoned if science showed some of the claims to be incorrect.

Religion is classified in the superstructure of culture along with language, worldview, and the arts, and it is based on belief. Three challenges immediately appear. First, religious beliefs are deeply felt. Anthropology does not judge whose beliefs are true. But scholars do examine religious beliefs and practices from an "etic" or outsider's viewpoint to understand all the variety of religious experience of all types of societies, not judging the "truth" of any particular religion. Second, studying religion requires us to step outside of our own ethnocentric "emic" perspective and personal experiences and examine other worldviews. Third, more objective ethnohistorical analysis of religious traditions often reveals facts that religions do not necessarily disclose or emphasize themselves in order to secure and retain advocates and may struggle to explain certain evidence.

FUNCTIONS OF RELIGION

Religion functions in a number of ways within a society. Religion is a major anchor for people facing adversity, e.g., slavery in the U.S. African-American churches fought segregation, preserved African traditions, and provided a message of deliverance to counter the oppression. Martin Luther King, the pastor of Ebenezer Baptist Church in Atlanta, Georgia, led a civil rights movement that changed the entire structure of American society. Anthropologists have identified at least ten functions of religion:

1. Order and Worldview. Religion provides a framework for understanding cultural identity and the structure and meaning of the world and existence. Many religions have beliefs in other spirit realms as well. Overall, religion provides a set of beliefs about the "why" of the universe.

2. Anxiety and Fear. By providing a set and often comforting way of looking at the world often with promises of salvation, heavenly rewards, or other benefits, religions reduce anxiety in their members. Prayer is a means to express desires and hope for rewards and rituals give members something they can do to try to control events.

3. Religious Experience and Altered States. Religion can provide a framework for seeking and interpreting altered states. For example, in the Thailand, the devotees of a deity show their courage and faithfulness by enduring multiple thick swordblades penetrating their cheeks and processing in honor of the deity during festivals. The Sufi Mevlevi Order dervishes twirl continuously in remembrance of God in a Sama ceremony. The story is their founder heard craftspersons beating gold in the marketplace and heard it as "there is no god but Allah" and he began to twirl in time to the rhythm to express God.

4. Meaning and Mortality: All cultures grapple with the meaning of life and death. Religious perspectives help people to see some purpose to suffering or inequality or some reward for good deeds, or the inevitability of death.

5. Healing: Religion also provides a number of prayers and rituals to address illness or to seek special favors. People offer prayers for someone dealing with cancer, a basketball player blesses himself before shooting the ball, or a hunter uses a magic spear that will find its target. People say prayers or engage in rituals for all sorts of occasions, even a broken down car.

6. Social Solidarity and Identity. Religion provides norms or standards of behavior for everyday life and backs those up with sacred promises or sanctions. Interestingly, all this external control also provides the benefit of removing the burden of each individual having to figure out how to live the good life.

A strong set of beliefs and rituals also provides great social cohesion and solidarity about what is right or wrong or important in a society. For example, a community coming together to pray and dance for rain or a good harvest reaffirms each individual role in the group effort and encourages "buy in" from members.

When societies want to wage a war or have a major goal of conquest they often invoke religious meaning to "win the game," "kill the infidels" or "bring salvation to the heathens." When Native Americans were promised that their "ghost shirts" would make them impervious to the white man's bullets, it was much easier to go into battle with confidence. Religions adopt special garments, colors, and symbols to identify themselves, e.g., crosses, yarmulke, special undergarments, or prayer beads. Identity is also formed with raising one's hands in praise, genuflecting, covering the body, and praying on a rug five times a day.

7. Enculturation. Religious education and training helps to enculturate the next generation. In many cultures, children go through stages or levels as they learn to be "human" in that society. They might also have to accomplish rites of passage and recite ancestry or scripture, and engage in dangerous deeds to prove their worth. Religious education includes learning the teachings, rituals, customs, major rites, and social hierarchies, roles, or gender duties. In some cases it also requires learning other languages or cultures.

ORIGIN OF RELIGION

The forms of religious beliefs and myths usually match the type of society in which they are found. This should not be surprising because religion is a part of the adaptation of a culture to its environment and the particular challenges of that time period.

PREHISTORY AND FORAGERS

Of course, without a written record and over millions of years, it's hard to know what was in the minds of our prehistoric ancestors or exactly when religion first began. However, a number of mental concepts had to be in place, first. There had to be a degree of intelligence to even begin reflection on the unknown. Appreciating causality and agency comes next—it's thundering because Thor is angry. Attributing intentions to others is called theory of mind. A third concept is the connectivity of existence—the fact that spirits or ancestors could even influence current events. A recent claim even suggests that humans possess a "God gene" called VMAT2 which predisposes individuals toward spirituality and feelings of oneness. Morality is often argued to be associated with the origins of religion, but scientists have found otherwise. Frans de Waal pointed out that great apes and other social animals clearly show restraint, altruism, cooperation, empathy, and other traits we associate with morality. In fact, great apes have social rituals of reconciliations following conflict involving hand holding, touching, and grooming. Apes and other intelligent animals will also act against others whom they perceive as unjust, when given a chance.

Going back at least a million years, we have an unusual bone pit dated to *Homo erectus* in Atapuerca, Spain. It contains bones of 30 humans causing speculation that it might have been intentional. Later sites also contain bones of cave bears and saber tooth tigers. It's interesting to note that the earliest known spirit beings or gods are in fact represented by predators or powerful beasts, e.g., Baal, the Semitic deity or the animal figures shown at Göbekli Tepe, discussed below. Think of the phrase, "the fear of God." We have many examples of prehistoric human skulls with canine teeth cut marks from predators so the fear of powerful forces outside our control was real. Burial of the dead, several hundred thousand years ago, also suggests at least attachment, and placement of grave goods might imply a possible afterlife. By 100,000 years ago, we begin to see marks on bone that may indicate sky observations and changing phases of the moon that may represent the first calendars and season markers. The Blanchard bone dated at 30,000 years certainly suggests counting of moon phases from new to cresent to full moon and back again.

Contemporary foragers live by hunting and gathering and see themselves as integrated into their environment. All of existence is sacred or energized by spiritual forces which can be either personal, called animism, or impersonal, called animatism. An example is the Ituri forest people of Africa and their notion of "molimo." It is about the connectedness of everything and it explains much of existence. Control of this force and rituals of healing and trance are also directed toward these powers.

HORTICULTURE AND PASTORALISM

Cultures who create gardens or raise animals focus on life cycles and sacrifice to affect food or rain. Early horticultural societies tended to be matrilineal where descent is determined through the mother's line. At Catalhoyuk in Turkey, an early Neolithic site, we have stone images of a mother goddess with human bones buried underneath her statue. There are many communal practices such as rain dances, harvest celebrations, and death rituals.

Fertility symbols are also important since people depended upon the renewal of life. The Men-An-Toi "hole stone" monument in Cornwall, England appears to be part of a larger circle of 18-20 stones which likely marked the summer and winter solstice. It consists of a doughnut shaped round stone with two standing stones, one in front and the other behind. By historic times, the stone represented fertility, childbirth, and curing of childhood rickets (actually caused by a lack of vitamin D). The belief was that if a woman passed through seven times backwards, local folklore said she would become pregnant.

AGRICULTURE AND COMPLEX SOCIETIES

As gardening and agriculture become more complicated, men did more of the cultivation and male and father gods and spirits dominated. As city states rose, central authorities were justified, and they developed pantheons of warrior deities that reflected local politics, warfare, and conquest. These societies created sacred scriptures and other writings that were studied, often with strict prescriptions for living, and severe consequences if not honored. With the division of labor and rise of elites, religion as well justified social injustice.

Agricultural societies developed priestly social classes who gave advice and oversaw the rituals of great rulers. Religions developed centralized spiritual figures like the Indian goddess Kali who has sharp fangs and wears tiger skins, or the Egyptian Apep, a giant serpent who "explained" the motion of the sun by swallowing the barge of the sun god Ra every night. With civilization, this was elaborated into polytheism where a pantheon or community of gods who reflect the social order of the society rule and must be appeased. Monotheism likely arose in Egypt with a pharaoh's emphasis on the sun god above all, and many scholars argue that this was carried over into Judeo-Christian traditions.

Today, 84% of people worldwide claim participation in a religion with Christianity representing 33% and Islam second with 21% (Islam is also the fastest growing world religion). But religion is not for all. At least 15% of people have a broad spiritual openness or no interest in religion. Many world religions have common global wisdom like the Golden Rule which is expressed as treating others as you would wish to be treated, in a reciprocal relationship. It requires empathy and perceiving someone else as a "self" much like yourself, instead of as "the other." Confucianism, a Chinese religion, states, "Never impose on others what you would not choose for yourself."

RELIGION AND CONTROL

Religion is also in the business of shaping and controlling its members. Foragers give individual prayers for success in the hunt; gardeners and agriculturalists do collective rituals for rain and a good crop, and members of contemporary complex societies sanction commercial holidays in big displays of wealth related to industry and corporate capitalism. Many organized religions have fundamental divisions or sects which advocate that their beliefs and rituals are the only way or that only they have the secret knowledge or path to the afterlife.

There is also a darker side to religion that has promoted much human suffering. Religions find reasons for sacred wars like the Crusades; requiring believers to sacrifice animals or people; cannibalism; torturing unbelievers—these are the dark side of religion. Often the conflicts have a gender or sociopolitical purpose related to support for the status quo, social inequality, conquest of other cultures, or increasing the wealth of elites. Thus, since the evolution of agriculture and civilization, religion has served to legitimize "the way things are" and the power of elites by claiming special divinity, powers of rulers, or sanctions against certain behaviors.

HERO MYTH

Joseph Campbell popularized hero myths in his classic *The Hero With a Thousand Faces* (1949). Campbell pointed out that myth addresses what many Native American cultures call "the good mystery" of the existence itself. For pre-modern societies myth functioned as a kind of proto-science giving explanations for weather, changing seasons, causation, meaning of life, and death. But, myths also explained and justified the social order—or challenged it in the hero's quest. Myths also taught young people about their culture and helped inividuals through the stages of life.

He noted that hero myths consist of 12 stages involving a challenge or situation in the real world that calls the hero to an adventure involving supernatural wonder.

The hero may hesitate but has a mentor who helps them with unusual forces, tests, and ordeals. The hero is victorious, is rewarded, and is reborn or resurrected. In the end, he returns with special or magical powers or gifts. Hero myths are found throughout the world and include Abenaki Gloscap, Abrahamic Noah, Celtic King Arthur, Eyptian Osiris, Greek Odysseus, and Aztec Quetsalcoatl.

Egypt had two important dieties, Osiris (right) who represented the sun and goodness, and Horus (left), who stood for the darkness and evil. Osiris would rise each morning and be killed by Horus at dusk, only to be reborn and resurrected the next morning. Other celestial bodies and measurements were also important. Cultures noticed the extreme and midpoints for the setting and rising sun and moon over the year, marking the summer and winter solstice, and the vernal and atumnal equinox.

They also named and personified star constellations as people or animal figures, and some cultures such as many Native American tribes believed that they were star travelers from the Pliedes or the belt of Orion. Early astrologers created a circle of 12 constellations marking the solstices and equinoxes inside in a cross form, later adopted by Christianity. The stars of Orion's belt alligned with the brightest star in the sky, Sirius, around December 21 the winter solstice, when the sun 'died' on the shortest days of the year.

Three days later the sun is reborn and rises from the dead around December 25. As a result, many ancient figures were said to be born on December 25, and scholars have noted festivals of light at that time. These include: Horus (Egypt, 2000 BCE), Mithra (Persia, 1200 BCE), Attis (Greece, 1200 BCE), Krishna (India, 900 BCE, and Jesus of Nazareth (Balilee, 3 BCE). Some deities were resurrected on horizon halfway mark of the vernal equinox around March 20th near Easter and Passover.

GOBEKLI TEPE

Most scientists assumed that elaborate religion and huge megalithic stone structures were introduced with agriculture to cope with the uncertainty of crops. However, we now know that religion pre-dates agriculture. The earliest sanctuary we know of, Göbekli Tepe, is 12,000 years old and located in Turkey. It is found on a barren plateau and consists of 200 stone pillars, each weighing 20 tons, formed in 20 circles, often with animal or human images on them. This means that our ancestors created spiritual sanctuaries before the wheel, pottery, or even villages! We assume its function was spiritual and involved communal rituals, but what was Göbekli Tepe? And why did hunter/gatherers, not agriculturalists, think to create it?

American archaeologist Robert Braidwood had proposed in 1948 that the origins of agriculture would be found in the hilly terrain of the Zagros and Taurus Mountains of southeastern Turkey. Göbekli Tepe was first discovered in an archaeological survey done between 1963 and 1972 to investigate the transition between Stone Age hunting and gathering during the Paleolithic Period to the settled villages of farmers and pastoralists of the Neolithic Period.

By 8,000 BCE, people were already gathering wild wheat from the fertile Harran plain just south of Göbekli Tepe and it was thought that farming started as a way to be sure that there would be enough food for all the people living in the new villages. The grass-covered hills near the plains were ideal for pasturing early flocks of sheep and goats. There was no water source near Göbekli Tepe and the land was not farmable, so the hill was not of much interest to archaeologists focused on the origins of agriculture and animal domestication. However, in 1994, a German archaeologist Klaus Schmidt with a different orientation discovered "strange stone-rings of dimensions barely moveable by men" at Göbekli Tepe.

Dated at 12,000 BCE, the t-shaped pillars that form the stone rings at Göbekli Tepe are almost 10,000 years older than Stonehenge, the best known megalith. Rock and mortar walls were built between the pillars to build circular buildings with terrazzo (colored rocks embedded in limestone paste) floors. Two free-standing pillars were placed in the center of each circle and the doorway for each structure was carved from a single large block of limestone. It probably took almost a year and a lot of people to build each circular building.

Many of the pillars have animals carved on them – foxes, lions, birds, spiders, and more. The most common animal image at Göbekli Tepe is that of the snake, sometimes pictured individually and sometimes in groups. Nearly all of the snakes are heading down the pillars and when grouped are parallel to one another. There are several mysteries about Göbekli Tepe. First, the meaning of the animal iconography image data incised on the stones. Are they totems, gods, or spirit guardians? Or are they possibly just art or better yet, hunter and gatherer graffiti?

Many of the Göbekli Tepe carvings – both animals and people – were depicted with an erect penis, and therefore, are obviously male. Numerous Venus figurines with exaggerated female reproductive body parts have been found at much earlier periods in the Paleolithic, 20,000 years in Europe. Could there have been a shift in beliefs from a gynocentric (female-centered) goddess religion possibly to an androcentric (male-centered) god? Since they are hunter/gatherers, perhaps they are focused on hunting the animals depicted.

So, an analysis of any animal bones present at the site is important. Zooarchaeologists (archaeologists who study animal bones) have found that most of the thousands of animal bones at Göbekli Tepe are from common food species such as gazelles, aurochs, boar, and deer, and not the more exotic animals depicted

on the pillars, with the exception of foxes. Though we may not think of foxes as food, cutmarks on meat-bearing bones of the foxes provides evidence that foxes were eaten. It is also possible that foxes were exploited for their fur, which is evidenced by a high frequency of toe bones.

All of the bones at Göbekli Tepe are actually from wild animals at the time, not used for food. Wild goats are also noticeably absent from Göbekli Tepe, although goats were an important food source that was later domesticated in the Middle East. Are the animal bones the remains of animal sacrifices or large communal religious feasts? Or are the bones just left over from feeding the many workers involved in the monolithic construction project?

A second major mystery of Göbekli Tepe is how nomadic hunter and gatherers managed to bring together the manpower and knowledge to build such impressive megalithic ("huge stone") monuments. It would require social coordination and planning we do not ordinarily associate with foraging societies, even ones living with rich resources. It also would have taken generations, but it turns out that Göbekli Tepe is one of more than one hundred stone circles still to be excavated.

It's a tantalizing story right on the edge of our understanding of religion before we become food producers. What were our ancestors thinking? How incredible that they put so much effort into a stone structure while still living as nomadic foragers. Most of the site is still not excavated. This is a reminder that there is so much more to learn from investigating prehistoric sites so we understand the human journey with a fuller understanding.

CRITICAL THINKING & WEBSITES

1. Can you find elements of religion or spirituality in other popular entertainment forms, e.g., sporting events, country music, or hip hop?
2. Analyze a religious or spiritual experience you or someone you know has had in terms of concepts used by anthropologists.
3. Define and describe the range of spiritual experience.
4. Contrast the religion of foragers with that of food producers.
5. Take a contemporary film, story or TV show—what elements of a hero myth can you find?
6. See the website of Bart Ehrman author of *Misquoting Jesus*, who explains his journey from a fundamentalist Christian to an agnostic at bartdehrman.com.
7. National Geographic has a video episode about Göbekli Tepe on YouTube at https://www.youtube.com/watch?v=IDXTmCwAETM.

REFERENCES

Alexander, Caroline. (2008). If the Stones Could Speak: Searching for the Meaning of Stonehenge. *National Geographic.*

Alves, William. (2012). *Music of the Peoples of the World,* 3rd ed. Belmont, CA: Cengage.

Anonymous, & George, Andrew. (2003). *The Epic of Gilgamesh.* New York: Penguin Classics Reissue Edition.

Ayali-Darshan, Noga. (2013). Baal, son of Dagan: In search of Baal's double personality. *Journal of the American Oriental Society*, 133, 4, 651-657.

Barber, Lynn. (2009). Shady lady: The truth about pop's Lada Gaga. *The London Sunday Times* (December 6, 2009).

Braidwood, Robert J. (1948). Prehistoric Men. Chicago, IL: Chicago Natural History Museum.

Callaway, Ewen. (2013). Hominin DNA baffles experts. Retrieved December 21, 2015 from: nature.com.

Coppens, Philip. (2009). Göbekli Tepe: The World's Oldest Temple. *Nexus Magazine* 16(4).

Hodder, Ian. (2006*). The Leopard's Tale: Revealing the Mysteries of Catalhoyuk.* London/New York: Thames & Hudson.

Kluger, Jeffrey, Chu, Jeff, Liston, Broward, Sieger, Maggie, Williams, Daniel. (2004). Is God in our genes? *Time,* October 25, 2004.

King, Barbara. (2007). *Evolving God: A Provocative View on the Origins of Religion.* New York, NY: Doubleday.

Lieberman, Philip. (1991). *Uniquely Human.* Cambridge, MA: Harvard University Press.

Lumholtz, Carl. (1903/1973). *Unknown Mexico.* London: McMillian & Company Ltd (reprinted Rio Grande Press).

Mann, Charles C. (2011). The Birth of Religion. *National Geographic.*

Montogomery, James. (2010). Lada Gag's Alejandro director defends video's religious symbolism. *MTV News,* (June 9, 2010).

Murray, Nick. How Tove Lo became Sweden's darkest pop export. *Rolling Stone* (October 15, 2014).

No author. (2012). The global religious landscape. *The Pew Forum on Religion & Public Life.* Pew Research Center (December 18, 2012).

Peters, Joris, and Klaus Schmidt. (2004). Animals in the Symbolic World of Pre-Pottery Neolithic Göbekli Tepe, South-eastern Turkey: A Preliminary Assessment. *Anthropozoologica* 39(1):179-218.

Preston-Jones, Ann. (1993). The Men-An-Tol Management and Survey. Historic Environment Service, Cornwall, UK: Cornwall County Council.

Ruggles, Clive. (2005) *Ancient Astronomy: An Encyclopedia of Cosmologies and Myth.* Santa Barbara, CA: ABC-CLIO.

Schmidt, Klaus. (1995). Investigations in the Upper Mesopotamian Early Neolithic: Göbekli Tepe and Gürcütepe. *Neo-Lithics* 2/95:9-10.

Schmidt, Klaus. (2000). Göbekli Tepe, Southeastern Turkey. A Preliminary Report on the 1995-1999 Excavations. *Paléorient* 26(1):45-54.

1. Describe Göbekli Tepe.

2. In what ways do you hypothesize that Gobekli Tepe might have been used by hunters/gatherers?

12 HUMAN FUTURE:
Sustainability and the Stars

When our ancestors began to produce food and live by technology and language, the Neolithic Revolution brought challenges of sustainability, social justice, and quality of life. We are headed for the stars—but this is only if we can become a Type 1 Civilization, first.

LEARNING OBJECTIVES

1. Describe how humans need to stay below the carrying capacity of the environment and what happens when humans don't as in the case of Easter Island.

2. Explain the mystery of the Nasca lines in the desert of Peru and how anthropologists explain them.

3. List and analyze global challenges faced by our species today.

4. Describe the goals of the United Nations in addressing immediate challenges faced by humans globally.

5. Define sustainability and what we need to do to become a Type 1 civilization.

6. Explain the challenges of creating colonies in space based on anthropological insights.

ADAPTATION

Like any other animal, humans have to adapt to the environment and find a means of making a living within the ecosystem. They have to use natural resources wisely, find food and shelter, and develop sustaining cultural practices that give a reason for living. Most importantly, cultures have to stay below the carrying capacity of the environment's resources, create new resources, alter the culture to live in sustainability with the earth, or terra-form other planets. It's as simple as that.

For example, the Dugum Dani who live in the highlands of New Guinea in the South Pacific must be careful not to overhunt the birds, lizards, and wild game they find. They stay below the carrying capacity of the mountainous area to ensure future sources of protein. They also cultivate sweet potatoes, cassava, and banana, but must clear the rain forest, fertilize with slash and burn practices, and move their gardens every few years to keep the land rich in nutrients.

This results in warfare with nearby groups as they compete for prime garden space. But here again if the warfare is too efficient, it might result in the collapse of the entire group. Instead, the conflict takes the form of ritual warfare where once someone is killed or wounded, all fighting stops. For several weeks the community engages in mourning, until the fighting starts up again—and stops again when someone is hurt, over and over for an estimated 10,000 years to date.

In sharp contrast, are the Rapa Nui, a Polynesian people who settled Easter Island in the South Pacific around 700 CE. The Rapa Nui are famous for the 887 tall "moai" stone statues that surround the island. Archaeologists calculate that it took 60 people a year to cut and sculpt the statue and then 250 people to lay it into place probably using logs and pulleys for transport. Many statues have mysterious images and other symbols in "rongo rongo" script.

But the art and wisdom of this culture may never be decoded because the Rapa Nui failed to live in balance with the environment. This was a ranked society and the elites had a highly developed system of ancestor worship so the statues probably represent ancestor spirits. However, the Rapa Nui over-exploited their natural resources which resulted in rapid deforestation. The population also experienced conflict, rat over-population, poor nutrition, disease, and stress.

Oral history and some inscriptions reported that the Rapa Nui were attacked by oppressed lower ranked warriors from their island as well as those from other islands. The warriors introduced a new religion, "Birdman," to replace the ancestor worship of the elites. The new cult targeted the stone symbols of the elites and toppled as many of them as it could. Eventually the whole culture collapsed in warfare and starvation and resorted to cannibalism, as some human remains confirm. It's a lesson in both ecology and social justice.

NASCA LINES

A fascinating UNESCO World Heritage Site is the Nazca Lines of southern Peru. They are on a high arid plateau, were made by the local Nazca culture and are dated between 500 BCE and 500 CE. The lines trace the shapes of hummingbirds, spiders, monkeys, fish, sharks, orcas, and lizards, and also consist of geometric shapes. The West became aware of them in the mid-20th century and pseudoscience speculation struggled with how a Native culture could create such huge images, and for what purpose? They jumped to the conclusion that there must have been extraterrestrial assistance and pointed to "landing strips" as evidence in support.

The Nazca culture was an agricultural chiefdom with regional centers of power associated with ceremonial sites of mounds, plazas, and avenues. It is also known for extensive crafts such as pottery ceramics and textiles, as well as an elaborate system of aqueducts they built to combat drought conditions in the extremely dry area. The aqueducts tapped into underground water along channels dug into the mountainside and brought down to the plateau. Interestingly, these channels are still in use by the people living there today.

The Nazca raised maize and cotton and may have exacerbated their changing environment by tree removal which created erosion. This suggested to archaeologists that the ceremonial areas and lines may have functioned for rituals and feasting related to agricultural concerns of providing water, harvest, and abundance. The presence of sea shells transported from the coast may also indicate the connection with water. Researchers find a number of skulls propped onto body shapes made with clothing. The holes in the skulls suggested that they were intentionally displayed or carried. Partial burials are also found with body parts or with the skull replaced by a jar. Some researchers have concluded that the Nazca engaged in headhunting or ritual sacrifices.

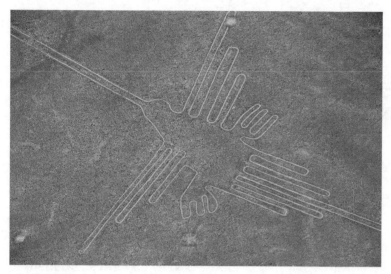

Images from pottery suggest that the Nazca believed in mythical spirit beings represented by the lines. Additional evidence suggests that they processed along the avenue and the lines in ritual activities linked to water worship. Caches of ritual offerings found in the corners of some glyph images supports this hypothesis. However, the claims that the lines are linked to extraterrestrial landing strips or that the Nasca received help from ancient aliens is without evidence and appeals to the supernatural which goes beyond the conclusions of science.

The 4-6 inch wide lines were likely made by stringing ropes over long distances and then wiping away surface rocks to reveal white chalk below, which made a dramatic outlines. Pseudoscientists have made claims that the line images cannot be seen from the ground, but they are actually visible from nearby hills and mountainsides. Although explanations have been offered that the lines are astronomical observatories most researchers conclude they are focused primarily on locations of water. Even the notion that you would have to see the lines in entirety reflects a cultural bias from a visual society. For Nasca, processing along the lines created the connection with the spirit beings of the images, whether seen or unseen.

The Nazca civilization eventually dissipated and it is a reminder of how humans have to work within an ecosystem, adapt to changes, and stay below the carrying capacity of the land to survive. The current use of the aqueducts is a tribute to the enduring ingenuity of the Nazca culture, nevertheless. Most of them have survived centuries. Communities in the area still use the aqueducts and still engage in water rituals as the area has continued to be dry due to climate change and the local geography.

GLOBAL CHALLENGES

Stonehenge's focus on the cycle of life and death described in an earlier chapter illustrates the basic challenge to a species: how to continue to adapt and survive. The struggles of Easter Island, and the Nasca concerns with water bring home some of the challenges to that adaptation. As a result of over-exploiting resources like the ****, climate change experienced by the Nasca, or producing food out of balance with nature, a species can live beyond the carrying capacity of its environment. Today, we are experiencing all three challenges. The question is what can we learn from the past and other cultures to help us now?

LAND AND WATER RESOURCES

More than half of the world's wetlands have been lost, 10% of the world population will be lost when sea levels rise, and since the Neolithic Revolution nearly half of the world's forests have been lost. That's a lot of loss, and the question is, can our earth absorb it?

Industrial agribusiness is resource-hungry, everything from crop irrigation, fertilizers, pesticides, packing, and transport. Scientists report that our current ecological footprint requires about 3 ecological units per person but the natural biological capacity of the earth provides only 2 units per person. This is a deficit of 30%, and something has to change.

Over-exploiting forests and the oceans as well as fossil fuels cannot continue indefinitely. China, India, and Africa all aspire to higher western standards of living which is a reasonable desire. However, resources are limited and this will require a simultaneous modification in western lifestyles which people currently seem reluctant to achieve.

DISTRIBUTION OF WEALTH

The sustainability goal is to have a good standard of living for all peoples, not just the West, without increasing the use of resources beyond sustainable levels. But, this will require cultural adjustments. A complicating factor is that in the century now less than 1% of the U.S. population holds more wealth than over half of the American people. Twentieth century Americans worked hard to achieve more than their parent's generation but now find themselves losing ground since the 1970s, producing children less well-off than their parents. CEOs of major corporations become billionaires while rustbelt workers' manufacturing centers move to Mexico or overseas and unions have to take cuts just to maintain employment. What will a world be like with such a political and economic divide between the haves and have-nots?

Global populations can be organized into groups based on their access to the world economy. The results are shocking. The "bankable" wealthy who can develop businesses, attend elite schools, and borrow monies for investments, development, or personal needs are only 20% of the world's population. Thirty percent are workers whose employment is insecure, seasonal, or dependent upon factors outside their control. A whopping 50% of the world's population are already essentially excluded from the global economic system and live in degraded environments, pollution, higher crime, resource depletion, dispossession, and war and conflict. They are nearly three billion people who live on two dollars a day.

Democracy requires a middle class to operate efficiently and the loss of the middle class globally, is potentially dangerous. Middle classes are important because they are more highly educated with better job skills, they purchase consumer goods, and they pay taxes. On the one hand, a global middle class has emerged in Brazil, Russia, India, China, and South Africa. But, on the other, the rising trend in global inequality means that three-quarters of the poor live in middle-income countries now experiencing widening income gaps, not middle class growth.

People begin to distrust government and the result is social upheaval. Governments have difficult meeting the daily needs of citizens, and fail miserably in dealing with major crises such as energy shortages or climate disasters such as hurricanes. The gap between the wealthy and the rest of the population builds strong resentment and social distance resulting in exclusion of the poor and blaming the victim. In the past, these social conditions have not resulted in stability, but in revolt and revolution.

OVER-POPULATION

Over population is affected by social factors such as wealth and birthrates and it will be a factor in determining our future. Most humans live in urban environments, and as cities grow, they must also provide quality of life. This is already a challenge for cities in India and China. For example, Hong Kong (left) is a major center for world commerce and one of the world's largest cities at nearly 8 million residents. It has the second highest density of skyscrapers in the world which provides a challenge for urban residences. It currently has urban citizens with the highest life expectancy but this is challenged by increasing pollution from mainland China and such a density of population that quality of life seriously declines.

NUCLEAR WAR

We also live in a nuclear age and without a clear path to prevent nuclear war most of us live in a degree of tension and fear of the other which does not facilitate working together to create quality of life for all. When the degree of intra- and inter-nation conflict rises people become concerned about the threat of nuclear war and the possibility that an impulsive nation might use them or the U.S. would be forced to use them in our defense. In the past, war was devastating to all populations but without weapons of mass destruction,

was contained. World Wars I and II took millions of lives away from their communities on an unprecedented scale. However, if a major nuclear war broke out, civilization itself might not continue or be so damaged by the destruction and radiation as to set back any survivors for centuries.

Predicting exactly the result of large scale nuclear war is difficult. Obviously, urban areas would be hardest hit with millions of city-dwellers facing immediate death. Most predictions note that rural communities might have a chance to survive although with difficulty. The Cold War even produced a document, Nuclear War Survival Skills. School children were taught to "duck and cover" and the U.S. still stockpiles chemicals that can be used to treat exposure to fallout. Public alert systems were developed, but the warning time for a nuclear attack might be three minutes or less, so most people would be helped relatively little. Most countries have plans for continuity of government and operations, and nuclear submarines have "letters of last resort" consisting of orders about actions to take in the event of a strike after a government has been destroyed. A price of living in the 21st century is a vague uneasiness and fear about nuclear war.

ROBOTICS

A less obvious challenge to our species is robotics, the design and construction of computerized systems of robots, a machine that can carry out automatic actions and controlled externally by humans (or other robots). Increasingly, robots are shaped to take on humanoid form and may become so perfected that it is hard to determine the difference. Some nano robots are so tiny they are microscopic. Either way they can even give the appearance of intelligence or independent thought, human style communication and reactions, and take on bio-robotic form called "soft robots."

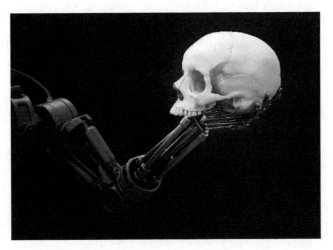

What effect will the increasing automation of work and introduction of drones and robots to our lives have? Obviously, there are many positives of efficiency and having robots do unsafe or routine jobs for humans. Robots are already cited as a cause of unemployment, and their use in military situations raises whole new issues. Will armies of the future be only my robot is "bigger and badder" than your robot, or will military robots be able to enter and obliterate a city of millions with only one command? Even if we consider only the positive aspects of robots, such as doing dangerous work, how will we interact with androids (robots designed to resemble humans) or cyborgs (part human, part machine)?

Vernor Vinge has described "the Singularity," the moment when computer-controlled robots become smarter than humans. Such artificial superintelligence might cause massive technological change that goes beyond the ability of human civilization to cope. Some scientists estimate that we might reach that point by 2040. This intelligence explosion might not have the mitigating features of human morality and ethics balancing sheer growth. On the other hand, the 1950s film, The Day the Earth Stood Still shows the earth being contacted by humanoid extraterrestrial Klaatu, who explains that other planets have created robots that are smarter and programmed to destroy all violence on the spot—as a means to keep intelligent life preserved.

PANDEMICS

What happens when it's not just a cold or flu that goes around the office or classroom, but a massive epidemic of infectious disease that spreads through a large region of a human population? A terrible pandemic of the past was the Black Death that killed over 75 million people in the Middle Ages.

A more recent example is the HIV-AIDS disease spread. Ebola and other hemorrhagic illnesses are current and future threats that could possibly become pandemic in nature. Rapid genetic mutations and resistance to known pathogens is also an issue. Zika has resulted in more than 1.5 million cases in the Americas and the World Health Organization (WHO) warned it could become global.

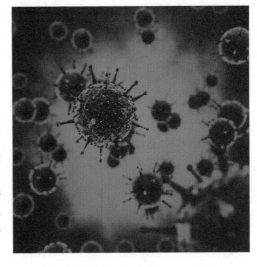

GLOBAL GOALS

What can we do to prepare to address more immediate threats to human society? The United Nations has been addressing these issues for decades. Getting many nations to cooperate on its initiatives has been a challenge and major countries such as the U.S. have often failed to sign important international agreements on the earth's resources. Recently, it developed a number of Sustainable Development Goals for the 21st century. This can be an important guide for the issues that all nations, rich and poor, need to address:

1. POVERTY AND HUNGER: One of the clearest problems to solve is extreme poverty due to climate, lack of energy, sociopolitical circumstances, and agricultural issues as well as structural violence and social inequality. Local production and distribution of food is necessary, e.g., the Slow Foods Movement draws food for homes and restaurants only within a 100 mile radius. The World Health Association is promoting the Mediterranean diet which is low in meat, rich in fruits and vegetables, low in sugar, salt, and saturated fatty acids; a Japanese diet is also desirable.

2. UNIVERSAL PRIMARY EDUCATION: In an age of computers those without access to basic primary education are doomed. Many parts of the world have the majority of its citizens unable to read or without basic educational skills. We are developing technology exponentially but without education, the majority of people will be left behind and the security of the ruling elites will be an issue. While technology might help the situation horror scenarios are also possible.

3. GENDER EQUALITY: The legacy of patriarchy is still with us. Women do not yet have equal pay in the U.S. and poor treatment and abuse of women in many countries as well as lack of economic opportunity must be changed if we are to achieve human rights. Where women lack basic rights they cannot control family size and contribute fully to the education and economic standing of their family, nor can they fully contribute to their community.

4. CHILD MORTALITY: More than half of the deaths of children globally are due to conditions that could be prevented or treated. Children in sub-Saharan Africa are more than 14 times more likely to die that children in developed nations. This extreme will continue to harm all nations because of geopolitical strife.

5. MATERNAL HELATH: Closely linked with child mortality is maternal health. Poor nutrition, poverty, stress, lack of medical care and medications, and lack of support for lactation all negatively affect maternal health, harming the quality of family life.

6. INFECTIOUS DISEASE: One of the biggest concerns in the medical community is the threat of pandemics and the overuse of antibiotics which has resulted in resistant strains of pathogens that threaten humans, easily spread today given extensive travel between nations.

7. SAFE WATER: Safe and clean water is a leading global issue since it is a limited resource. Currently 35% of human water use is unsustainable. In the last 50 years water demand doubled; agricultural use increased by 75%; industrial use by 200%, and domestic use by 400%. However, even in the U.S., Flint, Michigan was allowed to poison citizens with lead-filled water, which is a kind of structural violence and indirect genocide.

8. DEVELOPMENT PARTNERSHIPS: New methods and ideas for putting technical know-how and opportunity together are needed to solve many global issues facing humans in the 21st century.

SUSTAINABILITY

Anthropology's long six million year time perspective on our species gives an advantage here. While the Neolithic brought incredible challenges, it also provided solutions. Eighteenth century scholars speculated about "survival of the fittest" and considered if humans, like plants and other animals, had evolved from earlier life forms. However, the six million year story of our species suggests instead that we are the "survival of the generalist," meaning that the human way to adapt has been to be—adaptable.

From African swamps, dry cliffs, glacial mountains, and isolated islands, we have brought general cognitive skills, plasticity, and innovation to the challenges of survival—not increasingly specialized skills for only one ecosystem. We made Oldowan, Acheulean, Levalloisian, Neolithic, and now technological digital tools as well as environments we create ourselves. The core of this achievement is that we are generalists, not specialists suited to only one way of making a living. With this great history of being "*Homo adaptus*" we can face these challenges with energy, enthusiasm, empathy for others, and a new generation that is already highly aware of the need for sustainability.

An example of this adaptation is Astana, the capital of Kazakhstan. It is mall by urban standards, only about one million people but it is large in its vision. Astana is a planned city much like Brasilia in Brazil and our own Washington, D.C. Its stunning Bayterek Tower (above) resembles a spore and is part of the design of Astana as a "city of life," not a "city of the machine." Located on a steppe landscape, it is the second coldest capital city in the world, exceeded only by Mongolia, with minus 30 degrees common throughout the winter and massive mosquitoes in the summer. Yet, it has a high rate of economic development and futuristic buildings in its central area.

The most critical challenge to our species is whether we can become a Type 1 civilization on the Kardashev Scale—an idea that was introduced in Chapter 1. A Type 1 civilization is one with renewable use of earth's resources which includes not just fossil fuels, nuclear energy, air and water but also people. Despite the issues, there are many reasons for hope. In the words of Jane Goodall (Jane Goodall & Phillip Berman, 2000): "It is these undeniable qualities of human love and compassion and self-sacrifice that give me hope for the future. We are, indeed, often cruel and evil. Nobody can deny this. We gang up on each other, we torture each other, with words as well as deeds, we fight, we kill. But we are also capable of the most noble, generous, and heroic behavior."

Sustainability is the capacity to live in healthy renewable ways within the carrying capacity of the environment, and endure so that the earth can continue supporting life in a meaningful way. One environmental example is the effort to create both wind energy and desalinization of ocean water. Wind power as an alternative to burning fossil fuels is around us all the time with far fewer net effects on the environment. Offshore wind is stronger and more constant and production costs will come down. Right now, Denmark produces 40% of its electricity from wind, and nearly 100 other countries around the world are experimenting with wind power to support their grids. It is now 4% of the world's energy production, but that will grow.

As cities of the future attempt to meet the needs of their residents, they will develop roof top gardens and towers of plant communities so that much of their food will be local and at least some of the forests will be replenished. Many cities already have developed urban gardens on tiny lots and promote the slow foods movement where all food comes from a 100 mile radius of the community. More local and organic foods are provided even by big grocery chains as well.

MARS COLONY AND BEYOND

It's clear that humans will either need to, or likely choose to, take these new values and sustainable technologies with them into space. In order to do this, we must understand our evolution so far and promote or create environments, social conditions, and cultural systems that work. It also means that we must solve the wide range of social issues described above, including injustice, distribution of wealth, access to resources, and meaningful activities so life is worth living in the first place. Even here, anthropologists are contributing to how humans can create sustainable communities in space, starting with colonies in the solar system on nearby planets or even moons of Jupiter and Saturn.

A focus on human colonization has been on Mars because of its surface conditions and the presence of water in some form. The justification for such a colony includes space exploration, economic development, and military operations. Mars has about a 24 hour day with a similar land mass and seasons. However, there are challenges. Gravity is only 38% of earth's gravity, it gets less general sunlight and more ultraviolet light, and its temperatures are similar to Antarctica. Its atmosphere is 95% carbon dioxide and otherwise toxic to earth's lifeforms. Nevertheless, a number of technologies have been proposed to create an atmosphere with more oxygen, develop cyanobacteria as a food source—in short, terraform Mars and have humans become a two-planet species.

Babak Shakouri Hassanabadi (2016) has summarized some of the anthropological issues related to a Mars colony. Humans are foremost a social species with a great need for a sense of community, even in a society like ours that emphasizes the individual. We derive identity and meaning from our social community. So, the fist Martian colonies will need to provide that sense of community and affiliation in order to provide purpose and avoid depression and isolation. While the participants might be diverse in terms of age, gender, nationality, race, etc., the colony would need to feel "tribal" to succeed long-term. The ability to engage in teamwork and other collective action would be critical in addition to whatever skills individuals possessed. People will likely have to live in close quarters so a good balance of community and privacy would also be needed.

A Mars colony is also an opportunity to create a new culture, even a distinct extraterrestrial human culture. What will family life be like? Will people get married? How many genders will Mars have? How will we adapt? And what would the neo-Martians think about earth? Would they sometime in the future tell stories of a green and blue place away in space, a mythic land called Earth where great-great-grandparents came from?

CONCLUSION

In conclusion, the dinosaurs aren't here today because they did not have a space plan. We can. Given all the challenges of our six million year journey, and all its mysteries, anthropologists are hopeful that we will explore and solve these problems both on earth and Mars and beyond. No doubt an anthropologist will be part of the first expeditions if nothing less to document the adventure and the new mysteries our species will encounter. We will see *Homo sapiens* become *Homo adaptus*, and ultimately, *Homo cosmicus*. There may be many changes and challenges but hope is the best approach: it's pragmatic as well as visionary.

There will be mistakes and tragedies but opportunities to grow in ways we can't yet imagine. But such change and growth is within our nature, in fact, may be built into life itself. And anthropologists will be there to study it. As a U.S. President stated in a speech about a space shuttle failure, "...exploration and discovery is not an option we choose: it is a desire written on the human heart. We are that part of creation that seeks to understand all creation" (Scully, McConnell, & Gerson, 2003).

CRITICAL THINKING & WEBSITES

1. Design a civilization with social equality and no structural violence. What other problems might it have?

2. Are you hopeful about our species future? Why or why not?

3. Consider what an ethnography of a Mars colony might include. What do you think would be a major problem?

4. For an emerging anthropology of the future see: http://www.culanth.org/fieldsights/376-provocation-futurizing-memory.

REFERENCES

Belfer-Cohen, Anna. (1991). The Natufian in the Levant. *Annual Review of Anthropology* 20:167-86.

Bender, Barbara. (1977). Gatherer-Hunter to Farmer: A Social Perspective. *World Archaeology* 10: 204-22.

Hall, Stephen S. (2010). Nasca, Spirits in the Sand. *National Geographic*, March 2010).

Hassanabadi, Babak. (2016). Anthropological reflections on space colonization. The Space Review, November 14, 2016. Retrieved December 1, 2016 at: http://www.thespacereview.com/article/3104/1.

Haviland, William, Prins, Harald, Walrath, Dana, & McBride, Bunny. (2014). *Anthropology: The Human Challenge, 14th edition*. Belmont, CA: Cengage.

Hodder, Ian. (2010). Probing religion at Çatalhöyük: An interdisciplinary experiment. In *Religion in the Emergence of Civilization: Çatalhöyük as a Case Study*, Ian Hodder (ed.), pp. 1-31.

Hoffman, M. (1991). *Egypt Before the Pharaohs: The Prehistoric Foundations of Egyptian Civilization*, revised edition. Austin, TX: University of Texas Press.

Levanda, Robert, & Schultz, Emily. (2015). *Anthropology: What Does It Mean to Be Human?*, third edition. New York, NY: Oxford University Press.

Lykketoft, Mogens. (2015). *Transforming Our World: The 2030 Agenda for Sustainable Development*. United Nations General Assembly, August 12, 2015.

McMichael, Philip. (2017). *Development and Social Change: A Global Perspective*. Los Angeles, CA: Sage.

Odling-Smee, F., et al. (2003). *Niche Construction: The Neglected Process in evolution*. Princeton, NY: Princeton University Press.

Pearson, Mike Parker. (2012). *Stonehenge, Exploring the Greatest Stone Age Mystery*. London, UK: Simon & Schuster.

Schaffarczyk, Alois (ed.). (2014). *Understanding Wind Power Technology*. New York, NY: Wiley and Sons.

Scully, Matthew, McConnell, & Gerson, Michael. (2003). *Memorial Service in Honor of the STS-107 Space Shuttle Columbia*, National Aeronautics and Space Administration's (NASA) Lyndon B. Johnson Space Center, Houston, Texas, February 4, 2003.

Smith, Bruce. (1995). *The Emergence of Agriculture*. New York, NY: Scientific American Library.

Wenke, Robert & Olszewski, Deborah. (2006). *Patterns in Prehistory: Humankind's First Three Million Years*, 5th edition. New York, NY: Oxford University Press.

Zubrin, Robert. (1996). *The Case for Mars: The Plan to Settle the Red Planet and Why We Must*. New York: Simon & Schuster/Touchstone.

1. Rank order the top three global challenges we face today and explain why you think they are critical to solve for us to become a Type 1 Civilization.

Rank	Global Challenge
1	
2	
3	

2. What is your thinking about the human future and challenges faced by colonies in space?

PHOTO CREDITS

CHAPTER 8

p. 111, © Rastislav Ekkert/Shutterstock.com; p. 112, © LUCARELLI TEMISTOCLE/Shutterstock.com; p. 113, © Andy Lim/Shutterstock.com; p. 114, © vainillaychile/Shutterstock.com; p. 115 (top), © KalypsoWorldPhotography/Shutterstock.com; p. 115 (bottom), © Andrzej Kubik/Shutterstock.com; p. 116 (top), © Henry Tran/Shutterstock.com; p. 116 (middle), © Vicky Jirau/Shutterstock.com; p. 116 (bottom), © George W. Bailey/Shutterstock.com; p. 117 (top) © Phil Webb/Shutterstock.com; p. 117 (bottom), © Firdes Sayilan/Shutterstock.com; p. 118 (top), © Fedor Selivanov/Shutterstock.com; p. 118 (middle), © Kamira/Shutterstock.com; p. 118 (bottom), © Marzolino/Shutterstock.com; p. 119 (top), Shahril KHMD/Shutterstock.com; p. 119 (bottom), © pcruciatti/Shutterstock.com; p. 120, © Dietmar Temps/Shutterstock.com; p. 122 (top), © akphotoc/Shutterstock.com; p. 122 (bottom), © Rudra Narayan Mitra/Shutterstock.com; p. 123, © Peter Hermes Furian/Shutterstock.com.

CHAPTER 9

p. 127, © kaetana/Shutterstock.com; p. 128, © somersault1824/Shutterstock.com; p. 130, © LUCARELLI TEMISTOCLE/Shutterstock.com; p. 131, © Yuri Kravchenko/Shutterstock.com; p. 132 (top), © Arvind Balaraman/Shutterstock.com; p. 132 (bottom), © Kaetana/Shutterstock.com; p. 133, © tobkatrina/Shutterstock.com; p. 134, © Antonio Guillem/Shutterstock.com; p. 135, © Milind Arvind Ketkar/Shutterstock.com; p. 136 (top), © calmmindphoto/Shutterstock.com; p. 136 (bottom), © Liquorice Legs/Shutterstock.com; p. 137, © Stefano Tinti/Shutterstock.com.

CHAPTER 10

p. 143, © Kamira/Shutterstock.com; p. 144, © Alberto Loyo/Shutterstock.com; p. 145, © Ellya/Shutterstock.com; p. 147 (top), © Yevgen Belich/Shutterstock.com; p. 147 (bottom), © Alila Medical Media/Shutterstock.com; p. 148, © Benoit Daoust/Shutterstock.com; p. 149 (left), © sunxuejun/Shutterstock.com; p. 149 (right), © Milagli/Shutterstock.com; p. 150, © Sue Stokes/Shutterstock.com; p. 151, © Monika Wisniewska/Shutterstock.com; p. 152 (top), © Yuriy Vlasenko/Shutterstock.com; p. 152 (bottom), © Samuel Borges Photography/Shutterstock.com; p. 153, © Anneka/Shutterstock.com; p. 154, © Quick Shot/Shutterstock.com.

CHAPTER 11

p. 159, © Arturo Escorza Pedraza/Shutterstock.com; p. 160 (top), © Slazdi/Shutterstock.com; p. 160 (bottom), © sahua d/Shutterstock.com; p. 161, © Everett Collection/Shutterstock.com; p. 162, © Elena Schweitzer/Shutterstock.com; p. 163 (top), © SARIN KUNTHONG/Shutterstock.com; p. 163 (middle), © 1000 Words/Shutterstock.com; p. 163 (bottom), © Faraways/Shutterstock.com; p. 164, © szefei/Shutterstock.com; p. 165, © StockCube/Shutterstock.com; p. 166, © Bruce Au/Shutterstock.com; p. 167 (top), © Nejron Photo/Shutterstock.com; p. 167 (bottom left), © tan_tan/Shutterstock.com; p. 167 (bottom right), © tan_tan/Shutterstock.com; p. 168, © Linda Brotkorb/Shutterstock.com; p. 169, © Cornfield/Shutterstock.com; p. 170, © Cornfield/Shutterstock.com.

CHAPTER 12

p. 175, © iurii/Shutterstock.com; p. 176, © Sergey Uryadnikov/Shutterstock.com; p. 177, © Alberto Loyo/Shutterstock.com; p. 178, © John Kershner/Shutterstock.com; p. 180 (top), © leungchopan/Shutterstock.com; p. 180 (bottom), © Razvan Ionut Dragomirescu/Shutterstock.com; p. 181, (top), © Mopic/Shutterstock.com; p. 181 (bottom) © nobeastsofierce/Shutterstock.com; p. 183, © Ververidis Vasilis/Shutterstock.com; p. 184 (top), © artjazz/Shutterstock.com; p. 184 (bottom), © iurii/Shutterstock.com; p. 185, © Bruce Rolff/Shutterstock.com.